SECOND EDITION

MACROECONOMICS
Monetary, Search, and Income Theories

Charles W. Baird

Alexander E. Cassuto

*California State University,
Hayward*

SCIENCE RESEARCH ASSOCIATES, INC.
Chicago, Palo Alto, Toronto, Henley-on-Thames, Sydney, Paris
A Subsidiary of IBM

(312) 484 2000

**for Patti
and
for Barbara**

Acquisition Editor	Terry Baransy
Project Editor	Gretchen Hargis
Designer	Carol Harris
Technical Artist	John Foster
Compositor	Typothetae
Cover photographer	J. Eyerman, Black Star

Library of Congress Cataloging in Publication Data

Baird, Charles W.
  Macroeconomics.

  Includes bibliographical references and index.
  1. Macroeconomics.   I.   Cassuto, Alexander E.,
joint author.   II.   Title.
HB171.5.B19   1981   339   80-12002
ISBN 0-574-19400-2

10 9 8 7 6 5 4 3 2 1

CONTENTS

PREFACE

The preface to the first edition (1973) began with the assertion that "the field of macroeconomics is changing very rapidly." It still is. This edition includes much that was not part of any intermediate macroeconomics class in 1973. The Leijonhufvud-Clower restatement of Say's Principle (Chapter 3) and their reinterpretation of Keynes (Chapter 14) are indicative of the extent to which macroeconomic theory has developed in the last ten years. We believe that in the 1980s an intermediate macro theory class that does not include some consideration of these innovations is not complete. Similarly, an up-to-date intermediate class must, we believe, include some discussion of the Laffer curve and other "supply side" considerations such as the "tax wedge" (Chapter 11).

In 1974 F. A. Hayek was awarded the Nobel Prize in economics. Since that time there has been renewed interest in his work. It was none other than Sir John Hicks, the inventor of IS-LM analysis, who, in 1967, wrote:

> When the definitive history of economic analysis during the nineteen-thirties comes to be written, a leading character in the drama (and it was quite a drama) will be Professor Hayek. . . . [I]t is hardly remembered that there was a time when the new theories of Hayek were the principal rival of the new theories of Keynes. Which was right, Keynes or Hayek? . . . [M]any . . . (including the present writer) took quite a time to make up their minds.*

While this edition, like the first one, includes a model of inflationary recession based upon the quantity equation of exchange, it also (at the beginning of Chapter 12) discusses Hayek's model of inflationary recession. Hayek predicted in the 1930s that stagflation would inevitably result from the expansionary Keynesian policies financed by the creation of new money. Events since the late 1960s have borne out his prediction.

Nevertheless, Hicks' IS-LM model continues to dominate the intermediate macro theory class. In our judgment many useful insights can still be derived from a careful use of that model. In Chapter 10 we develop the model in its standard (fixed price) form, but we manipulate it with careful attention to the

---

*Sir John Hicks, "The Hayek Story," *Critical Essays in Monetary Theory* (Oxford: Oxford University Press, The Clarendon Press, 1967), p. 203.

constraints of Say's Principle; and in Chapter 11 we develop its more useful (variable price) version.

Perhaps the most widely acclaimed feature of the first edition of this text was its treatment of the labor market and unemployment within the context of positive information costs and search. That discussion has been extended in this edition to include the effects of unanticipated inflation on employers as well as employees in the job search process (Chapter 7). Moreover, the long-run and short-run Phillips curve analyses are immediately integrated into the labor market discussion instead of being deferred, as in the first edition, to the last chapter.

This edition, like the first, has an overall monetarist perspective. We believe that Milton Friedman and his colleagues from the University of Chicago Workshop on Money and Banking have done more than any other group to develop and clarify macroeconomic relationships. Unlike the first edition, this edition includes numerous references to empirical investigations of those relationships. Many of those investigations were carried out in the Research Department of the Federal Reserve Bank of St. Louis. We consider the St. Louis model, developed by Andersen and Carlson, to be the best overall statement of the monetarist framework; and, in Chapter 13, we include the same geometric representation of the model that was in Chapter 16 of the first edition.

The most obvious difference between the editions is that the second edition has a coauthor—Alexander E. Cassuto. The division of labor in the production of the revision was as follows. Baird was solely responsible for Chapters 1, 3, 7, and 14 as well as all the references to Hayek. Cassuto's job was to revise, expand, and update the exposition in the first edition that was relevant to the rest of the second edition, paying particular attention to opportunities to simplify the discussion and to add empirical material. Throughout the revision we have substantially reduced the dependency on math that characterized some of the first edition, and we have made a conscious effort to present the issues separating the Keynesians and monetarists more even-handedly than they were discussed in the first edition.

Because of increasing time constraints on busy instructors and the rapid turnover in course assignments, we have supplied an *Instructor's Guide* to facilitate the use of the second edition. It contains suggested answers to all discussion questions at the ends of the chapters and test items for each chapter.

We wish to express our appreciation to the following people who provided useful comments and suggestions in the early stages of the development of the manuscript: Ujagar S. Bawa (Bloomsburg State College), George H. Blackford (University of Arkansas), C. A. Christofides (East Stroudsburg State College), D. Larry Davis (Indiana University Northwest), F. Trenery Dolbear,

Jr. (Brandeis University), C. H. Farrell (University of North Carolina at Wilmington), C. Grootaert (University of Hawaii at Manoa), Curtis E. Harvey (University of Kentucky), Anthony K. Lima (California State University, Hayward), Bruce D. Mann (University of Puget Sound), Warren Pillsbury (Lehigh University), and Maurice Weinrobe (Clark University).

A special note of thanks is due to Jack Carr (University of Toronto), Fred L. Harder (Union College), David C. Klingaman (Ohio University), and Robert J. Michaels (California State University, Fullerton), who read the final manuscript page by page and helped immeasurably in making the book more accurate, clearer, and pedagogically sound.

All textbook writers know how vital are the efforts of the editor who shepherds the project through the multiple stages of production. We are grateful to Terry Baransy for his patience, good humor, punctuality, and plain hard work on behalf of the revision. He made the job seem easy.

As project editor Gretchen Hargis had the responsibility of converting our final draft into a more logically ordered, easily readable manuscript. Her thoughtful editing contributed significantly to the quality of the final product.

As on numerous other occasions, Sandra Anderson provided speedy, thorough, and accurate typing and clerical services. We hope she was only kidding when she said this was the last time, for she really would be next to impossible to replace.

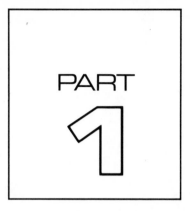

PART

1

THE ANALYTICAL
FRAMEWORK

Setting the Stage

The main topics of this book are inflation and unemployment. It is next to impossible to find an edition of any major daily newspaper that does not contain several stories concerning these two problems. Much of what is written in the general press about inflation and unemployment is misleading and contradictory. It is our hope that after you have read this book, you will understand the causes, consequences, and remedies of inflation and unemployment at least well enough to see why most of the measures governments use to combat them are counterproductive.

1-1 INFLATION AND UNEMPLOYMENT

Inflation is a sustained increase in the average level of money prices. There are hundreds of thousands of individual prices in the economy. At any time some are falling (e.g., the price of minicalculators) and others are rising (e.g., the price of gasoline). Prices that fall do so at different rates, as do also prices that rise.

Inflation is reported as a *rate*—so much change per specified time period (usually a year). An inflation rate of 10 percent, for example, means that, on the average, prices are rising at the rate of 10 percent a year. It does *not* mean that *all* individual prices are rising at 10 percent a year. Nor does it mean that, on the average, prices have increased by 10 percent and now are steady. If, on the average, prices increased by 2 percent each month, the (annual) inflation rate would be 24 percent. In reality, the rate at which average price level changes is different from month to month. The inflation rate for a year is computed by measuring the average price level at the beginning of a 12-month period and again at the end of the 12-month period and finding the percentage difference between the two. We will see in the next chapter how the average price level is computed.

You are unemployed if you don't have a job. Not all unemployment is bad, however. Some people (e.g., the retired and students) *choose* to be without a job. It is involuntary unemployment that most people complain about, but not all involuntary unemployment is bad either. If a college alumna offers to work for $100 an hour and can't find an employer willing to pay that price, is she "involuntarily" unemployed? Would you feel sorry for her? What if her asking price were $50 an hour? $25? $2.50? At what prices does a person's unemployment become a matter of social concern? As we will see in Chapter 7, the terms "employed" and "unemployed" as they are used by the Department of Labor's Bureau of Labor Statistics (BLS) have very precise meanings. The BLS reports the "unemployment rate" each month. This rate is the percentage of the active labor force (people either employed or actively seeking employment) that is unemployed.

Most people consider increases in either the inflation rate or the unemployment rate to be undesirable. Governments at all levels, but especially the federal government, devote much time and energy to trying to keep these two rates as low as possible. As we will see, economists used to think that there was a trade-off between these two rates—the lower the inflation rate, the higher the unemployment that must be tolerated. We now know that no such trade-off exists except in the very short run. Over a longer time, high inflation rates cause high unemployment rates.

1-2 THEORY AND REALITY

The data on inflation presented in Figure 1-1 shows that the average price level in the United States climbed throughout the 1970s. The inflation rate (the annual rate of climb of the average) is indicated by the percentages associated with the brackets. For example, between the first quarter of 1975 and the fourth quarter of 1977 the annual inflation rate was 5.7 percent. Inflation has become worse since then.[1]

During the 1930s the unemployment rate got as high as 25 percent. Since the end of World War II the average unemployment rate has been around 5.5 percent. Figure 1-2 depicts unemployment rates in the United States for the 1970s. The large jump over 1974 and into 1975 has been described as the worst recession since the Great Depression. A recession is a period when the unemployment rate is above average, and a depression is a very bad recession. (Someone

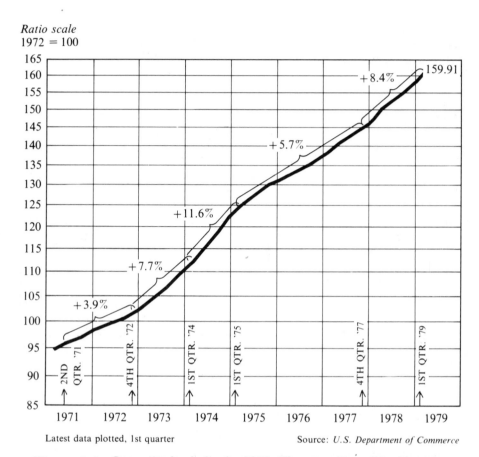

Ratio scale
1972 = 100

Figure 1-1 General price index for 1971—79 as used in national income accounts. The percentages are the annual rates of change for the periods indicated. (Prepared by Federal Reserve Bank of St. Louis, "National Economic Trends," June 29, 1979, p. 14)

quipped that a recession is when your neighbor is unemployed, and a depression is when you are unemployed.)

Since the late 1960s the United States, as well as some other Western industrialized countries, has experienced what some call "stagflation," and what others call "inflationary recession"—periods of high inflation rates and high unemployment rates together. At first this was a puzzle to economists. We usually

*Percent of civilian
labor force*

Latest data plotted, April   Source: *U.S. Department of Labor*

**Figure 1-2   Unemployment rate, seasonally adjusted, for 1971–79.
(Prepared by Federal Reserve Bank of St. Louis, "National
Economic Trends," June 29, 1979, p. 3)**

thought of inflation as something that happens when there is too much dollar
spending relative to the amount of real goods and services that are available to
be purchased. (If you spend $1000 on four camera lenses, their average price is
$250; while if you buy only two for $1000, their average price is $500.) And we
usually thought of high unemployment rates as something that happens when
there is too little dollar spending relative to the amount of real goods and
services available for purchase. (If four camera lenses are purchased and their
average price is $250, $1000 is spent; if only $500 is spent, only two lenses are

purchased, and so some camera lens makers may be laid off.) In brief, we used to think of inflation and excessive unemployment as opposite problems.

Economists recommended that the federal government take steps (called monetary and fiscal policy) to alter total dollar spending whenever either of the two problems appeared: in times of high unemployment, increase total dollar spending (by creating more money or by spending more than it collected in taxes); in inflationary times, decrease total dollar spending (by reducing the amount of money in circulation or by collecting more in taxes than it spent). It all seemed so simple. But it didn't always work, and it seems to work less and less. Why? That is what this book is about. We will have much to say about the nature, consequences, and cures of recession and inflation in this book.

1-3 DISTINGUISHING MACRO FROM MICRO

Economics is divided into two primary parts—microeconomics and macroeconomics. This book is about the latter, but in it we will use some of the techniques and frames of reference of the former. Microeconomics is concerned with the implications of the fact that people act purposefully to attain their goals. It focuses on the decision-making process whereby individual households and individual firms plan their purchases and sales. It also focuses on how changes in the pattern of individual prices act to coordinate the plans and actions of the individual households and firms.

Macroeconomics focuses on the economy as a whole. Of course, what happens in the economy as a whole depends on the plans and actions of the individuals that make up the economy, but it is possible by using averages (e.g., the average price level) and summary statistics (e.g., the national unemployment rate) to describe broad characteristics of the entire economy and to analyze how these broad characteristics relate to each other. Such description and analysis, together with careful consideration of government policy measures designed to affect the economy as a whole, constitute macroeconomics.

Our analysis of the relationships between averages and summary statistics (which are, of course, the outcomes of individual human action) is carried out using the microeconomic notion of "markets." A *market* is the interaction of two groups of human actors—buyers and sellers. The plans of buyers are represented by "demand curves," and the plans of sellers are represented by "supply curves."

A *demand curve* shows how much of some good (e.g., gasoline) buyers will want to buy at each different price of the good. Each person has some upper limit on the price he or she is willing and able to pay for a gallon of gasoline, depending on the person's income, tastes, and preferences. Since people have different incomes and different attitudes toward gasoline's significance, they will have different upper limits on what they are willing to pay for a gallon of gasoline. The lower the price that a seller charges, the larger the quantity of gasoline that the seller will be able to sell. If the price is $2 a gallon, the person will only sell to those whose upper limits are greater or equal to $2. If the price is $1, all those whose upper limits are greater or equal to $1 will buy. Since those who have upper limits greater than or equal to $1 include those whose upper limits are greater than or equal to $2, there will be more sales at $1 than at $2.

A *supply curve* shows how much of some good (e.g., gasoline) sellers will want to sell at each different price of the good. When the price that sellers can get from buyers goes up, more of the good will be offered for sale. This is because the sellers already selling some of the good will want to sell more if the higher price means more profit, and because people who were selling something else or simply looking for a business to get into will be attracted by the higher price to selling the good in question.

Consider Figure 1-3. The line labeled D is the demand curve. It slopes downward, showing that at a high price (e.g., p_1) the quantity buyers want to buy

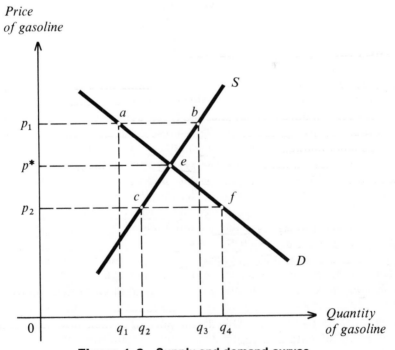

Figure 1-3 Supply and demand curves.

is relatively small (q_1), while at a lower price (e.g., p_2) buyers will want more (q_4). The line labeled S is the supply curve. It slopes upward, showing that at a high price (e.g., p_1) sellers would like to sell a relatively large quantity (q_3), while at a lower price (e.g., p_2) sellers will want to sell less (q_2). If the price were p_1, there would be an *excess supply* (ES) indicated by *ab*, because the quantity sellers would want to sell (q_3) would exceed the quantity that buyers would want to buy (q_1). In such a situation sellers would have to lower the price to get rid of the surplus. If the price were p_2, there would be an *excess demand* (ED) indicated by *cf*, because the quantity that buyers would want to buy (q_4) would exceed the quantity that sellers would want to sell (q_2). In such a shortage sellers would see that they could raise the price and still sell all they wanted to sell.

Only if the price is p^* would there be a match between the amount that sellers want to sell and the amount that buyers want to buy. Neither supply nor demand would be in excess. There would be what is called "equilibrium." The market would "clear"—all that is offered for sale is bought, and all buyers have bought as much as they planned to buy. p^* is called the *market-clearing price* and it is also called the *equilibrium price*. It is the price that coordinates the plans and actions of buyers and sellers. The coordination is indicated by the fact that point e represents the plans of both buyers and sellers.

1-4 THE FRAMEWORK OF THIS BOOK

A large part of microeconomics consists of examining the implications of price movements toward market-clearing values in individual markets. In macroeconomics we talk about excess supplies and excess demands and market-clearing prices in four highly aggregated markets—the commodities market, the bond market, the labor market, and the money market.

The *commodities market* refers to the aggregate of all the goods and services produced in the economy each year. In the next chapter we will see how this aggregate (called gross national product) is formed, and in Chapters 4 through 6 we will see how aggregate demand and supply for commodities are analyzed.

The *bond market* refers to the supply and demand for all financial securities except money. Stocks, bonds, and savings account passbooks are lumped together and called "bonds." The interest rate that we will refer to throughout the book is the rate of return on this composite financial security. The sellers of bonds are governments and business firms that want to borrow funds. The buyers of bonds are households who lend the funds to the firms and government. Households purchase bonds with the portion of their incomes that they save. Putting funds into a savings account is really buying a savings passbook credit. It is the same as buying stocks and bonds. It is a claim on funds that others (primarily business firms and governments) are using. Our composite bond is a claim on a fixed amount of money. A $1000 bond entitles the person to $1000 when the bond matures. In addition, each bond pays to the holder a fixed amount of money each year as an interest payment on the funds the household has tied up in the bond (has put in the bank). The rate of return that the bond buyer earns depends on the price paid for the bond.

Suppose a particular $1000 bond (one that pays $1000 at maturity) pays $50 each year as interest, or 5 percent of $1000. If other bonds are earning 10 percent for their owners, a buyer would not be willing to pay $1000 for this bond that pays only $50 a year interest. If the price of the bond were $500, the $50 would represent a 10 percent rate of return.[2] Thus the $1000 bond would sell for only $500. The price of the bond must fall below its face value (the amount it pays at maturity) in order to bring the rate of return on the bond up to the rate of return earned on other bonds. For any given face value and interest payment each year, the higher the price paid for the bond the lower will be the rate of return the fixed interest payment represents. Throughout this text, the *rate of interest* is the rate that is determined by the supply and demand for bonds. The supply and demand for bonds determine the market-clearing price of bonds and therefore also the equilibrium interest rate. There are no chapters devoted exclusively to the bond market. Its role in macro theory is made explicit in conjunction with the other markets.

The *labor market* refers to the supply of and demand for all types of labor time lumped together. The *wage rate* that is referred to in the text is the price of this imaginary homogeneous labor. It is determined by the interaction of the buyers of labor time (firms and government) and the sellers of labor time (households). The labor market is fully discussed in Chapter 7.

The *money market* refers to the supply of and the demand for the actual things that serve as media of exchange. A *medium of exchange* is something that sellers accept in payment from buyers of what they sell and then in turn use to pay for what they buy. In the United States that is currency and coins and checking account deposits. (We will see later why credit cards are not included.) When you buy something, either currency passes from you to the seller, or a checking account credit goes from your account to his or her account. In turn, the seller uses the currency or checking account credit to pay for his or her purchases. The money market is fully developed in Chapters 8 and 9.

In Chapter 3 we will see that interaction between individual markets is crucial to an understanding of the determination of all economic magnitudes. In Chapters 10 through 12 we will see how interaction between the four highly aggregated macro markets is carried out to determine such things as the average level of prices and wages, the interest rate, employment, and unemployment.

1-5 THE NATURE AND ROLE OF THEORY

It may seem silly to lump together all the diverse kinds of labor services that are bought and sold in the real world and analyze only one supply and one demand for this aggregate—or to lump together all the various kinds of financial securities or all the various kinds of goods and services that are produced. By doing this much aggregation we lose a lot of detailed information. Then why do we do it?

The justification for any approach in economic theory is that it works. That is, an analytical approach is good if it answers the questions that the investigator wants answered and if those answers are corroborated by real world experience. The approach is not good if it fails to give answers to the questions of concern or if the answers given are inconsistent with real world observation.

The facts of experience are simply too numerous and too complex to organize themselves. We cannot understand the United States economy, for example, simply by recording and observing what happens in it over time. We need an organizing framework within which the facts we observe and the relationships between those facts can be understood. We call that organizing framework economic theory. Any theory necessarily is abstract—that is, it ignores some details of reality. A road map is abstract because it doesn't tell you the location of every house and tree on the landscape; it ignores those details and focuses on the more important (to travelers) characteristics of the landscape, namely the paths followed by roads.

In macroeconomics our organizing framework consists primarily of the four macro markets outlined above. The high level of aggregation is an abstraction from reality. Whether this organizing framework is a good one depends on how well it works. Does it help us better to understand the two main macroeconomic maladies—inflation and too high unemployment rates? Is our understanding consistent with real world experience? In the next chapter we begin the inquiry that will answer these questions.

NOTES

1. The chart records the average price level on a "ratio scale." This type of scale is compressed as it goes up so that if the average increases at a constant percentge rate, the line that keeps track of the average is a straight line. If the scale were not compressed, a constant percentage growth rate would cause the line to get steeper and steeper; 10 percent, for example, of a number that gets bigger and bigger, itself gets bigger.

2. Actually, if the price of the bond were $500, the rate of return would be slightly higher than 10 percent because when the bond matures, there would be a $500 capital gain (the maturity value is $1000 and the person paid only $500 for it). That capital gain would have to be apportioned over each year the bond is held to get the actual rate of return.

$$c = \text{coupon rate}$$

$$r = \frac{c \cdot F + \frac{F - pb}{m}}{pb}$$

$$m = \text{number of years this matures}$$

$$F = 1000$$
$$pb = 500$$

$$\frac{60 + \frac{1000 - 500}{10}}{500}$$

$$\frac{60 + 50}{500} = \frac{110}{500}$$

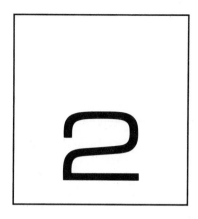

National Income Accounting
and Price Indices

Since the basic aggregate of concern in the commodities market is total income, or gross national product (GNP), the first task to which we must turn is national income accounting. What is GNP, and how does the Department of Commerce generate the number that it calls GNP for any given year?

In this chapter we will also discuss how the total dollar amount of economic activity that occurs in some time period (e.g., a year) is divided into "real" and "price" magnitudes. Is $1000 of economic activity the result of producing four real things that cost an average of $250 each, or the result of producing 100 real things that cost an average of $10 each? We will discuss the two main price indices that are used to answer such questions.

2-1 WHAT IS GNP?

Gross National Product (GNP) is defined as the dollar value of all final goods and services newly produced during a calendar year. We specify a calendar year because GNP is a *flow variable,* involving so many dollars *per unit of time.* If we say that the U.S. GNP for 1978 was $2 trillion, we mean that $2 trillion worth of new final goods and services were produced in 1978. If GNP became $2.2 trillion in 1979, that would mean $2.2 trillion worth of new final goods and services were produced in 1979. A *stock variable,* on the other hand, lacks any time dimension. If I say that I now own five sport coats, I don't have to specify in what time period I own them in order to convey an accurate impression of my current supply of sport coats. I don't say that I own five sport coats per year. If I state that my income is $5, nobody can know how well off I am until I specify the relevant time period. If I make $5 a minute I am better off than if I make $5 a year. Thus it is clear that income, like GNP, is a flow variable.

A *final good* is any good that is in the hands of its ultimate user or consumer. Suppose a farmer produces some wheat and sells it for 10¢ to a miller. The miller then grinds the wheat into flour and sells it for 20¢. The miller's activity has added 10¢ of value to the wheat. The baker who buys the flour bakes bread and sells it to a retailer for 35¢. The value added by the baker is 15¢. The retailer then sells the bread to a customer for 40¢, adding 5¢ of value to the baker's bread. (Table 2-1 summarizes these transactions.) This 40¢ is the dollar value of the final product, and this whole production sequence adds only 40¢ to GNP. We do not add together the dollar value of the wheat, the flour, the baker's bread, and the retailer's bread when we compute GNP because these are intermediate goods; not final goods. An *intermediate good* is something that is produced and fully used up in the production of some other good during the accounting period. By counting only the final good we add together the value added at each stage of production.

THE PRODUCTION STATEMENT

Each firm in the economy has an income statement for a year's activity. The right-hand side (RHS) of the statement lists all sales made during the year—to households, firms, governments, and foreigners. The left-hand side (LHS) of the statement lists the costs of goods that are sold. This side also includes indirect business taxes, such as sales taxes or business property taxes, collected by the government from the firm. The amount by which sales exceed the cost of goods sold is called *profit* (or *loss*).

The income statement can be changed into a *production statement* by adding to the sales on the RHS the products that were not sold but were added to inventories. On the LHS the figures for the cost of goods sold must be adjusted upward to include the cost of producing those goods added to inventories. The

Table 2-1   Calculation of value added

Agent	Value Added	Selling Price
Farmer	10¢	10¢
Miller	10¢	20¢
Baker	15¢	35¢
Retailer	5¢	40¢
Total	40¢ = cost to consumer	

resulting statement will look like Table 2-2, a production statement for a typical firm in the economy.

This statement is meant to be perfectly general in the sense that any expense incurred by a firm can be put into one of the categories on the LHS. In the case of a partnership or proprietorship, profit is simply income to the owners of the firm. If the firm is a corporation, however, profit must be divided into three subcategories: corporate profits tax, retained earnings, and dividends. Corporate profits tax is always a fixed percentage of earned profit. A maximum of 46 percent of corporation profits is taxed away by the federal government, and most states also impose a tax on corporation profits. Corporations retain a portion of what is left after taxes for growth purposes; this is called retained earnings. The remaining profit is given out to stockholders as dividends.

Imagine adding together the production statements of *all* firms in the U.S. economy, regardless of whether the firm produces intermediate goods or final goods. The result, with hypothetical numbers, is pictured in Table 2-3. It is called a *consolidated production statement*.

ELIMINATING DOUBLE COUNTING

In Table 2-1 the baker's bread represents "raw materials and supplies" sold to the retailer for 35¢. This 35¢, however, is also the sum of the value added at each stage of production up to the final (retail) stage. Wages, salaries, and other expenses paid by the farmer, plus a profit, equal the 10¢ of value added by the farmer. The expenses (except for the wheat) plus profit of the miller equal the

Table 2-2   Production statement for any firm

Costs of Production	Production
Wages and salaries	Sales
Rent	To households
Interest	To firms
Raw materials and supplies	To governments
Services	To foreigners
Indirect taxes	Changes in inventory (production
Depreciation	minus sales)
Profit	
Corporate profits tax	
Retained earnings	
Dividends	

**Table 2-3 Consolidated production statement
(in billions of dollars)**

Costs of Production		Production	
Wages and salaries	$1100	Sales	
Rent	160	To individuals	
Interest	190	New housing	$ 54
Raw materials and		All other	835
supplies purchased			
From U.S. firms	480	To U.S. private firms	
From foreigners	50	Services	96
Services purchased		Raw materials and supplies	415
From U.S. firms	120	Plant and equipment	370
From foreigners	15		
Indirect taxes	150	To government firms	
Depreciation	58	Services	24
Profit	225	Raw materials and supplies	65
		Plant and equipment	92
		To general government	
		(all levels)	242
		To foreigners	140
		Changes in inventory	215
Total	$2548	Total	$2548

Omit to avoid double counting

10¢ of value added by the miller. The expenses (except the flour) and profit of the baker equal the 15¢ of value added by the baker. Since the consolidated production statement includes *all* firms (the farmer, the miller, the baker), the *total* figure for wages and salaries, other expenses, and profit includes the 35¢ of wages and salaries, other expenses, and profit generated by the production of the "raw materials" sold for 35¢ to the retailer.

In a production statement we want to count only the value added at each stage of production. We do this by looking at the wages and salaries, other expenses, and profit figures. The figures that are explicitly labeled "raw materials and supplies" must be eliminated if we want to find out what GNP is.

In Table 2-3 the entry on the LHS of $480 billion in raw materials and supplies bought from U.S. firms corresponds to the entries on the RHS of sales of $415 billion in raw materials and supplies to U.S. private firms and of $65 billion to U.S. government firms. These entries are actually counted *twice on each side.* On the LHS they appear directly as themselves and are also incorporated in the figures for wages and salaries, rent, interest, and profit. On the RHS the entries for raw materials and supplies are counted once as such and once included in the value of sales of final products such as new houses to individuals, plant and equipment to private and government firms, and loaves of bread to households (the "all other" category). To eliminate this double counting, we eliminate the explicit entries for sales of raw materials and supplies to U.S. private firms and to government firms. Since entries that total $480 billion have been eliminated from both sides, the LHS still equals the RHS.

The same double counting elimination process can be carried out for services (such as insurance), which also appear twice on each side of the statement. These services are intermediate products; they are sold in the current accounting period and are used up by firms who are producing something else. For instance, the miller's flour and the baker's fire insurance are both inputs into the manufacture of the bread. The insurance company is one of the firms included in the consolidated production statement; its wages and salaries, other expenses, and profit come from its sales of insurance. Thus on the LHS this insurance service appears as services bought from U.S. firms and is also embodied in the figures for wages and salaries, other expenses, and profit. On the RHS the services appear as such and are also embodied in the final products. The entries for these services on both the LHS and the RHS are eliminated. Since these entries equal each other, the LHS still equals the RHS.

Finally we must eliminate the entries on the LHS for raw materials and supplies and services purchased from foreigners. Although they appear only once, we don't want to count them at all, because GNP is a measure of U.S. economic activity only. On the RHS these foreign raw materials and supplies and services are counted just once—in the dollar prices of the final products of U.S. firms. Again we don't wish to count them. We shall therefore make a new entry on the RHS for imports of intermediate products and give it a negative numerical value equal to the positive value of the entries eliminated on the LHS. The resulting statement (as in the hypothetical example presented in Table 2-4) is an account of the value added *by the business sector.*

On the RHS in Table 2-4 the only entries remaining under sales by U.S. firms to other U.S. firms (whether private or government-owned) are sales of plant and equipment. To avoid double counting, we have eliminated $530 billion of raw materials and supplies and $135 billion in services from the LHS (the numbers in italics in Table 2-3). On the RHS, reductions in sales to U.S. private firms were $511 billion; to government, $89 billion (again, the numbers in italics in Table 2-3); and to foreigners, $65 billion (the negative entry in Table 2-4). The totals of both the RHS and LHS of Table 2-3 were reduced by $665 billion, leaving $1883 billion on both sides of Table 2-4.

ACCOUNTING FOR ADDITIONAL SERVICES

We have not yet arrived at a number that we can call U.S. GNP. One omission is the services that individuals sell to other individuals. A piano teacher, for example, sells music services to interested persons, and a landlord sells housing

**Table 2-4   Value added by business sector
(in billions of dollars)**

Income Generated by Production		Production	
Wages and salaries	$1100	Sales by U.S. firms	
Rent	160	To individuals	
Interest	190	New housing	$ 54
Indirect taxes	150	All other	835
Depreciation	58	To U.S. private firms	
Profit	225	Plant and equipment	370
		To government firms	
		Plant and equipment	92
		To general government	242
		To foreigners	140
		Imports of intermediate	
		products	−65
		Changes in inventory	215
Total	$1883	Total	$1883

services to tenants. So far we have not taken this into account because the piano teacher and some landlords are not considered business firms. If we want to change the statement of value added by the business sector into a statement of total value added, we must include the services of individuals such as the piano teacher and the landlord. We must also include the value of housing services consumed in owner-occupied housing. This is determined by estimating the rental income the owners of such houses would receive if they rented them out to others. Wages and salaries on the LHS must be increased to account for the piano teacher's fee, and on the RHS sales to individuals of "all other" must be increased by the same amount. The rent paid and the rental value of owner-occupied houses would increase the figure for rent on the LHS and the figure for "all other" on the RHS.

Individuals also sell services to government; in fact, this represents the largest part of "general government" expenditures. These are the salaries of all government employees from the President to the faculty and staff at a public university. "Wages and salaries" on the LHS and "general government" on the RHS must be increased to reflect these services.

Individuals also sell to foreigners. The fee for an economist hired as a consultant by a foreign government, for example, would have to be added to wages and salaries on the LHS; sales to foreigners on the RHS would be increased by an equal amount. Returns earned on investments by Americans abroad would

Table 2-5   Total value added or GNP statement
(in billions of dollars)

Income Earned by U.S. Factors		Production	
Wages and salaries	$1312	Sales	
Rent	170	To individuals	
Interest	200	New housing	$ 54
Indirect taxes	150	All other	852
Depreciation	58	To U.S. private firms	
Profit	225	Plant and equipment	370
		To government firms	
		Plant and equipment	92
		To general government	442
		To foreigners	155
		Imports of intermediate	
		products	−65
		Changes in inventory	215
Total	$2115	Total	$2115

increase interest on the LHS and sales to foreigners (of the services of capital) on the RHS.

Table 2-5 presents our total GNP or total value added. Using hypothetical numbers we can easily show the differences between Tables 2-4 and 2-5. Assume that wages and salaries of government employees are $200 billion, transactions in the private sector between households are $17 billion (e.g., piano lessons and housing rentals), while sales by individuals to foreigners are $15 billion (e.g., consulting fees and capital services). The RHS of Table 2-4 would be increased by $232 billion. The LHS would then be increased by a corresponding amount. In our example wages and salaries would increase by $212 billion ($200 billion for government employees plus $7 billion for the wage portion of interhousehold services plus $5 billion for the consulting fees portion of sales to foreigners), rents by $10 billion, and interest (from sale of capital services to foreigners) by $10 billion. When all of these additions have been made, we have a total value added, or GNP, statement as illustrated in Table 2-5.

Conceptually, we are done, and we say that GNP is $2.115 trillion. Although the steps we have taken are those that should logically be taken in order to discover what GNP is, the resulting number is still only an approximation. The only goods and services we have counted are those that are bought and sold in the marketplace or, in the case of the rental value of owner-occupied houses, for which market values are imputed. The services of housewives have been omitted, as have projects carried on by weekend do-it-yourselfers, although these are newly produced final goods and services and should be counted. We have also eliminated illegal goods and services, although these are as useful to those who purchase them as are legal goods and services and should be included if we want a truly inclusive measure of newly produced final goods and services. However, the services of housewives and do-it-yourselfers are difficult to measure, and illegal goods and services are not reported.

2-2 CATEGORIES OF EXPENDITURE

We must now find out how the U.S. Department of Commerce actually goes about generating the number it reports as GNP. The approach is simply to add together data of the types that appear on the RHS of our conceptual statement. The department uses the following categories of expenditure:

- *Consumption expenditures (C)* include all expenditures by individuals (or households) except purchases of new houses.

- *Investment expenditures (I_A)* are purchases of new houses, expenditures by private firms on plant and equipment, and changes in inventories held by private firms. The subscript A signifies that we are talking about *actual* investment expenditures. (In Chapter 4 we will use the letter I by itself to stand for *planned* investment expenditures as distinct from actual investment spending.)

- *Government expenditures (G)* include all general government expenditures, purchases of plant and equipment by government firms, and changes in inventories held by government firms. Government transfer payments—payments made to some people out of revenues received from others, which are not payments for goods or services—such as welfare payments are not included in G.

- *Net foreign expenditures ($X - M$)* are the difference between sales to foreigners and purchases from foreigners, or exports (X) minus imports (M).

The data collected for C, I_A, and G include expenditures on final products produced by foreigners. The entries in our conceptual GNP account include only expenditures on final products produced by U.S. firms. The data used by the Department of Commerce will therefore be overstated. This does not present a problem as long as we can find a separate account of imports of final products.

Such information is available from the balance of payments accounts; all we must do is deduct the figures for imports of final products from the sum of C, I_A, and G reported by the Department of Commerce, and we will have a total that corresponds to the $2.115 trillion in our conceptual GNP statement. In other words, to correct for the overstated figures for consumption (C), investment (I_A), and government expenditures (G), we increase the M portion of net foreign expenditures by the amount of the overstatement of C, I_A, and G. GNP data as well as data on many other variables can be found in *Business Statistics* and *Survey of Current Business*, two publications of the Department of Commerce.

2-3 THE NATIONAL INCOME ACCOUNTING IDENTITY

We have seen that the entries on the RHS of the GNP statement can be labeled either C, I_A, G, X, or M. The entries on the LHS can be labeled either disposable income (Y_d), business saving (S_b), or taxes (T).[1] Wages and salaries, rents, and interest are income received by individuals; a part of this income is retained and can be used however the individual wishes—this is Y_d. The other part, T, is taxed away. Indirect taxes are part of T, depreciation is part of S_b, and profit of non-corporations is either Y_d or T for their owners. The portion of corporation profit that is taxes is T; the portion that is held as retained earnings is S_b; and the portion that is distributed as dividends is either Y_d or T to the stockholders.

Since the RHS of the GNP statement is always equal to the LHS,

$$Y_d + S_b + T \equiv C + I_A + G + (X - M) \qquad (2\text{-}1)$$

The symbol $\equiv$ means that the right-hand side and the left-hand side of the relationship must always be equal. They are merely different expressions for the same thing, GNP. The sum of consumption, investment, government expenditures, and net foreign expenditures we can label as total expenditures. These expenditures must, from our equality, generate an equal amount of income.

We can illustrate this equality using Figure 2-1. Expenditures, $C + I_A + G + (X - M)$, are measured on the vertical axis, while income, $Y_d + S_b + T$, is measured on the horizontal axis. The 45° line depicts the equality between income and expenditures. Since expenditures, measured by the distance OA, must equal income, OB, point C is located on the 45° line.

We have illustrated, both mathematically and graphically, the basic national income accounting identity. Expenditures must result in an equal amount of income. In Chapter 4 we will use this identity to develop the Keynesian cross diagram, with which we can identify and define the equilibrium values of all these variables.

*Aggregate
expenditures*

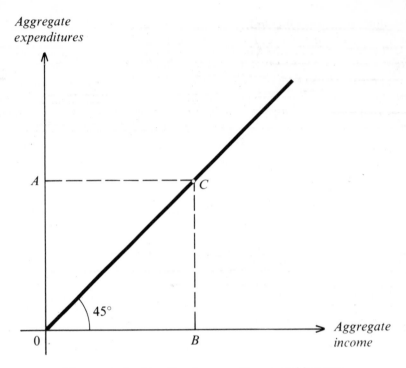

Figure 2-1 Identity of expenditures and income.

2-4 PRICE INDICES AND THEIR BIASES

The second aggregate variable, after GNP, that must be defined is the price level. In fact, there is no such thing as "the price level"—all we have is a weighted average of literally millions of individual prices. The two weighted averages in most common use today are the consumer price index (CPI) and the GNP deflator.

All price indices are based on a comparison of the dollar cost of a particular collection of goods and services at one point in time with the dollar cost of the same collection of goods and services at another point in time. The ratio of these dollar amounts indicates the magnitude of price changes that have occurred over the time interval.

CONSUMER PRICE INDEX (CPI)

The CPI is formed by pricing a basket of representative goods and services. This "market basket," as it is called, is developed by statisticians at the Bureau of Labor Statistics (BLS) who sample family buying habits throughout the United States. From expenditure surveys, the BLS picks a collection of goods and services that represents the way a typical household spends its money. It then sends out representatives to stores and service establishments to see what prices are charged for the items in the market basket. The cost of the market basket in the year of the sample (the base year) is the basis of all subsequent calculations. At a later date, say year t, representatives of the BLS again go out to stores and service establishments and see what prices are *then* being charged for the items in the market basket. The CPI is then formed as a ratio of the cost of the market basket in year t to the cost of the same market basket in the base year.

$$\text{CPI}_{(\text{for year } t)} = \frac{\text{Cost of market basket in year } t}{\text{Cost of market basket in base year}} \times 100 \qquad (2\text{-}2)$$

The ratio is multiplied by 100 to put the index in percentage terms. If the CPI for a given date were 157, for example, the dollar cost of the market basket for that date would be 157 percent of what the cost of the same basket was in the base year. In other words, prices at the later date were, on the average, 57 percent higher than they were in the base period.

We can illustrate these calculations with an example. To keep the illustration simple, we assume that the market basket consists of three goods: pens, milk, and meat. The quantities of each good in the basket and the prices in the base and current years are listed in Table 2-6.

Using these figures, the CPI is calculated as:

$$\text{CPI} = \frac{(5 \times \$.60) + (15 \times \$.45) + (25 \times \$2.50)}{(5 \times \$.50) + (15 \times \$.40) + (25 \times \$1.50)} = \frac{\$72.25}{\$46.00} \times 100 = 157$$

Table 2-6 Prices and quantities for CPI calculation

Good	Quantity	Base Price	Current Price
Pens	5	$ .50	$ .60
Milk	15	$ .40	$ .45
Meat	25	$1.50	$2.50

This basket costs 57 percent more in the current year than it did in the base year. Notice that the CPI is a weighted average of individual price changes. The price of pens increased 20 percent, of milk, 12.5 percent, and of meat, 66.7 percent, while the index rose 57 percent. Obviously, the index is sensitive to the relative quantities in the basket as well as to the relative prices. Meat was the largest component dollar-wise in our basket, and the percentage change in the cost of the basket was pulled up by this item.

In January 1978, the BLS created two new CPIs. Prior to this there was one consumer price index. The new indices are the CPI for all urban consumers, an index representing about 80 percent of the noninstitutional civilian population, and the revised CPI for urban wage earners and clerical workers. Each of these new indices contains different baskets of goods and may very well reflect different general price increases. Changes in either of the CPI measures will affect the income levels of millions of people. Many labor unions have cost of living adjustments built into their contracts. Social Security payments (affecting 34 million people), school lunch programs (affecting 25 million people), food stamp payments (affecting 16.7 million people) also are tied to the CPI.[2] The CPI is a very important statistic.

It is apparent that the CPI is deficient as a measure of changes in the "cost of living" because it assumes that the basket of the base year represents the way people live and spend their money in the later year. But individuals may be buying items today that didn't exist last year, and the quality of today's products is likely to be higher than the quality of the same products in earlier years. For instance, while buyers may pay more for a 1981 car than they did for a 1971 car, they presumably get more for their money. A 1971 automatic washing machine was somewhat less automatic than a 1981 washing machine. Thus the CPI is likely to have an upward bias.

Another major reason for this bias is that the index ignores substitution effects. When we say we want to compare the cost of living in two time periods, what we really want to do is to compare the costs of attaining a given level of satisfaction in those two time periods. Using our example, the cost of meat has risen *relative to* the cost of pens and milk. Consumers will change their consumption patterns as relative prices change. They willingly do so in order to attain the highest possible levels of satisfaction. Persons whose income rose 57 percent from the base year to the current year could still purchase the same basket of goods. They will not do so, however, because relative prices have changed. They will consume less meat and more milk and pens because the latter goods have become relatively less expensive. Thus the 57 percent change in prices overstates the increased cost of acquiring the same level of satisfaction in the current year. Because of the method of calculating the CPI, pricing a basket of goods in the base year and the same basket in the current year, the index will overstate inflation.

THE GNP DEFLATOR

All goods and services that are counted in GNP in a given time period (called time period t for convenience) are priced in that same time period. That is, the current dollar amount for GNP is calculated in the manner described in the first section of this chapter—by determining total value added in period t dollars. This is called *nominal* or *money GNP* for period t. Next, the same goods and services that are included in period t's nominal GNP are priced according to the prices that existed for them in some earlier (base) year. The currently used base year for the calculations is 1972. The technique used by the Bureau of Labor Statistics to get period t's goods and services expressed in 1972 prices is the following:

1. Put all goods and services counted in GNP into categories such as machinery, fuels, and textiles.
2. Calculate a price index (similar to the CPI but using 1972 as the base year) for each of these categories of goods and services.
3. Divide the current (period t) dollar amount in each category by the corresponding index.
4. Add the resulting inflation-corrected dollar amounts. The sum is called *real GNP*. It is merely current GNP expressed in base year dollar amounts.

The GNP deflator for period t is calculated by dividing nominal GNP for period t by real GNP for period t. If P is the GNP deflator, then

$$P = \frac{\text{nominal GNP for period } t}{\text{real GNP for period } t} = \frac{Y}{Q} \qquad (2\text{-}3)$$

where Q is real GNP. Note that P is *not* used to calculate Q. We have to know Q before we can calculate P.

Current GNP in base year dollars is "real" because if the value of Q in 1982 is different from the value of Q in 1981, all of the difference must be ascribed to changes in the actual output of real goods and services. After all, both the 1982 and the 1981 figures are in terms of 1972 prices. None of the change can arise, therefore, from prices. It all has to arise from different physical amounts of output.

As you can see, there is a fundamental difference between the CPI and the GNP deflator. The quantities used as weights in the CPI are *base year* quantities, and those used in the GNP deflator are *current year* quantities.

We saw that the CPI will overstate any inflation because it ignores substitution. The GNP deflator *understates* any inflation becaute it too ignores substitution. Goods that were produced in a certain proportion in 1980 were purchased and consumed based upon 1980 relative prices, which are different from the relative prices that existed earlier. If a basket of goods produced and consumed this year was $150, and the cost of the same basket last year was $125, it costs 20 percent more this year. But consumers would not have bought the same mix of goods and services in the previous year. They would have substituted goods that were less expensive (relative to the current year). Thus the dollar cost of what would actually have been bought would be lower than the dollar cost of what the index assumes people bought. Thus the GNP deflator will not measure all of the increase in expenditure actually called for between last year and this year. The GNP deflator underestimates any change in the cost of living. The true rate of inflation lies somewhere between the rates indicated by the CPI and the GNP deflator. The annual rate of change of prices in 1978 as indicated by the CPI was 9.4 percent, while that indicated by the GNP deflator was just 7.1 percent.

2-5   REAL AND NOMINAL VALUES: AN INTRODUCTION

The dollar value of GNP consists of two components: the actual goods produced and the prices of each of the goods. The general vigor of the economy is not well measured by changes in the dollar value of GNP. If the dollar value of GNP were to increase by 10 percent in any one year, this change could be the result of any of the following:

- 10 percent rise in output and no rise in prices
- 10 percent rise in prices and no rise in output
- 15 percent rise in prices and 5 percent fall in output

Actually, an infinite number of combinations are possible, and we as consumers may prefer some of these possibilities to others. The President, Congress, and the Federal Reserve Board are concerned with both output changes and price changes. Sustained increases in prices are called inflation, and decreases in real output often imply increases in unemployment. From the fourth quarter of 1973 to the first quarter of 1975 the U.S. economy experienced its most severe and protracted decline since the 1930s. Profits declined, inventories rose, and the unemployment rate exceeded 9 percent. Industrial production declined at an annual rate of 11.2 percent; real GNP, the output of goods and services in the economy, declined at an annual rate of 5.3 percent. Yet, during the same period the dollar value of GNP *rose* at an annual rate of 5.3 percent. Obviously, prices were rising so rapidly that a decline in real output was accompanied by increases in dollar expenditures on that output. Which figure was the more accurate representation of the health of the economy, a 5.3 percent rise in nominal GNP or a 5.3 percent fall in real GNP?

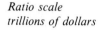

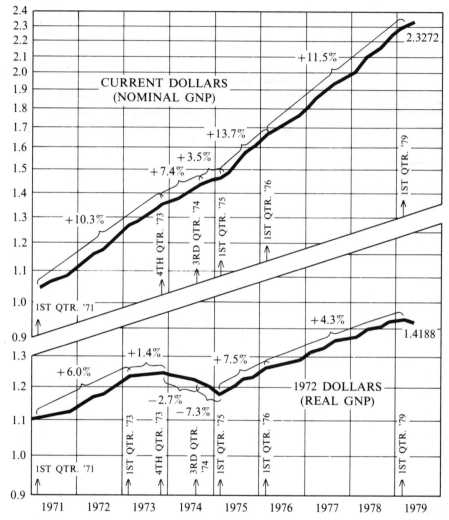

Figure 2-2 Gross national product for 1971–79 in current dollars and in 1972 dollars. (Prepared by Federal Reserve Bank of St. Louis, "National Economic Trends," July 31, 1979, p. 13)

Figure 2-2 presents, from 1971 to 1979, the two GNP time series that we have been discussing. GNP in current dollars measures the dollar value of GNP in each of the years. GNP measured in 1972 dollars reflects only the increase in output, not prices, in the same period. (If GNP, in dollars of 1972 purchasing power, is $1.2 trillion one year and $1.5 trillion the next year, the total quantity of real goods and services *had* to increase. More can be bought with 1.5 trillion 1972 dollars than with 1.2 trillion 1972 dollars.) The two series present different pictures. Nominal GNP has been rising very steadily throughout the period. Real GNP has had its ups and downs and presents a much clearer picture of the state of the economy. We can clearly see the expansion of real economic activity from the beginning of 1971 to the beginning of 1973, a decline (which many have called the worst decline since the 1930s) from the first quarter of 1973 to the first quarter of 1975, followed by an expansion that lasted into 1979. In the second quarter of 1979 the economy began another decline in real GNP. Just as in Figure 1-1, the percentage numbers associated with the various bracketed time periods are all *annual* rates of change.

SUMMARY

In this chapter we have defined and explained three important macroeconomic variables—total income, the average price level, and real income—which will be used over and over in the text. Total income is the current dollar value of all productive activity within a specified time period. The average price level is the ratio of what goods and services cost today to what those goods and services cost in some earlier time period (the base year). We can think of goods and services actually purchased in the base year (the CPI), or goods and services actually purchased in the current year (the GNP deflator). Both indices have shortcomings, but in our further analyses we will rely on the GNP deflator because it is more inclusive than the CPI. Real income is defined as total income adjusted for price changes. This is the best guide to such current economic conditions as total production and employment.

QUESTIONS

1. If we were to calculate the cost of a basket of goods in the United States and then calculate the cost of the same basket in Japan, would a comparison of the two costs be an accurate representation of the relative cost of living in these two countries?

2. Demonstrate that services (such as insurance) are counted twice on each side of the consolidated production statement. Construct a numerical example.

3. The national income accounting identity says that supply creates its own demand. Do you agree or disagree? Why?
4. The sale of intermediate goods is not included in GNP. Does this mean that the salaries paid to workers employed in the production of these goods is also not included in GNP?
5. If a used car dealer buys a used car for $500 and sells it for $800, what part of this transaction is included in GNP? In what categories of GNP would these transactions be included?
6. If the CPI was 205.1 (1967 = 100) in January 1979 and 187.5 in January 1978, what was the rate of inflation (as measured by the CPI) during that period?
7. If a corporation sells new shares of stock to the public, is this transaction included in GNP? If so, where?

NOTES

1. In our use of the term "disposable income," we are including only income payments included in GNP; we are ignoring government transfer payments.
2. Numbers taken from "The Consumer Price Index" by Brian Richey, *Texas Business Review* (October 1978), p. 1.

Say's Principle

With this chapter we begin our discussion of macroeconomic theory per se. The main message of the chapter is that it is not legitimate, for the purposes usually pursued in macroeconomics, to analyze only one market at a time. All markets, whether viewed from a macro or micro perspective, affect and are affected by other markets. These necessary (logical) links between markets provide us with the organizing framework for all macroeconomic theory. They are based on a simple proposition that has been called Say's Principle (SP).[1] To quote Axel Leijonhufvud, a generally recognized authority on SP, "This principle, though elementary and outwardly trivial, is crucial for clear understanding of macro-theory. Indeed, there is hardly a single problem in macro-theory (or, for that matter, in micro-theory) that can be consistently analyzed without it. . . . It is essential, therefore, that students acquire a clear understanding not only of what SP means and does not mean, but also of what it implies and does not imply."[2]

3-1 WHAT THE PRINCIPLE IS ALL ABOUT

If we assume that no transactors (independent decision-making units such as households, firms, and individuals) are either thieves or philanthropists, we can say that any transactor who plans to acquire some amount of any commodity or service must at the same time plan to supply some other commodity or service in exchange.

31

AN EXAMPLE OF THE EXCHANGE PROCESS

If you are not a thief, and if no one else is going to give you anything without receiving something in exchange, when you plan to acquire a pair of shoes you must at the same time plan how (or with what) you will pay for the shoes. (To be sure, some people steal and other people give things away. However, our goal is to build an analysis that will shed light on macroeconomic issues. We will do that by focusing on a particular, and pervasive, mode of human action: voluntary exchange.)

Let Δq_{shoes} be the difference between the quantity (number) of pairs of shoes you want to have (given what you must pay to get them) and the number of pairs of shoes you in fact have. If Δq_{shoes} is positive, that means you want to acquire additional pairs of shoes. If Δq_{shoes} is negative, that means you have more pairs of shoes than you want, and you are planning to supply the extra pairs (perhaps in a flea market) in exchange for some other commodity or service, such as money or records. If you have three pairs of shoes and, taking into consideration what you are able and willing to pay to get more, you want to have five pairs of shoes, Δq_{shoes} would be $5 - 3 = 2$. Economists would say that you have a *positive planned excess demand* for shoes. On the other hand, if you already have ten pairs of shoes (a couple of which you have not worn), and, taking into consideration what you can obtain for them, you decide you want only eight pairs of shoes, Δq_{shoes} would be $8 - 10 = -2$. In this case economists would say that you have what is called either *negative planned excess demand* for shoes or a *positive planned excess supply* of shoes. These are merely two ways of saying the same thing: you have more shoes than you plan to keep; but since you don't give things away, you are planning to offer the excess in exchange for something else.

Of course, the purchase and sale plans that a transactor makes at any time depend on the prices for the goods that are to be traded. Movements of the prices of all the individual goods induce people to alter their purchase and sale plans until the plans of any one transactor are consistent with the plans of all other transactors. In other words, it is movements of prices that coordinate the plans and actions of all the independent transactors.

Suppose that you have a positive planned excess demand for shoes. At existing prices you are planning to acquire more pairs of shoes; but you are not a thief and so you must also plan to give up something in exchange for the shoes. Moreover, you must plan to give up a sufficient amount of some thing (or things) to pay for the shoes. Perhaps you are planning to give up some of your leisure time so that you can work and get paid enough to acquire the shoes. Perhaps you are planning to work directly for the shoes (e.g., you are planning to do the shoe supplier's gardening in direct exchange for the shoes). In either case you need to know what quantity of your time is necessary to pay for the additional shoes.

TWO ROLES FOR MONEY

In every modern economy there is something that serves as a *medium of exchange* and as a *numeraire.* What we call money serves both purposes. Money is a medium of exchange because it is accepted by those who sell things and is later used by those sellers to pay for what they would like to acquire. It is *intermediary* between the act of selling something and purchasing something else. Money is a numeraire because the market value of each and every good (whether commodity or service) is expressed as a number of (say) dollars that must be given up to acquire the good. We can calculate how many hours of your time must be given up to get a pair of shoes precisely because we can observe the money price of each hour of your time and the money price of each pair of shoes. Money is the basic unit of account. (Just imagine the chaos that would result if there were no prices expressed in terms of a general unit of account. How could people calculate exchange equivalents and make plans on the basis of those equivalents?)

Since in our analysis no transactor is a thief or a philanthropist, when transactor A has a positive planned excess demand for any good, A must at the same time have a positive planned excess supply of some thing (or things). Moreover, the money value of the positive planned excess demand must be identical to the money value of the planned excess supply. Let p_{time} be the money value (price) of an hour of A's time (the wage rate), and let p_{tv} be the money value (price) of a television set. If A has a positive planned excess demand for two television sets, and if A is planning to sell labor time for money and then use the money to pay for the television sets, it must be the case that the dollar value of A's positive planned excess demand for television sets equals the dollar value of A's positive excess supply of labor time. If Δq_{tv} is the number of additional television sets desired by A, and if Δq_{time} is the number of hours A plans to work to pay for the television sets, then

$$p_{tv}\Delta q_{tv} = p_{time}\Delta q_{time}$$

The left-hand term, $p_{tv}\Delta q_{tv}$, is the planned use of funds, while the right-hand term, $p_{time}\Delta q_{time}$, is the planned source of funds. If there are no thieves and no philanthropists, for each transactor the sum of the planned uses of funds must be equal to the sum of the planned sources of funds.

Any transactor, such as A, could at any time be planning to acquire additional amounts of several goods. If so, A must, at the same time, be planning to supply enough of some other good or goods to raise enough funds to pay for all of the planned acquisitions.

SAY'S PRINCIPLE AT THE INDIVIDUAL TRANSACTOR LEVEL

Suppose there are n goods (including services as well as commodities) that can be exchanged in the economy. (If there are 2,098,456 exchangeable goods in the economy, then $n = 2,098,456$; if there are only 125 exchangeable goods in the economy, then $n = 125$. n can be any number you wish it to be.) Instead of giving these goods names, let's give them numbers. For example, the money price of the first good will be p_1, and the quantity of transactor A's planned excess supply (or demand) for the first good will be Δq_1; the money price of the second good will be p_2, and the quantity of A's planned excess supply (or demand) for the second good will be Δq_2; and so on. Since money exists and is exchanged from transactor to transactor, it must be one of the n goods. If we agree that money will be the last good in our list of goods (i.e., the nth good is money), then the quantity of A's planned excess supply (or excess demand) for money will be Δq_n, and the money price of money will be p_n. (Since the dollar price of a dollar is 1, $p_n = 1$.)

Let's say that transactor A is perfectly happy with the amount of most of the n goods A has. A plans neither to add to nor subtract from the amounts of these goods. However, A does plan to add to A's holdings of the third, the eighth, the ninth, and the twelfth goods. To pay for these acquisitions A plans to offer for sale some of the twentieth, the thirtieth, and the fifty-first goods. Then it must be the case that

$$\text{planned uses of funds} \quad = \quad \text{planned sources of funds}$$

$$p_3\Delta q_3 + p_8\Delta q_8 + p_9\Delta q_9 + p_{12}\Delta q_{12} = p_{20}\Delta q_{20} + p_{30}\Delta q_{30} + p_{51}\Delta q_{51}$$

The left-hand side (LHS) is the sum of the planned uses of funds (the sum of A's positive planned excess demands), and the right-hand side (RHS) is the sum of the planned sources of funds (the sum of A's positive planned excess supplies).

If now we bring the planned uses and source of funds together on the LHS of the equality, remembering that the positive excess supplies are negative excess demands, we get

$$p_3\Delta q_3 + p_8\Delta q_8 + p_9\Delta p_9 + p_{12}\Delta q_{12} + p_{20}\Delta q_{20} + p_{30}\Delta q_{30} + p_{51}\Delta q_{51} = 0$$

In words rather than symbols, *the sum of A's planned excess demands, taking positive and negative excess demands together, must be zero.*

The general symbolic representation of this proposition, which is Say's Principle at the individual transactor level, is

$$p_1\Delta q_1 + p_2\Delta q_2 + p_3\Delta q_3 + \cdots + p_n\Delta q_n = 0 \qquad (3\text{-}1)$$

This equation includes each of the n exchangeable goods in the economy, beginning with the first good and ending with the nth good (money). The three dots in the equation mean that all of the goods between the third good and the nth good are understood to be included in the equation. Such an equation can be written for every transactor. Of course, any particular Δq for any particular transactor could be zero. This would merely mean that the transactor is happy with the amount of that good he has—even if the amount is zero; in that case the transactor neither has any of the good nor wants any.

One of the n goods is IOUs. One way an individual can pay for planned acquisitions is to borrow the money. In this case we would say the person involved had a planned excess supply (negative excess demand) of IOUs. The person plans to sell IOUs (borrow the funds). Similarly, a corporation or a government could raise funds needed to finance planned purchases by selling IOUs. In this case the IOUs are called bonds. A bond is a piece of paper with a fixed "face value," usually $1000, printed on it. This face value is the amount of money that the issuer of the bond must pay to the holder of the bond at some specific date in the future when the bond matures. At maturity, then, the issuer of the bond buys it back from whoever holds it. So a corporation or government borrows funds by selling bonds and pays back the loan by buying the bond back.

When transactors save, they do not spend all of their receipts on ordinary goods and services. They can save by simply holding on to money, in which case the saving would show up in Equation 3-1 as a planned excess demand for money; or they can save by purchasing credits in bank passbooks or by purchasing bonds, in which case the saving would show up in Equation 3-1 as a planned excess demand for bonds. The "bond market" in macroeconomic theory includes the planned purchase and sale of all financial assets (stocks, bonds, IOUs, savings account credits) other than money itself.

SAY'S PRINCIPLE AT THE AGGREGATE LEVEL

There is an Equation 3-1 for every transactor in the economy. To derive SP at the aggregate level, we must consider all of these equations at once.[3] Suppose that there are k (as many as you like) transactors in the economy. There would be k equations like Equation 3-1—one equation for each transactor. In Figure 3-1 these k equations are put in rows. Each row refers to one transactor. For example, in the second row, $p_1\Delta q_{1,2}$ is the (money value of the) second transactor's planned excess demand for good 1; $p_2\Delta q_{2,2}$ is the second transactor's planned excess demand for good 2. Note that the subscript on q that comes before the comma refers to the good, and the subscript that comes after the comma refers to the transactor. Thus, for example, $p_2\Delta q_{2,k}$ is the kth transactor's planned excess demand for good 2. We know that the sum across any row must be zero, and that is indicated in the column headed "sum."

	Good 1	Good 2	$\cdots$	Good $_{n-1}$	Good n (money)	Sum
Transactor 1	$p_1\Delta q_{1,1}$ +	$p_2\Delta q_{2,1}$ +	$\cdots$ +	$p_{n-1}\Delta q_{n-1,1}$ +	$\Delta q_{n,1}$	= 0
Transactor 2	$p_1\Delta q_{1,2}$ +	$p_2\Delta q_{2,2}$ +	$\cdots$ +	$p_{n-1}\Delta q_{n-1,2}$ +	$\Delta q_{n,2}$	= 0
.	.	.		.	.	.
.	.	.		.	.	.
.	.	.		.	.	.
Transactor k	$p_1\Delta q_{1,k}$ +	$p_2\Delta q_{2,k}$ +	$\cdots$ +	$p_{n-1}\Delta q_{n-1,k}$ +	$\Delta q_{n,k}$	= 0
Market excess demands	$p_1 X_1$ +	$p_2 X_2$ +	$\cdots$ +	$p_{n-1}X_{n-1}$ +	X_n	= 0

Figure 3-1   Tabulation for deriving the aggregate version of Say's Principle.

Now let's add up the entries in the column for good 1. That is, let's add transactor 1's planned excess demand for good 1 to transactor 2's planned excess demand for good 1, and add that to transactor 3's planned excess demand for good 1, and so on. The result would be the aggregate or "market" planned excess demand for good 1. The planned market excess demand for good 1 is indicated in the bottom row as $p_1 X_1$. If we add up the entries in a column, the result will be the planned market excess demand for the good in that column. Thus $p_2 X_2$ is the planned market excess demand for good 2, $p_{n-1} X_{n-1}$ is the planned market excess demand for good $n - 1$, and X_n is the planned market excess demand for money. (p_n is omitted because it equals one.)

Any single planned market excess demand could be zero, positive, or negative. It is conceivable, for example, that all transactors are planning to acquire some of good 1, in which case the planned market excess demand for good 1 would be positive. Or, all transactors could be planning to reduce their holdings of good 1. In this case the planned market excess demand for good 1 would be negative. Or, some transactors could have a positive planned excess demand while others have a negative planned excess demand. On balance, the planned market excess demand could be positive, negative, or even zero. But what if we add up all the planned market excess demands? That is, what would we get if we added up the bottom row marked "market excess demands"? Clearly we must get zero, for we would in effect be adding all the zeros in the sum column.

Now we have Say's Principle at the aggregate level: *the sum of the planned market excess demands over all exchangeable goods including money must come to zero.* That means, for example, that if on balance there is a planned market excess supply of one of the goods (such as labor services), there must be a corresponding planned excess demand for some other good or combination of goods such that the total of the planned market excess demands (both positive and negative) is zero.

If households have a planned excess supply of labor services—i.e., if they plan to sell more labor services than firms plan to hire at the existing wage rate— they must also exhibit a planned excess demand for some other goods. The households would in effect be saying, "If we could sell all of the labor services we would like to sell at the prevailing wage rate, we would plan to use the proceeds of the sale to purchase other goods such as records, bread, cars, and refrigerators."

SAY'S PRINCIPLE AND GENERAL EQUILIBRIUM

The bottom row in Figure 3-1 depicts planned market excess demands. It must sum to zero, no matter what the individual money prices, p_1 through p_{n-1}, are. Say's Principle holds for *any* list of prices. When there is zero planned excess demand in every market, there is what economists call *general equilibrium* (GE). GE exists only if the list of money prices, p_1 through p_{n-1}, is exactly right—that is, only if the price in each market has the value that establishes equality between quantity demanded and quantity supplied.

Say's Principle, on the other hand, holds, no matter what the list of prices looks like. But we can see from Say's Principle that if one price is not at its GE value, there has to be at least one other price that is also not at its GE value. Specifically, if one price is above its GE value, there must be at least one other price that is below its GE value. The reason for this is that when a price is above its equilibrium value, there will be a planned market excess supply for that good. When there is a planned market excess supply of a good, there has to be a planned market excess demand for some other good to go with it. We get a planned market excess demand for a good when its price is below its equilibrium value.

Ordinarily we would expect the price of the good for which there is a planned market excess supply to fall and the price of the good for which there is a planned market excess demand to rise. The falling price will tend to eliminate the excess supply, and the increasing price will tend to eliminate the excess demand. Movements of prices tend to move each market into equilibrium. When all markets are in equilibrium—in other words, when there is GE—all of the separately made plans of the independent transactors can be carried out. There are no buyers who cannot buy all they want to of each good at existing prices for those goods. Moreover, all sellers can sell all they want to of each good at the existing prices for those goods. The economic activities of all of the independent transactors are fully coordinated. Price changes are the mechanism that establishes this coordination. When the price of a good goes up, some transactors respond by planning to purchase less of the good, and other transactors respond by planning to supply more of the good; hence a planned excess demand will diminish. When the price of a good goes down, some transactors respond by planning to purchase more of the good, and other transactors respond by planning to supply less of the good; hence a planned excess supply will diminish.

3-2 WHAT SAY'S PRINCIPLE MEANS AND DOES NOT MEAN

There is, as we just pointed out, a difference between Say's Principle and general equilibrium. The sum of the market planned excess demands of all exchangeable goods in an economy must be zero, no matter what list of prices happens to exist. It could be, for example, that the price for each good is different from the price that would establish equality between the quantity wanted and the quantity made available in its market. In no sense could this situation be called equilibrium. It is not general equilibrium; it is not overall equilibrium; it is not even partial equilibrium. Yet the *sum* of the market planned excess demands will be zero. Say's Principle simply has nothing to say about the extent of equilibrium in an economy.

Throughout Section 3-1 the term "planned" was used. Say's Principle is only about planned excess demands. It says nothing about effective or actual excess demands. If there is a market planned excess supply for labor services, for example, we know by SP that those households that would like to sell more labor services than they are now selling at the existing wage rate will have corresponding planned excess demands for those goods they would like to acquire more of than they now have. However, if these households are unable to find buyers of the additional labor services they would like to sell, and if the only source of purchasing power they have is the receipts from the current sale of labor services, they will not be able to execute their planned excess demands. They will not have, following the language of Leijonhufvud, *effective excess demands.*

SUPPLY CREATES ITS OWN DEMAND?

Sometimes Say's Principle is stated as the proposition that "supply creates its own demand." In a sense this is true, but in another sense it is false and misleading. It is true in the sense that whenever there is a planned excess supply of any good or goods there *must* be a planned excess demand for some other good or goods. The act of planning to supply can, if you like, be said to "create" plans to demand. It is clearer, however, to say that the act of planning to supply necessarily carries with it plans to demand. If people are neither thieves nor philanthropists, no one plans to supply anything without at the same time planning to acquire something else of equal market value.

If "supply creates its own demand" is taken to mean that the act of offering something for sale on the market creates an equal demand for that thing in the market, then SP clearly does not mean supply creates its own demand. There is no principle in all of economic theory that implies the supply of a good creates an equal demand for that same good.

Moreover, if "supply creates its own demand" is taken to mean that any actual offers to sell something in the market will result in actual equal demands for other goods, SP does not imply that supply creates its own demand. It is possible for any transactor to *plan* to sell something but find that those plans cannot be executed. If the sale plans cannot be executed, it is quite possible that the corresponding buy plans will not be carried out. Clearly, a planned supply does *not* necessarily create an equal *actual* demand for other goods.

AGGREGATE SUPPLY EQUALS AGGREGATE DEMAND?

Sometimes it is asserted that Say's Principle implies that aggregate supply equals aggregate demand. Here again, there is a sense in which this is true and a sense in which it is false. It is true in the sense that if we add together all of the positive market planned excess demands and call this "aggregate demand," this sum must equal the sum of all of the negative market planned excess demands, which we might call "aggregate supply." But the terms "aggregate demand" and "aggregate supply" are not used in these senses in the macroeconomic literature. *Aggregate demand* usually means the sum of all actual expenditures on newly produced final goods (the goods included in GNP), and *aggregate supply* usually refers to the quantity of those goods made available by sellers.

As we will see in the next chapter, when any final goods are not bought by customers of firms, those firms will "buy" them themselves by adding them to inventories; therefore, aggregate demand must equal aggregate supply. But Say's Principle is a statement about *planned* excess demands for *all* exchangeable goods, not just that subset of exchangeable goods called final goods and included in GNP. Say's Principle implies nothing about the supply and demand for final goods in isolation from all other goods. Furthermore, the fact that aggregate demand for final goods equals aggregate supply of final goods in the sense that what is not bought by buyers is "bought" by sellers implies nothing about overall equilibrium in the markets for final goods. It is merely a semantic convention with no operational content whatsoever.

3-3 SAY'S PRINCIPLE AND DEPRESSIONS

It is often suggested that economists, prior to the publication of John Maynard Keynes' *General Theory of Employment, Interest and Money* in 1936, were blinded by Say's Principle to the possibility of large-scale unemployment. After all, if one believes that supply creates its own demand, one must believe that it can never be the case that jobs can be *generally* hard to get. If the demand for some things declined, the demand for other things would expand.

In fact, there is absolutely nothing in Say's Principle that precludes unsold goods in most markets at the same time. Look back at Figure 3-1. Recall that the nth good is money. There is nothing to prevent negative planned market excess demand for thousands of goods other than money, providing that there are offsetting positive planned market excess demands for other goods. In particular, it could well be that the only good for which there is a positive planned market excess demand is money itself. Sellers could be planning to sell (and therefore producing) more than buyers are planning to purchase of all goods other than money. This would indicate merely that the incomes resource owners earn when their resources (including labor time) are employed in production were being used to build up their own holdings of money. Goods would be produced, and incomes would be paid, but the money would not be spent on goods. It would be spend on money—i.e., it would be hoarded. If this were the case, unsold goods would accumulate, production would be cut back, and people would be laid off. This laying off of workers is the visible sign of an excess supply of labor. There would be widespread unemployment—a depression.

One way this situation could be remedied would be for the money prices of all the goods for which there is a planned excess supply to fall. As that happened, the purchasing power of money would increase (the average money price level would fall) until people generally became content with the amount of money they were holding. With the average money price level lower, any given quantity of money can do more for its holder than it could before the price fell. It can purchase more, and it can provide more protection against unforeseen economic troubles. Thus, as the money price level falls, more and more people become satisfied with the average balances they carry in their checking accounts and in cash. They cease trying to build up their balances. They cease hoarding, and so the market excess demand for money becomes zero. At that point the link between production, the earning of incomes, and the expenditure of those incomes on what is produced would be restored. In short, what is called for in periods of widespread unemployment is a general deflation—a decline in the average money price level.

Prior to Keynes' *General Theory* the above explanation for depression was the only one that economists had. It was used by both classical economists such as John Stuart Mill and neoclassical economists such as Alfred Marshall. These economists believed in Say's Principle and in depressions. They saw (and rightly so) absolutely no contradiction in these views. Keynes' major contribution in *The General Theory*, according to Axel Leijonhufvud, was to provide an alternative explanation for depressions. We will discuss this alternative explanation in Chapter 14, when we consider the modern interpretation of *The General Theory.*

SUMMARY

In this chapter we have seen that the plans transactors make with respect to buying or selling in one market have their counterpart in other markets. The prices that exist in each market affect the plans that are made. In all analyses of questions that involve more than one market, the necessary linkage between markets must be explicitly acknowledged.

Much of what has been written about Say's Principle is either false or misleading. Several people have tried to read more into the idea than is really there. The most common misconception is that belief in Say's Principle makes it impossible to believe in the possibility of depressions. In fact, all reputable adherents to the principle, from Say himself to Keynes and contemporary economists such as Leijonhufvud, have been able, in a manner consistent with the principle, to explain widespread unemployment.

═══ APPENDIX ═══

SAY'S LAW AND WALRAS' LAW

In 1942 Oscar Lange wrote an influential article entitled "Say's Law: A Restatement and Criticism."[4] In that article Lange called "Say's Law" (SL) the proposition that the sum of the market excess demands (the word "planned" was not used) for all goods other than money must be zero. Look back again at Figure 3-1. If we ignore the fact that SP is concerned only with planned excess demands, what Lange called SL is a proposition that requires the market excess demand for money to be zero. After all, if the sum of the market excess demands for all exchangeable goods including money must be zero, and if the sum of the market excess demands for all goods other than money is also zero, the market excess demand for money must be zero. Lange asserted that many pre-Keynesian economists actually believed, or assumed, that the quantity of money demanded always equaled the quantity of money supplied, and because they believed this obviously false proposition they were incapable of explaining depressions. It was this silly belief that, according to Lange, Keynes attacked in *The General Theory.* But Lange was wrong on both counts. No reputable economist prior to Keynes believed in SL as it was stated by Lange, and all reputable economists could very easily explain depressions in the manner we discussed in this chapter.

It is true that what we, following Leijonhufvud, call Say's Principle used to be called Say's Law. But what Lange calls Say's Law is nothing but pure nonsense. Lange labeled the proposition that the sum of the market excess demands for *all* exchangeable goods must be zero Walras' Law (WL). He claimed that Keynes agreed with WL and attacked SL. Again Lange was in error. As we will see in Chapter 14, it was precisely Walras' Law that Keynes attacked.

It may seem that WL is merely another name for what we now call SP, but that is not so. In his statement of WL, Lange made no distinction between planned and effective excess demands. SP refers *only* to planned excess demands. This distinction, as we will see in Chapter 14, is the basis of the modern interpretation of Keynes' *General Theory*. Throughout the next ten chapters of this book, however, we will use Say's Principle to guide our analysis whenever we discuss the interaction of two or more markets. The analysis we will cover is established and generally accepted macroeconomic theory. The reinterpretation of Keynes has not yet become generally accepted. Nor is it necessarily desirable that it should. Reinterpreting the work of a major figure in any discipline is interesting in its own right apart from any practical implications of the reinterpretation. Our major task in this text is to achieve understanding of the macroeconomic analysis that is in fact used in the real world to inform the policy decisions of the President, the Congress, and the Federal Reserve Board (which oversees the nation's central banking system).

QUESTIONS

1. From macroeconomics we know that the prices that affect the plans and actions of individuals are relative prices. In the discussion of SP we referred to "money prices." That expression does *not* mean current prices expressed in current dollars. What does it mean? How can a money price be a relative price?

2. Does Say's Principle imply that in the real world prices are always tending toward their general equilibrium values?

3. In what sense is it true that "supply creates its own demand"?

4. If the money price of a dollar is $1, how could the money market *ever* be out of equilibrium? After all, an ES implies a price that is too high, and an ED implies a price that is too low. What is the price that changes to establish equilibrium in the money market? (The interest rate is the price of *credit*, not money.)

5. What is the difference between Say's Principle and Walras' Law?

NOTES

1. The principle is named for J. B. Say, a French economist of the early nineteenth century, who was the first to call attention to the principle.
2. R. W. Clower and Axel Leijonhufvud, "Say's Principle, What It Means and Doesn't Mean," *Intermountain Economic Review*, 1974.
3. The remainder of this section and the next subsection is reprinted by permission from *Elements of Macroeconomics* by Charles W. Baird (St. Paul: West Publishing Company, 1977).
4. In Oscar Lange et al., eds., *Studies in Mathematical Economics and Econometrics* (Chicago: University of Chicago Press, 1942).

PART

2

THE COMMODITIES MARKET

The Keynesian
(Income-Expenditure) Model

In this chapter we will develop the first of our four markets. The commodities market consists of four categories of expenditures: consumption, investment, government, and foreign.

For convenience of exposition we will initially ignore government. That is, we will initially assume that government spending and taxes are zero. This assumption will be dropped after Section 4-4 of this chapter when we have thoroughly discussed the model in its most simple form—with only households and firms. Households supply labor services to firms and purchase the output of firms with most of the income they thereby earn. Such purchases are called *consumption expenditures*. Households also save some of the income they earn. This portion of income is made available to firms (through the purchase of bonds and deposits into savings accounts) to use to acquire investment goods (plant and equipment) from other firms. Of course, firms also save directly (through depreciation accounts and retained earnings) to generate funds to acquire investment goods. Without government there are no taxes, and without taxes disposable income equals gross income. Thus although aggregate household consumption expenditure logically depends on how much disposable (spendable) income households have rather than total income earned, until we introduce government later in the chapter we need not worry about this distinction.

4-1 PLANNED AND ACTUAL EXPENDITURES

As we saw in Chapter 2 (Section 2-3), if we consider a closed economy (one without international trade), the actual total value of expenditures in this market must, by definition, equal the actual value of income. This is simply the equality between the LHS and the RHS of our national income accounts (excluding X and M). This equality is depicted by the 45° line in Figure 2-1. At the end of any accounting period (the period for which GNP is calculated) this equality must hold true, regardless of the expenditure plans formulated by consumers, firms, and governments during that period.

The Keynesian model that is used most of the time is based on the assumption of a direct relationship between aggregate (disposable) income and aggregate consumption expenditures. As aggregate income increases, it is assumed to call forth increases in aggregate consumption. Extra income *causes* households to increase consumption expenditures. (While that may seem reasonable at the individual household level, one must be careful in making the assertion for all households together. For example, in spite of an increase in aggregate income some households may actually lose income. In order for such an increase in aggregate income to cause an increase in aggregate consumption, the extra consumption of those households that have received additional income must be greater than the decrease in consumption on the part of the households that lost income. This problem is called the *aggregation problem*.)

Moreover, the Keynesian model most frequently used assumes that the rate of increase in aggregate consumption for every extra dollar of aggregate income is constant, and that the rate is less than one. For example, if a $10 billion increase in aggregate income would cause aggregate consumption to increase by $8 billion, it would do so whether the initial aggregate income was $100 billion or $300 billion. Statistical studies of the relationship between aggregate income and aggregate consumption seem consistent with these assumptions.

Of course, factors other than aggregate income also affect aggregate consumption. Interest rates (or the hypothetical single interest rate of macro theory) are the most important of these other variables, as we will see in later chapters. Changes in aggregate spending not caused by changes in aggregate income are called autonomous changes.

The relationship between aggregate consumption expenditures and aggregate income is depicted in Figure 4-1. Notice that the consumption line starts above the zero on the vertical axis. Where it starts is called the *vertical intercept of the line*. The vertical intercept indicates the amount of consumption spending that is unrelated to aggregate income—i.e., the amount of autonomous consumption spending. It is labeled C in the diagram. The consumption line has a positive slope (meaning it rises from left to right), indicating that as aggregate income

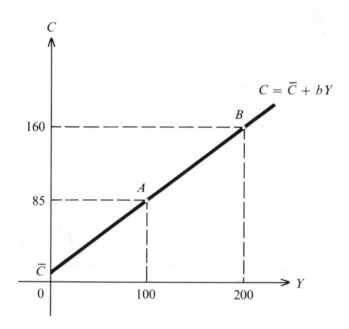

Figure 4-1   The consumption function.

(the variable plotted on the horizontal axis) increases, the result is an increase in aggregate consumption (the variable on the vertical axis). The arithmetic value of the slope of the line is found by increasing aggregate income by some amount (e.g., 100) and seeing how much extra consumption is thereby generated. (In the diagram consumption increases by 75 when income increases by 100.) The slope is then the extra consumption divided by the extra income (.75 in the diagram). In general, the symbol for a change in consumption is ΔC, the symbol for a change in income is ΔY, and thus the slope is $\Delta C/\Delta Y$. In our example $\Delta C/\Delta Y$ is less than one, in keeping with the usual Keynesian assumption and the statistical evidence.

The slope of the consumption line is called the *marginal propensity to consume (MPC)*. The equation for this line is

$$C = \bar{C} + bY$$

where b is $\Delta C/\Delta Y$, or the MPC. We call this relationship the consumption function and it represents the sum of planned consumption expenditures of all consumers at different levels of income.

If we use $\bar{C} = 10$ and $b = .75$ as an example, at income level $Y = 100$ planned consumption expenditures would be 85 (point A). At $Y = 200$, C would be 160

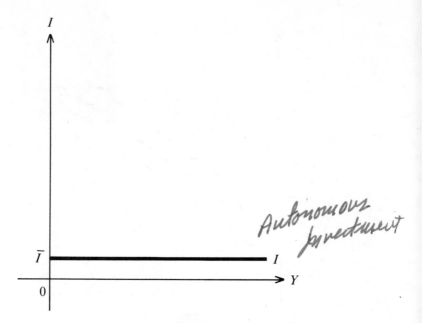

Figure 4-2 Planned investment expenditures.

(point *B*), Notice that, as *Y* changed by 100, *C* changed by 75 and $\Delta C/\Delta Y$ equals .75.

The ratio *C/Y* is called the *average propensity to consume (APC)*. Clearly this ratio is falling as *Y* increases in Figure 4-1. At point *A*, *C/Y* = .85, while *C/Y* = .80 at point *B*. The APC is falling because the constant term, $\overline{C}$ (determined by all variables other than income that affect consumption), is positive.

The other component of planned expenditures in this model without government is illustrated in Figure 4-2. We assume (for the moment) that producers decide on their planned investment expenditures without considering the value of *Y*. That is, *I* is autonomously determined (i.e., determined by factors other than income). This autonomous level is shown as $\overline{I}$.

Combining Figures 4-1 and 4-2, Figure 4-3 depicts planned expenditures (E_p) at each level of income. Planned expenditures or aggregate demand are *C* + *I*. We can now summarize the relationships that we have discussed.

$$C = \overline{C} + bY \qquad \text{consumption function} \qquad (4\text{-}1)$$

$$I = \overline{I} \qquad \text{planned investment} \qquad (4\text{-}2)$$

$$E_p = C + I \qquad \text{planned expenditures} \qquad (4\text{-}3)$$

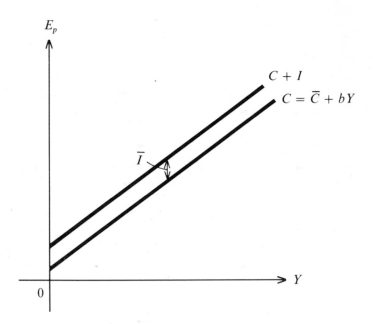

Figure 4-3 Total planned expenditures.

All of the variables in this model are in current dollar (nominal) terms, and prices are assumed to be fixed.

Planned investment expenditures include purchases of plant and equipment along with planned inventory changes. A planned addition to inventory is a positive investment expenditure, and a planned inventory reduction is a negative investment expenditure. However, some inventory changes are unplanned. If we define actual investment (I_A) to include purchases of plant and equipment and *all* changes in inventory, whether planned or not, we can define the total of *actual* expenditures as consumption, plus actual investment:

$$E_A = C + I_A \tag{4-4}$$

Notice that the C term in Equations 4-3 and 4-4 is the same. The difference between the two equations is the difference between planned and actual investment. Firms plan to undertake certain investments (I), but these may not be the ones that have actually been undertaken (I_A) by the end of the accounting period. Firms plan to invest in plant and equipment; we assume that these long-range plans are carried out. Firms also plan to increase or decrease their inventories according to expected sales levels; these plans may not be fulfilled. Inventories act as a buffer for firms against unexpected sales levels. If sales exceed expected levels, firms will initially meet this demand by drawing down their inventories. This is unplanned inventory decumulation or disinvestment. If sales were to fall below expected levels, inventories would increase by more than was expected. This increase would represent unplanned inventory investment or accumulation. We can then define $I_A - I$ as unplanned inventory investment.

We know from the national income accounting identity in Chapter 2 that, ignoring government,

$$Y \equiv Y_d + S_b \tag{4-5}$$

or GNP always equals the sum of disposable income and business saving. Since Y_d is either spent (C) or saved (S_p, personal saving),

$$Y \equiv C + S_p + S_b \tag{4-6}$$

If $S = S_p + S_b$, then

$$Y \equiv C + S \tag{4-7}$$

Since E_A (the RHS of the total value added statement such as we used in Table 2-5) must also equal Y (the LHS of the total value added statement), we can write

$$C + I_A \equiv C + S \tag{4-8}$$

Actual expenditures ($C + I_A$) are not equal to planned expenditures ($C + I$) at *all* levels of income. When the two are equal, the level of income (which we shall call the *equilibrium level of income*) will be the only one at which unplanned investment is zero. This concept will be developed in the next section.

4-2 THE KEYNESIAN CROSS DIAGRAM AND EQUILIBRIUM INCOME

We can now proceed to develop the traditional Keynesian "income-expenditure" model. The key assumptions of this model are that the price level is constant and that there are unemployed productive resources (e.g., labor, plant, and equipment). All adjustments to changes in the level of aggregate demand are assumed to be made through changes in real output. Any extra real output comes from using resources that were previously unemployed, while any reduction in real output implies that some resources have ceased to be employed.

The basis of the Keynesian income-expenditure model is a stable relationship between the level of nominal income and the level of consumption expenditures. We have called this the *consumption function*. Since the price level is constant, this function is the same as a stable relationship between real consumption expenditures and real income. *Nominal income*, remember, is the product of the average price level (P) and real income (Q). If P does not change, any change in nominal income (Y) must come about through a change in Q. Nominal consumption expenditures are the product of real consumption expenditures (consumption expenditures in base year prices) and the average price level. If the average price level does not change, any change in nominal consumption expenditures must come about through changes in real consumption expenditures.

In a two-sector model (households and firms) the RHS of a total value added statement would include only consumption and actual investment expenditures. The LHS would include only disposable income and business saving. That is,

$$Y \equiv Y_d + S_b \equiv C + I_A \tag{4-9}$$

If we assume that $S_b = 0$,

$$Y \equiv Y_d \equiv C + I_A \tag{4-10}$$

and since

$$Y_d \equiv C + S_p$$

$$Y \equiv C + S_p \equiv C + I_A \tag{4-11}$$

Income is equal to the sum of either consumption spending and personal saving or consumption spending and actual investment.

We shall continue with the assumption that planned investment expenditures (I) are determined by variables (such as the interest rate) other than Y. The Keynesian cross diagram for this two-sector model appears in Figure 4-4. Equilibrium income is Y^*; the equilibrium condition is

$$Y = C + I \tag{4-12}$$

Equation 4-11 points out that at all levels of income the sum of consumption and actual investment equals the level of income. Equation 4-12 points out that only at a particular level of income does consumption plus planned investment equal income. The equals sign in Equation 4-12 signifies an equilibrium condition. The three horizontal lines in Equation 4-11 indicate that the relationship is always true—in or out of equilibrium.

Suppose that the consumption function (C) is $10 + 3/4Y$ and that planned investment expenditures ($I = \bar{I}$) are 20. Then, using Equation 4-12, we get

$$Y = 10 + \frac{3}{4}Y + 20$$

$$\left(1 - \frac{3}{4}\right)Y = 10 + 20$$

$$Y = \frac{1}{1 - \frac{3}{4}}(10 + 20) = 120$$

Equilibrium income is 120.

In general, the equilibrium condition, consumption function, and investment function will be in the form

$$Y = C + I \tag{4-13}$$

$$C = \bar{C} + bY \tag{4-14}$$

$$I = \bar{I} \tag{4-15}$$

These relationships are depicted in Figure 4-4. These three equations together are called the "structural form" of the model; that is, they fully define all behavior (consumers and firms) in the model. $Y*$ in Figure 4-4 is equilibrium income.

In order to solve for $Y*$ we must construct the "reduced form" of the model. This is done by substituting Equations 4-14 and 4-15 into Equation 4-13 to get

$$Y = \bar{C} + bY + \bar{I}$$

$$(1 - b)Y = \bar{C} + \bar{I}$$

$$Y = \frac{1}{1 - b}(\bar{C} + \bar{I}) \tag{4-16}$$

Equation 4-16 is the reduced form. It will always have the form of a coefficient, in this case $1/(1-b)$, multiplied by the sum of the autonomously determined

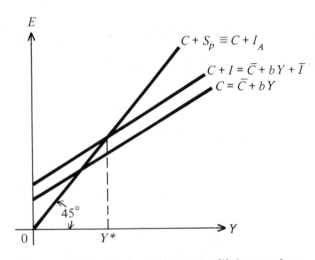

Figure 4-4 Equilibrium income with two sectors.

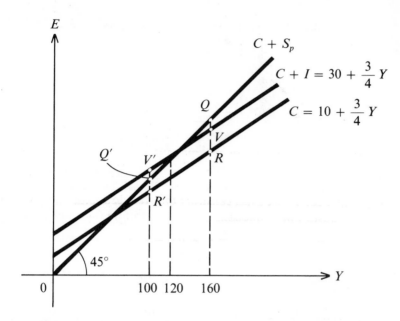

Figure 4-5 A numerical example of equilibrium income.

spending numbers on the RHS, with Y by itself on the LHS. In this case both $\bar{C}$ and $\bar{I}$ are determined outside the model.

In the numerical example given above the equilibrium income level was 120, as shown in Figure 4-5. The height of the 45° line above any value of Y is equal to $C + S_p$ (from now on, personal saving will be denoted by S). At income level 160,

$$C = 10 + \frac{3}{4}(160) = 130$$

Point R is at height 130; hence S and I_A (or distance RQ) equal 30. Distance VR, which is planned investment (I), equals 20. Distance VQ is unplanned investment, I_u, and it is equal to 10. At income level 100, $C = 85$, $I = R'V' = 20$, $I_A = S = Q'R' = 15$, and $I_u = Q'V' = -5$. These calculations are summarized in Table 4-1. The planned expenditure line, $C + I$, has an intercept of 30 ($\bar{C} + \bar{I}$) and a slope of 3/4 (i.e., $b = 3/4$).

Great caution should be used when applying this model. The consumption function was developed as an aggregate representation of the plans of millions of consumers, and the investment function as an aggregate of the plans of millions of producers. Since information is neither perfect nor available instantaneously,

Table 4-1 Relationship between planned and actual expenditures

Y	C	I	I_A	I_u
100	85	20	15	−5
120	100	20	20	0
160	130	20	30	10

it is quite likely that the plans of consumers and producers will not match actual production. Inventories may well rise above or fall below expected levels. We will deal with the reactions of producers in disequilibrium (income levels of 100 or 160 in our example) at great length in later chapters.

4-3 THE MULTIPLIER AND THE SAVING FUNCTION

At income level 160 in Figure 4-5 the deficiency between production and planned expenditure is distance QV, or an amount equal to 10. This deficiency is called a *deflationary gap*. It will induce producers to cut back production to income level 120, since only at this level will there be no unintended inventory accumulation. This relationship suggests that if we could somehow raise the $C + I$ line by 10, we could support an equilibrium production (or income) level of 160. If an increase of only 10 in planned investment brings about an increase of 40 in equilibrium income, it appears that we are getting something for nothing. In fact, however, all that is happening is that the increase of 10 in autonomous spending causes, or induces, an increase of 30 in consumption expenditures.

Consider Figure 4-6. An increase in I of $I_2 - I_1$ raises equilibrium income from Y_1 to Y_2. This increase in income has two parts: the change in I (DF) plus the induced change in C (AB). In our numerical example the change in I equals 10. The induced change in C is

$$10 + \frac{3}{4}(160) - 10 - \frac{3}{4}(120) = \frac{3}{4}(40) = 30$$

This induced increase in C may be thought of as a process whereby the initial increase in Y, which equals ΔI, causes those who have received the additional Y to increase their spending by $b(\Delta I)$. This represents additional income to others, who in turn increase their consumption spending by $b^2(\Delta I)$, and so on. The total increase in consumption spending induced by the initial ΔI is

$\Delta I + \dfrac{\Delta I b}{1-b}$

$\dfrac{1.75}{1-.75}$

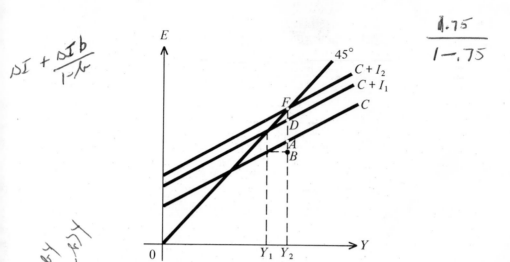

Figure 4-6 The multiplier with autonomous investment.

$\delta I b + \delta I b^2 + \delta I b^3$

$$\Delta C = \Delta I(b + b^2 + b^3 + \cdots)$$

$$= \frac{b}{1-b}\Delta I \qquad (4\text{-}17)$$

$\Delta I + \Delta I \dfrac{b}{1-b}$

$\Delta Y = -\Delta I \dfrac{b}{1-b} = \Delta I$

The total change in income is

$$\Delta Y = \Delta C + \Delta I = \left(1 + \frac{b}{1-b}\right)\Delta I$$

$$= \frac{1}{1-b}\Delta I \qquad (4\text{-}18)$$

$\Delta Y = \Delta I = \dfrac{\Delta I}{1-b}$

$\Delta Y - \Delta I \left(\dfrac{\Delta I}{1-b}\right)$

Growth in income causes growth not only in consumption expenditures but also in saving:

$$S = Y - C = Y - \overline{C} - bY$$

$$= -\overline{C} + (1-b)Y \qquad (4\text{-}19)$$

At income level 120, $S = 20$ and at income level 160, $S = 30$. Thus saving has increased by 10.

This *multiplier process* is best understood in the following way. In equilibrium it must be the case that $I = S$. Starting from equilibrium, we raise I above S. This causes income to start growing, and it will continue to grow until it causes saving to increase by the same amount that investment has increased. When I and S are again equal, the multiplier process stops.

Algebraically the multiplier is easy to derive. The reduced form of our simple model is

$$Y = \frac{1}{1-b}(\overline{C} + \overline{I}) \tag{4-20}$$

Suppose $\overline{I}$ is increased by $\Delta \overline{I}$. This will result in a new level of income:

$$Y + \Delta Y = \frac{1}{1-b}(\overline{C} + \overline{I} + \Delta \overline{I}) \tag{4-21}$$

Subtracting the original reduced form from this last equation, we get

$$\Delta Y = \frac{1}{1-b}(\Delta \overline{I}) \tag{4-22}$$

The coefficient $1/(1-b)$ is the multiplier for this simple model; it is equal to $1/1$ minus the slope of the planned expenditure line. We multiply the change in investment spending by this number to get the resulting change in income.

We could have obtained 160 as an equilibrium level of income by increasing $\overline{C}$ by 10 instead of increasing $\overline{I}$. In that case we would start with $I = S$, and reduce S by 10. Therefore investment will be greater than saving $(I > S)$, and income will grow. It will continue to grow until S returns to its previous level. Since

$$\Delta S = (1 - b)\Delta Y = \frac{1}{4}(\Delta Y) \tag{4-23}$$

income must grow by four $[1/(1 - b)]$ times the amount that saving must grow.

Of course, as we pointed out before, this analysis assumes that there are unemployed resources at income equal to 120. With fixed prices, all of the income that is generated by the multiplier process is new real output. Without unemployment, if income were to increase to 160, all of the increase would be in the form of higher prices.

4-4 INVESTMENT AS A FUNCTION OF INCOME

Now we shall drop the assumption that investment is entirely autonomous. Suppose the investment function were $I = \overline{I} + vY$. The coefficient v is the rate at which I grows as Y grows. The $C + I$ line no longer parallels the C line. The equation of the $C + I$ line is $C + I = \overline{C} + \overline{I} + (b + v)Y$ and the slope of the $C + I$ line is $(b + v)$. The slope of the C line is only b. Assuming that $(b + v) < 1$, the diagram looks like Figure 4-7.

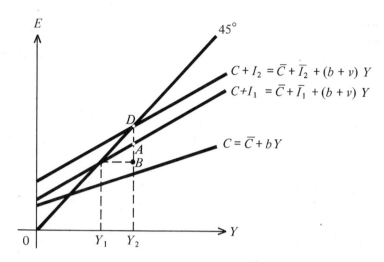

Figure 4-7   The multiplier with induced investment.

Starting with equilibrium income level Y_1, increase the autonomous portion of the investment function from $\bar{I}_1$ to $\bar{I}_2$. This results in an increase in equilibrium income from Y_1 to Y_2. This increase in income has two parts, the increase in autonomous spending, DA, and an increase in induced spending of AB. This time, however, the added induced spending includes induced investment spending as well as induced consumption spending. The existence of induced investment spending when investment depends on income indicates that the multiplier will be higher than it was before.

The structural form of our model is now

$$Y = C + I \tag{4-24}$$

$$C = \bar{C} + bY \tag{4-25}$$

$$I = \bar{I} + vY \tag{4-26}$$

The reduced form is

$$Y = \frac{1}{1 - b - v}(\bar{C} + \bar{I}) \tag{4-27}$$

The multiplier for this model is $1/(1 - b - v)$ and this is clearly larger than $1/(1 - b)$ since v is greater than 0. Again, the multiplier is equal to $1/1$ minus the slope of the planned expenditure line.

Now the multiplier process may be viewed in the following way. Starting with $I = S$, increase the autonomous part of I. Therefore investment is greater than saving, and so income will increase. As income increases, S will increase, but so will I. However, if $(b + v) < 1$, a new equilibrium can be established. If $(b + v) < 1$, $v < (1 - b)$. Here v is the rate at which I grows with respect to income and $(1 - b)$ is the rate at which S grows with respect to income. Even though investment increases as income increases, saving increases at a faster rate. Therefore saving can catch up with investment and establish a new equilibrium (such as Y_2 in Figure 4-7).

If $v = .05$, $b = .75$, $\overline{C} = 10$, and $\overline{I} = 20$, then the new equilibrium level of income is 150. The multiplier is now $1/1 - .75 - .05 = 1/.2 = 5$, and so an increase of 10 in either $\overline{C}$ or $\overline{I}$ would lead to an increase in income of 50. A larger multiplier always results in a larger change in income when there is a change in the autonomous components of planned expenditures.

4-5 ADDING THE GOVERNMENT SECTOR TO THE MODEL

We can expand our model by adding the government sector to our simple two-sector model, but we shall continue to ignore the foreign sector. From the total value added statement we know that when we include the government sector we are adding government expenditure (G) to the RHS, and to the LHS we are adding personal income taxes, indirect taxes, and corporate profits taxes, which are lumped together here and called taxes (T).

The variables on the axes of the Keynesian cross diagram are changed somewhat. The variable on the horizontal axis of Figure 4-8 is still "income" or Y, but now it is the sum of disposable income Y_d, business saving S_b, and taxes T. Total expenditures, including unintended inventory accumulation, equal $C + I_A + G$, and this must necessarily equal $Y_d + S_b + T$. The 45° line represents the necessary equality. The height of the 45° line for any value of Y is both $Y_d + S_b + T$ and $C + I_A + G$. The planned expenditure line is the sum of $C + I + G$, where I is *planned* investment. For the value of Y where $I_A = I$, or where $I_u = 0$, we have equilibrium. Y_1 is equilibrium income. We have drawn the $C + I + G$ line parallel to the $C + I$ line because we are assuming that G is an autonomous variable.

We must be very careful when we specify the structural form. Consumption spending logically depends on *disposable* income, Y_d, not on Y (or GNP). Yet we want to draw the consumption line against Y. We must therefore specify the relationship between Y and Y_d in our structural form. Assume that G, S_b, and T are autonomously determined. C and I are specified as before. The structural form of our model is then

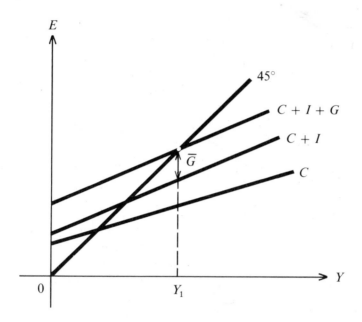

Figure 4-8 Three-sector aggregate demand and equilibrium income.

$$Y = C + I + G \tag{4-28}$$

$$C = \overline{C} + bY_d \tag{4-29}$$

$$Y_d = Y - S_b - T \tag{4-30}$$

$$T = \overline{T} \tag{4-31}$$

$$S_b = \overline{S}_b \tag{4-32}$$

$$I = \overline{I} + vY \tag{4-33}$$

$$G = \overline{G} \tag{4-34}$$

The reduced form is

$$Y = \frac{1}{1 - b - v}(\overline{C} - b\overline{S}_b - b\overline{T} + \overline{I} + \overline{G}) \tag{4-35}$$

The impact of taxes and business saving shows up in a downward shift of the consumption function relative to its height when $T = S_b = 0$. The magnitude of the shift at each value of Y is $b(S_b + T)$, as indicated in Equation 4-35 and depicted in Figure 4-9.

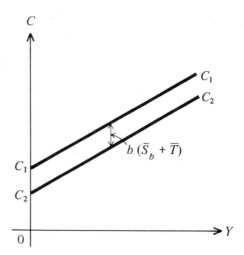

Figure 4-9 **The effect, on consumption line, of adding
autonomous taxes and business saving.**

To illustrate the impact of adding the government sector more completely, assume initially that $G = S_b = T = 0$, that $C = 10 + 3/4 Y_d$, and that $I = 20 + .05 Y$. We know that this implies an equilibrium income of 150. Suppose government spending increases from zero to 10 at each value of Y. This would mean that the aggregate demand line would become $C_1 + I + G$ in Figure 4-10 and that equilibrium income would become 200. (The student should check these calculations.) Now let's suppose that taxes increase from zero to 10. The consumption function $(10 + 3/4 Y_d)$ now becomes $10 + 3/4(Y - 10)$ or $2.5 + 3/4 Y$. The impact of adding a lump sum tax of 10 is to shift the C line downward by $3/4(10)$ or by $b(\Delta T)$ at each income level. The $C + I + G$ line becomes $C_2 + I + G$. The whole aggregate demand line is lowered by 7.5 because one of its components, C, is lowered by 7.5.

What is equilibrium income now? The best way to find out is to calculate the change in the height of the aggregate demand line relative to what it was when $T = 0$. We have just seen that the height was *lowered* by 7.5. We know that the multiplier for this model is $1/1 - (b - v)$ or 5; therefore we know that the change in equilibrium income will be $5(-7.5) = -37.5$. The new equilibrium income level is $200 - 37.5 = 162.5$.

4-6 TAXES AND AGGREGATE DEMAND

In the last section we saw that the effect of adding government spending was to push up the aggregate demand line by the amount of the spending, while the

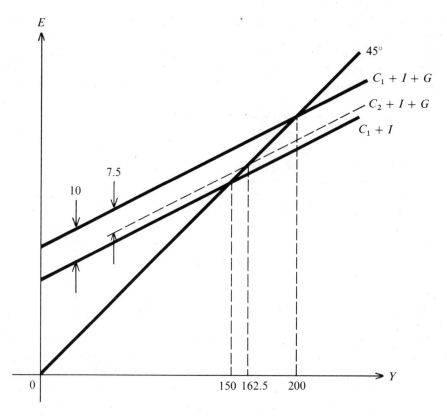

Figure 4-10   The impact of adding government.

effect of adding taxes was to pull down the consumption function (and therefore the aggregate demand line) by an amount smaller than the taxes. Specifically, the consumption function was shifted down by the marginal propensity to consume (which is always less than one) times the amount of the taxes. In our numerical example the addition of taxes equal to 10 lowered the consumption function by 7.5 because the MPC equaled 0.75. This effect of taxes on consumption is logical. After all, if the MPC is 0.75, any change of 10 in disposable income will cause a corresponding change in consumption of 7.5. Disposable income declines by 10 at each level of gross income (Y) whenever taxes equal to 10 are imposed at each level of gross income. Thus, the consumption number that goes with each level of gross income depicted on the horizontal axis of the Keynesian cross diagram will be 7.5 lower than it was before.

However, the effect of the tax on aggregate demand is not limited to its effect on consumption. Even if the taxes are directly imposed only on households and

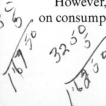

not on business firms, the taxes will reduce investment spending as well as consumption spending. This will be true even if investment spending is entirely autonomous. The reason for this lies in the relationship between investment and saving. If taxes of 10 are imposed on households and households respond by reducing consumption by 7.5, the households are paying 7.5 of the tax with income that otherwise would be spent on consumption. The remaining 2.5 of the tax must be paid with income that would have been saved. But if saving is reduced, and if saving is the source of funds used for investment (as it in reality is), then investment must decline along with saving. Therefore, the effect of adding taxes to the two-sector Keynesian model is to affect investment as well as consumption. *Both* the consumption function and the investment function shift down. We will return to this insight in the next chapter when we discuss fiscal policy.

SUMMARY

In this chapter we developed the Keynesian income-expenditure model. This model is used to represent the commodities market in macroeconomic theory. The aggregate demand line is the sum of planned consumption, investment, and government spending. Actual consumption and government spending are always assumed to be the same as that planned. Planned investment spending, however, can be different from actual investment. The latter is all expenditure on plant and equipment, new houses, and changes in inventory. Some actual changes in inventory can turn out to be surprises. If firms underestimate sales, inventories will fall below planned levels; while if firms overestimate sales, inventories will accumulate above planned levels. When there are no unplanned inventory changes, actual investment equals planned investment and aggregate demand equals aggregate supply.

The 45° line can be thought of as the aggregate supply line in the sense that it shows at each level of income the aggregate dollar value of goods and services producers would be pleased to supply if there were an equivalent dollar volume of spending. When the aggregate demand line intersects the 45° line, the dollar value of the goods and services supplied (the 45° line) is matched by intended purposeful spending by households, firms, and government (the $C + I + G$ line).

When there is a sustained increase in any component of autonomous spending that does not come about at the expense of any other spending, the multiplier process is set in motion. The extra income caused by the new autonomous spending in turn calls forth additional consumption and investment spending. Thus the flow of spending grows, or is "multiplied."

The effect of an increase in government spending is to push the aggregate demand line up by the exact amount of the spending. G is simply added to $C + I$. Changes in taxes also affect aggregate demand. The effect shows up as shifts in the consumption and investment lines. So even though there is no T explicitly in $C + I + G$, C and I are affected by T. The effect of T on I exists even if investment does not depend on income—i.e., is entirely autonomous.

QUESTIONS

1. Suppose the economy could be characterized by the following structural form:

$$Y = C + I$$
$$C = 10 + 0.75Y$$
$$I = 5 + 0.25Y$$

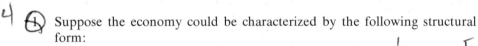

$$Y = \frac{1}{1 - .75 - .25}\left[10 + 5\right]$$
$$Y = \frac{1}{0}\left[30\right)$$

What is equilibrium income? Draw this situation in a Keynesian cross diagram. Explain the dynamics of this situation.

2. A deflationary gap will cause deflation, and an inflationary gap will cause inflation. Only prices change when aggregate spending changes, and so a change in nominal income does not involve changes in real output and employment. Under what circumstances would these statements be true?

3. The multiplier analysis assumes that when one kind of spending increases, other kinds of spending do not change. Do you agree?

4. What is the difference between the 45° line and the planned expenditure line?

5. What is the difference between the multiplier process when $v = 0$ and when $v > 0$? Explain this added dimension to the basic Keynesian model.

6. In our numerical example, increasing government expenditures by $10 increased the equilibrium level of income from $150 to $200. If taxes are not increased by a corresponding amount (as in the latter part of our example), how can the government pay for its increased expenditures? Can the means of payment have a feedback effect on consumption and investment?

Fiscal Policy
in the Keynesian Model

It was, and to some extent still is, the view of Keynesians that the private economy is inherently unstable. In the absence of countervailing government action, they believed, the economy will suffer alternating periods of recession and boom. A more recent view is that the private economy *is* inherently (fairly) stable and that most, if not all, of the depressions, recessions, and inflations the economy has experienced have been the result of faulty government policy. However, the Keynesian view has dominated the policy making of the federal government since the 1930s. The economists to whom most politicians still listen subscribe to the Keynesian view; hence it is incumbent upon us to examine the Keynesian view of fiscal policy.

5-1 THE ROLE OF GOVERNMENT

The main thrust of the "Keynesian revolution" was the role it gave to government in the maintenance of nominal aggregate demand (total dollar spending in the economy) through fiscal policy. *Fiscal policy* refers to attempts to alter nominal aggregate demand by changing the relationship between government expenditures (injections into the income stream) and taxes (leakages from the income stream). Keynes and his followers developed and expanded upon the idea that government intervention in the economy was both necessary and desirable to dampen economic cycles. In other words, alternating periods of boom (expansion, inflation) and bust (contraction, deflation) need not be simply endured.

Keynesians hoped that adroitly managed government policies would flatten out, although not necessarily eliminate, the business cycle. Figure 5-1 illustrates this idea. The business cycle can be viewed as a continuous movement of expansions and contractions in economic activity. Increases in government spending relative to taxes when the economy was on the downswing and decreases in government spending relative to taxes when the economy was too active would, the Keynesians thought, iron out the cycle.

HISTORICAL BACKGROUND

Pre-Keynesian economists discussed the role of government in promoting economic activity through public works programs, but had not integrated the idea into a generally accepted theory of economic policy. Pre-Keynesian economic policy was concerned mostly with microeconomic issues such as antitrust rather than with affecting aggregate demand (macroeconomic policies). What changed all of this was the Great Depression of the 1930s, commonly regarded as the

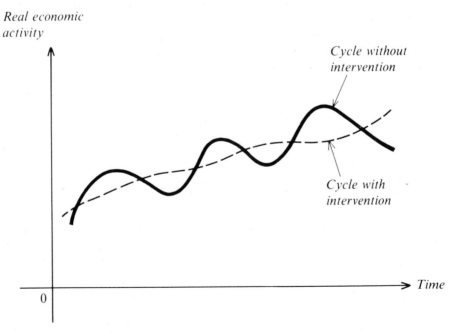

Figure 5-1 Hoped-for effects of fiscal policy.

worst in the history of the world. In the United States the Great Depression involved two serious contractions. The first, and more severe, occurred between 1929 and 1933, when GNP fell over 30 percent, unemployment rose to around 25 percent, and over 9000 banks had to close. The recovery, which began in 1933, lasted until 1936. In 1936 a second decline set in that lasted until 1938. A long period of recovery began in 1938 and continued throughout World War II.

In England (Keynes' homeland) the initial contraction began somewhat before 1929 and lasted throughout the 1930s. Keynes was struck by the long-term inability of the British economy to recover from declining production and income. The solution, he suggested, was to promote private spending by an infusion of public spending. Government would buy things from the private sector, and those who sold things (including labor time) to government would spend the receipts in the private sector. Thus government spending would have a "multiplier" effect on private spending.

FINANCING GOVERNMENT EXPENDITURES

How will the government get the money that it spends? The budget of the government consists of expenditures (G) and taxes (T). The difference between them is either a deficit (if $G > T$) or a surplus (if $T > G$). Keynes and his followers proposed that in times of contraction G be increased without a corresponding increase in T. Injections into the income stream would be higher than before and this would increase the equilibrium level of income. How, though, can any transactor—government, consumer, or firm—spend more than it receives? The answer, of course, is through increased borrowing. The government deficit must be financed, and it is financed by borrowing from the private sector. (It could also be financed simply by creating new money, but that involves monetary policy, which we will consider later.)

The government borrows from the private sector by selling bonds to households and firms. The funds that are used to buy the bonds pass from the private sector to government. The private sector has less to spend, and the government has more to spend. Of course, this cannot alter total spending unless the funds in the hands of the private sector would have been idle—i.e., hoarded or not spent. If transactors in the private sector would have used the funds (which they turned over to government by buying government bonds) to buy private sector bonds (from corporations) or to buy investment goods directly, the government deficit would simply cause government spending to be higher and investment spending to be lower. The government spending would simply "crowd out" an equivalent amount of private spending. Keynesian economists usually ignore this crowding-out effect. They, at least implicitly, assume that the funds the private sector uses to buy government bonds would not otherwise be spent.

5-2 FORMS OF FISCAL INTERVENTION

An increase in government spending or a decrease in taxes is expansionary, whereas a decrease in government spending or an increase in taxes is restrictive.

CHANGING GOVERNMENT SPENDING

Using the foregoing Keynesian assumption and ignoring the effect of taxes on investment, we can use the Keynesian income-expenditure model of Chapter 4 to see that both a reduction in taxes and an increase in government spending would increase aggregate demand. Using the general equations in Chapter 4 (Equations 4-28 through 4-34), assume that the specific values for b, v, I, G, and T are such that:

$$Y = C + I + G$$
$$C = 10 + .75\,Y_d$$
$$Y_d = Y - T$$
$$T = 10$$
$$I = 20 + .05\,Y$$
$$G = 10$$

The reduced form is

$$Y = \frac{1}{1 - b - v}(\overline{C} - b\overline{T} + \overline{I} + \overline{G})$$

Substitution of the appropriate terms yields the following:

$$Y = \frac{1}{1 - .75 - .05}(10 - (.75)(10) + 20 + 10)$$

$$Y = 162.50$$

Substituting the equilibrium value for Y into the structural equations we see that

$$C = 10 + .75(162.50) = 131.875$$
$$I = 20 + .05(162.50) = 28.125$$

If government expenditure were to increase by 10, the new equilibrium level of income would be increased by the multiplier $(1/(1 - b - v))$ times ΔG. The multiplier equals $1/(1 - .75 - .05)$, which is merely $1/.2$, or 5. Thus the change in the equilibrium level of income will be 5 times the change in government spending, or 5 × 10, or 50. The new equilibrium level of income is 162.50 plus 50, or 212.50. The additional government spending increases the height of the aggregate demand line (the $C + I + G$ line) by 10. The new aggregate demand line intersects the 45° line at an income level that is 50 greater than before. In other words, the multiplier process works by calling forth 40 of additional consumption and investment spending. (As income increases due to the new spending, consumption and investment are made to increase.) In symbols:

$$\Delta C = b(\Delta Y) = .75(50) = 37.5$$

$$\Delta I = v(\Delta Y) = .05(50) = 2.5$$

$$\Delta G = 10$$

and

$$\Delta C + \Delta I + \Delta G = \Delta Y$$

A change in government expenditures (10) induces a change in income (50) much greater than the increase in G. This implies that if unemployment existed when income was 162.50 and it was known that full employment (at existing prices and wages) occurred at 212.50, the government would not need to increase its expenditures by the full 50. A mere 10-unit increase in expenditures would call forth an additional 40-unit increase in spending from the private sector, and the total of the new direct and induced spending would add up to the desired change in income. Of course, this result depends on the assumption that there is no crowding out.

CHANGING LUMP-SUM TAXES

A tax reduction would operate in a similar fashion. In our example, if taxes were reduced from 10 to zero while government spending was maintained at 10, the resulting equilibrium income would be (ignoring the effect of taxes on investment and crowding out):

$$Y = \frac{1}{1 - .75 - .05}(10 - .75(0) + 20 + 10) = 200$$

A cut in taxes of only 10 increased income by 37.50 (200 − 162.50).

ASYMMETRY OF EFFECTS

You will notice that the results of the two policies are not the same. Creating a deficit by increasing government spending by 10, while holding taxes constant, increased income by 50. Creating the same size deficit by decreasing taxes by 10, while holding government spending constant, increased income by only 37.50. Moreover, if government spending were increased by 10 and if taxes were also increased by 10, the result would be an *increase* in income of 12.50. Try it.

Spending changes do not have the same impact as tax changes. When government spending increases by 10, 10 is added to the height of the $C + I + G$ line; a decrease in taxes by 10, however, results in an addition of only 7.5 (which is the marginal propensity to consume times the change in tax) to the height of the $C + I + G$ line. This difference occurs because in the reduced form of the equations the entry within the parentheses for tax is $-b\overline{T}$. Less formally, and more directly, it occurs because the effect on total spending of changes in taxes is assumed to show up *only* through the resulting changes in consumption. Since people change consumption spending by the marginal propensity to consume times any change in their *disposable income*, and since tax increases (decreases) reduce (increase) disposable income, the effect of a change in tax is to shift the consumption line in the opposite direction of the tax change, but by only a fraction of the tax change. The heights of the other components of the aggregate demand line (other than the consumption component) are assumed to be unchanged when taxes change.

When taxes are increased by 10, how are they paid? Since the marginal propensity to consume is .75, 75 percent of the taxes will be paid out of money that otherwise would have been spent on consumption. This means the consumption line is lower than it would be without the tax increase. But how is the other 25 percent of the taxes paid? It must be paid out of money that otherwise would have been saved. If the government didn't take and spend this money that would have been saved, what would have happened to it? If it would have simply lain idle in a cookie jar or in a mattress, then the government's taking and spending it would cause aggregate spending to be higher than it otherwise would be. But suppose that saving does not take the form of hoarding idle pools of cash; suppose instead that the money that would have been saved, had the tax not been imposed, would have gone to buy corporation bonds or credits in savings account passbooks. The corporations that would have sold the bonds would have spent the money on investment goods, and the banks would have loaned the saved funds to other businesses for the purchase of investment goods. Thus when the tax is imposed and 75 percent of it shows up as reduced consumption, the other 25 percent of it shows up as reduced investment spending. Empirical studies of the U.S. economy indicate that a small portion of the saving that is used to pay taxes comes from idle funds, but the great majority of it would otherwise have been spent in the private sector. This implies that an equal increase in government spending and taxes will have *zero* net effect on the height of the aggregate demand line, and therefore no effect on equilibrium income.

EFFECTS OF IMPOSING AN INCOME TAX

The imposition of an income tax affects the consumption function not only by shifting the C line down but also by making it less steep, as in Figure 5-2. If $C = \overline{C} + bY_d$, $Y_d = Y - T$, and $T = \overline{T} + tY$ (where $\overline{T}$ is the amount collected from taxes other than the income tax, and t is the percent that tax increases when income increases), and if $S_b = 0$, we can rewrite the consumption equation as

$$C = \overline{C} + b(Y - \overline{T} - tY)$$

or

$$C = \overline{C} - b\overline{T} + b(1 - t)Y \qquad (5\text{-}8)$$

Since taxes vary with income, at any value of Y the vertical separation between the old and the new C line is b times the amount of tax *for that level of income.*

The structural form of the model is now (ignoring the effect of taxes on investment)

$$Y = C + I + G$$
$$C = \overline{C} + bY_d$$
$$Y_d = Y - T$$
$$T = \overline{T} + tY$$
$$I = \overline{I} + vY$$
$$G = \overline{G}$$

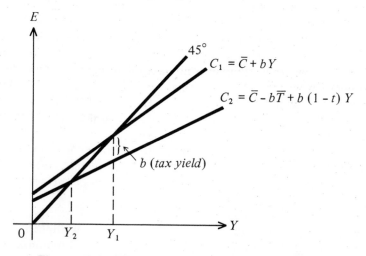

Figure 5-2 Effect of income tax on consumption.

The reduced form of the model is

$$Y = \frac{1}{1 - b(1 - t) - v}(\overline{C} - b\overline{T} + \overline{I} + \overline{G})$$

The multiplier is $1/[1 - b(1 - t) - v]$, which is clearly less than $1/(1 - b - v)$. In the multiplier process, income grows until this growth generates sufficient leakages to offset the injections into the income stream. The injections in a three-sector model are investment and government spending $(I + G)$; the leakages are saving and taxes $(S + T)$. Starting from an equilibrium income level, where $I + G = S + T$, let us raise either I or G. Since injections are larger than leakages, income will grow. Now, in addition to saving growing, we have taxes growing. Thus the leakage will catch up sooner to the higher rate of injections. This means that equilibrium income will not grow as much as it would if taxes did not increase when income increased; in other words, the multiplier is smaller.

In Figure 5-2, if $I = G = 0$, equilibrium income would be Y_1 before the imposition of the income tax. When the income tax is imposed, Y becomes Y_2. The fall in income, $Y_1 - Y_2$, equals the multiplier times b times the tax yield at Y_1, or the multiplier times the change in height of the aggregate demand line at the initial income level.

5-3 OTHER GOVERNMENT-INDUCED CHANGES IN THE PRIVATE SECTOR

Government policies can affect investment or consumption directly rather than through the induced effects discussed above. These policies can have a tremendous impact on economic activity, but would not be the result of changes in G or T. A rise in the legal minimum wage may, for example, make some investment projects seem unprofitable because of higher wage costs. If this occurs, either $\overline{I}$ or v or both of them may fall, resulting in a decrease in the equilibrium level of income.

Similarly, if the government were to require a minimum down payment of 50 percent on the purchase of all durable goods by consumers, both $\overline{C}$ and b may fall, resulting in a decrease in income. This, in fact, was the case during both World War II and the Korean War.

In the late 1960s and throughout the 1970s the federal government imposed several new regulations on private sector transactors. For example, the Occupational Safety and Health Administration (OSHA) and the Environmental Protection Agency (EPA) were created and given tremendous regulatory powers. The EPA instructed investors to spend a lot of money on pollution abatement programs and equipment. These funds were, therefore, not available for the creation and expansion of new plants and equipment. OSHA imposed rules that required investors to spend a lot of money altering the work environment in the interests of safety and health. Although OSHA records show no improvement in safety and health performance, the funds used for these purposes were not available for normal investment spending. In the late 1970s many people came to believe that the costs of such regulations, including reduced investment and economic growth, were larger than the benefits. It came gradually to be recognized that many programs thought by some to have admirable social intent also may have undesirable economic results.

5-4 AN ILLUSTRATION OF FISCAL POLICY FROM A KEYNESIAN PERSPECTIVE

As we said before, most of the economists to whom most politicians listen on the issues of inflation and unemployment are Keynesians. The Keynesian view of how fiscal policy works ignores the crowding-out phenomenon and ignores the effect of taxes imposed on households on aggregate investment spending. Following that perspective, suppose the height of the aggregate demand line is such that equilibrium income is less than the income (production) level that brings about full employment *at existing prices*, as in the aggregate demand line $C_1 + I_1 + G_1$ of Figure 5-3. We would say that at Y_f (full employment nominal income at existing prices) there is a deflationary gap equal to AB. Suppose

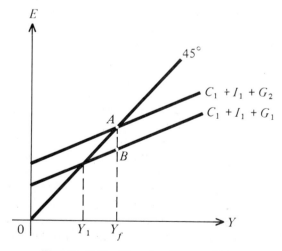

Figure 5-3 Fiscal policy problem.

government officials don't want to wait for prices to adjust because this takes too long and the interim unemployment is too costly politically. The interim unemployment period could be avoided if aggregate demand could be increased so that at Y_f it is AB higher than before. Accomplishing this task by changing government expenditure and/or tax levels is called "expansionary fiscal policy." For instance, suppose the tax function does not change (remember, the tax equation is embodied in the consumption function) but government expenditures increase by AB. If the C and I lines do not change position, the new aggregate demand line is $C_1 + I_1 + G_2$, and full employment is restored at Y_f.

Assuming that the saving taken by taxes would not have been spent on bonds or investment goods, another way to accomplish the same end is to lower the tax yield at Y_f by an amount greater than AB. We know that the change in the height of the aggregate demand line at income level Y_f will be $\Delta G - b$ times the change in the tax yield at Y_f. The change in height that we want is AB, and we wish to achieve this by lowering taxes and keeping G unchanged ($\Delta G = 0$). Therefore

$$AB = -[b \cdot \Delta T(Y_f)]$$

and

$$\Delta T(Y_f) = -AB/b$$

Given the tax equation, the value of Y_f, and the value of b, we can see what is necessary to achieve the fiscal policy goal. For instance, suppose the tax equation is

$$T = 2 + 0.25Y$$

$$Y_f = 160$$

$$b = \frac{3}{4}$$

and

$$AB = 9$$

At Y_f, with the present tax structure, $T = 2 + 1/4(160) = 42$. We wish to reduce T by $9/(3/4) = 12$ at income level 160. One way to do this would be to change the constant term in the tax equation to -10—in other words, to institute a negative income tax. Another way would be to change the slope of the tax equation, reducing it to 7/40. Since we want the tax yield at $Y = 160$ to be 30 (or $42 - 12$), we would simply solve for t in $2 + t(160) = 30$. We find that $160t = 28$ and $t = 28/160 = 7/40$.

In Figure 5-4, use of the first technique would shift the aggregate demand line to $C_2 + I_1 + G_1$, and the second technique would shift it to $C_2' + I_1 + G_1$.

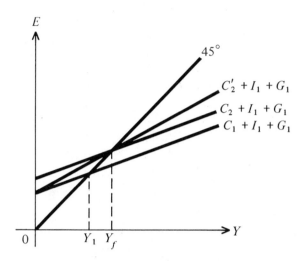

Figure 5-4 Changes in lump-sum tax versus changes in income tax.

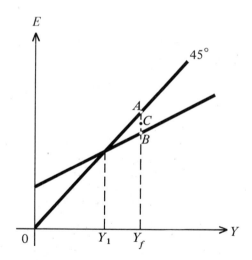

Figure 5-5 Fiscal policy choices.

Aggregate demand can be pushed up by AB at the full employment income level, Y_f, in an infinite number of ways. Given that $AB = \Delta G - b\Delta T$, for any ΔG we can solve for the value of ΔT that will make the above equation hold. In addition to increasing G by AB and decreasing T by AB/b, we can, for any point such as C in Figure 5-5, increase G by BC and decrease T by AC/b.

If the aggregate demand line intersects the 45° line at an income level greater than Y_f, there will be an inflationary gap at level Y_f. In this situation, the indicated fiscal policy steps are exactly the reverse of those for a deflationary gap.

You should make certain that you can write out the various possible fiscal policy prescriptions for the inflationary gap case. If you really understand the deflationary gap situation, the inflationary gap case should give you no problems.

The correct list of fiscal policy prescriptions in the case of an inflationary gap of AB units (here you should be certain that you know why this is the proper procedure) is:

1. Lower government spending by AB units.
2. Change the tax equation so that at the desired equilibrium level of income the tax yield is AB/b higher than it was before.
3. . Use any combination of the first two items. For example, if $AB = 9$ units, we could lower government spending by 5 and raise taxes by $4/b$.

SUMMARY

Fiscal policy is the attempt by government to alter the level of nominal aggregate demand, so that it becomes consistent with full employment at existing prices, by changing government spending relative to taxes. The Keynesian view of the impact of changes in government spending relative to taxes ignores both the crowding-out phenomenon and the effects, on aggregate investment spending, of changes in taxes imposed on households. Nevertheless, it is the Keynesian perspective that has informed almost all fiscal policy since the 1930s, and it is within that perspective that we examined the implementation of fiscal policy.

With this chapter we have completed the rudiments of the commodities market of macroeconomic theory. Throughout the remainder of the book the 45° line Keynesian cross diagram will be used to represent the commodities market. In the next chapter we will discuss some developments in the theory of the consumption function and examine the relationships between the interest rate and consumption and investment.

===================== **APPENDIX A** =====================

FULL EMPLOYMENT BUDGET CONCEPT

So far we have noted that an increase in government spending or a decrease in taxes is expansionary, while a decrease in government spending or an increase in taxes is restrictive. Suppose we want to determine whether an *existing* tax structure and spending level are restrictive or expansionary. Since we have income taxes, the size of the budget deficit that results from a given level of government expenditure is inversely related to the level of income. It will not suffice to say that, because the budget is in deficit today, fiscal policy is expansionary. Such a deficit is consistent with a restrictive fiscal policy if the budget goes into surplus before full employment is attained.

In Figure 5A-1, income is measured on the horizontal axis and the size of the budget surplus is measured on the vertical axis. At zero the budget is balanced, above the horizontal axis the budget is in surplus, and below the horizontal axis the budget is in deficit. We wish to compare two fiscal programs. Program A (represented by line AA') includes a given level of government expenditures and a given tax structure. Program B (line BB') includes the same level of government expenditures but a different tax structure. Tax structure B involves less taxation at each level of Y than does tax structure A. Fiscal program A yields a balanced budget at income level Y_1, while fiscal program B yields a balanced budget at Y_2. Relative to program A, program B is expansionary. For example,

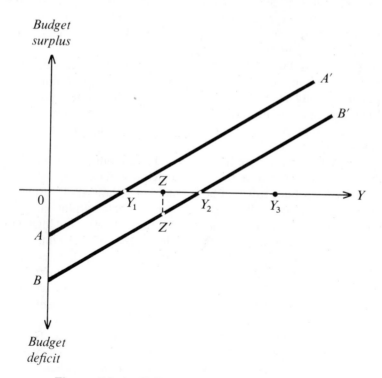

Figure 5A-1 Full employment budget concept.

suppose program A consists of $G = 20$ and $T = 10 + .1Y$, while program B consists of $G = 20$ and $T = 5 + .1Y$. Program A generates a balanced budget at $Y = 100$, but at that income program B generates a deficit of 5. Program B generates a balanced budget at $Y = 150$. If the tax equation of program B were $T = 10 + .05Y$, program B would yield a balanced budget at $Y = 200$. Moreover, the line that represents program B in Figure 5A-1 would intersect the vertical axis at the same place as the line that represents program A. (Why?)

In Figure 5A-1 as drawn, if full employment were to be at income level Y_2, program B would yield a balanced budget at that level of income. If income were Y_1 and program B were in effect, a deficit would occur; if income were Y_3, a surplus would occur. This is important in understanding the use (or misuse) of the full employment budget concept. Depending upon where full employment is *assumed* to be, a given program can be viewed as being expansionary, contractionary, or neutral. Let's assume that Y_2 represents full employment income and that full employment represents a 5 percent unemployment rate.

Program B is neutral; that is, if we were at full employment, the budget would be balanced. If conditions change (social, economic, or otherwise), we may decide that Y_3 is, in fact, full employment income. Income Y_3 may represent a 4 percent unemployment rate. Now program B is contractionary; the redefinition of full employment income would give Congress or the President ammunition for increasing expenditures or decreasing taxes.

Economists do not know what full employment is in a practical sense. The theoretical concept will be discussed in Chapter 7. But a determination of the full employment budget necessitates the choice of a specific unemployment rate. In the 1960s that rate was arbitrarily set at 4 percent. Any downward change in this rate calls for more expansionary policies while upward revision calls for contractionary policies.

In Figure 5A-1, with program B in effect, if Y_2 were full employment income and Z the actual level of income, the actual deficit would be given by ZZ', while the full employment budget would be balanced. The last actual surplus in the federal budget occurred in 1969, and that was the only surplus in the 1960s. According to the Office of Management and Budget (OMB), the high employment budget, as they call it, would have had a surplus of $1.1 billion in 1974. Table 5A-1 presents some results for the years 1970–77. The high employment budget tells quite a story. Federal policies became more and more expansionary from 1970 to 1972. By 1972 the economy had developed a severe case of inflation, and contractionary policies to decrease inflation were instituted. Unfortunately, by late 1973 the economy was headed for a recession. It was not clear at the time that the recession would be as severe as it became. This realization in 1974 did lead the government to try expansionary fiscal policy to restore employment. The later years did not see contractionary fiscal policies in spite of a vigorous expansion in economic activity.

Table 5A-1 **Actual and full employment budgets (in billions of dollars)**

Year	Actual	High Employment
1970	$ − 12.1	$ 2.2
1971	− 22.0	− 7.8
1972	− 17.3	− 15.5
1973	− 6.7	− 4.6
1974	− 10.7	1.1
1975	− 70.6	− 24.3
1976	− 53.8	− 18.6
1977	− 48.1	− 24.5

NOTE: Negative numbers mean deficits and positive numbers mean surpluses.

APPENDIX B

AUTOMATIC STABILIZERS

With an income tax, tax yields increase as income increases. If the government expenditure level is fixed, a budget deficit decreases and eventually could turn into a surplus. As we have seen, this movement is along a line such as AA in Figure 5A-1. If something depresses aggregate demand, an existing fiscal program will automatically become expansionary. In addition, since we have unemployment compensation laws, as income (and therefore—with fixed prices and wages—employment) decreases, government expenditures increase. As income grows, such transfer payments decrease and income tax yields increase.

These automatic changes are always countercyclical. However, discretionary policy changes may not be. Decision makers can make the wrong decision and pursue an expansionary policy when a restrictive one is called for. They may react to inaccurate data or think that observed changes are transitory when in fact they are permanent. In contrast, actual economic conditions themselves, rather than some decision maker's perception of these conditions, determine the automatic changes. Remember, it is changes in the level of aggregate demand that cause fluctuations in the unemployment rate. Any level of nominal aggregate demand can be a full employment level as long as prices adjust to their equilibrium values. It is the relative inflexibility of prices due to information costs that gives rise to unemployment. If policy makers make mistakes in their perceptions of the level of aggregate demand, they may cause unnecessary fluctuations in its level. If we relied only on the automatic stabilizers, the amount of fluctuations in aggregate demand would be reduced.

Of course, if some exogenous force shifts aggregate demand downward, we may want to take deliberate steps to force it back up so that we won't have to wait for prices to adjust. The important point is that we must try to avoid unnecessarily changing the level of aggregate demand by implementing policy measures based on mistaken perceptions of economic conditions.

=========================== **APPENDIX C** ===========================

GENERALIZED THREE-SECTOR MODEL

At this stage you should be able to take any specified structural form, put it into reduced form, and determine the multiplier. For instance, suppose the structural form is:

$$Y = C + I + G$$
$$C = \overline{C} + bY_d$$
$$Y_d = Y - S_b - T$$
$$S_b = \overline{S}_b$$
$$T = \overline{T} + tY$$
$$I = \overline{I} + vY$$
$$G = \overline{G}$$

What is the reduced form and what is the multiplier for this model? The answers to these questions (you should be certain you can find them for yourself) are

$$Y = \frac{1}{1 - b(1 - t) - v}(\overline{C} - b\overline{S}_b - b\overline{T} + \overline{I} + \overline{G})$$

and

$$\frac{1}{1 - b(1 - t) - v}$$

respectively.

Changes in any of the components will cause a change in the aggregate demand line. Table 5A-2 illustrates each of the possible changes. The only component that changes both the slope and intercept is a change in the marginal

Table 5A-2   Factors influencing aggregate demand

Factor	Slope	Intercept
b increases	Increases	Decreases
v increases	Increases	No change
t increases	Decreases	No change
$\overline{C}$ increases	No change	Increases
$\overline{S}_b$ increases	No change	Decreases
$\overline{T}$ increases	No change	Decreases
$\overline{G}$ increases	No change	Increases

propensity to consume (MPC). Although this result is obvious from the reduced form, the student should go back to the structural equations and determine why this is so.

QUESTIONS

1. What is the economic significance of the difference between *investment* as we have been using the term and *investment* in the sense of purchasing stock, bonds, and other financial instruments on one of the organized securities markets such as the New York Stock Exchange?

2. Suppose the economy could be characterized by the following structural form:

$$Y = C + I + G$$

$$C = 20 + 0.8 Y_d$$

$$Y_d = Y - T$$

$$T = 10, I = 20, G = 10$$

a. What is equilibrium income?

b. If G were increased by 10 and T were increased by 5, what would be the change in equilibrium income?

c. If $T = 10 + 0.15Y$, what would equilibrium income be? What is the multiplier in this case?

3. One additional direct control the government is authorized to use is to vary margin requirements on the purchase of stocks and bonds. Margin requirements determine the minmum down payment that an individual must make to buy the financial asset. For example, if the margin requirement is 60 percent, an individual who purchases $10,000 in stock must put down at least $6000. The remaining $4000 may be borrowed. Would a change in margin requirements have any effect on economic activity?

4. A national sales tax would raise prices (i.e., would be inflationary), but an increase in income taxes would be deflationary. Do you agree?

5. Using the following government sector equations, determine the budget surplus or deficit for income levels of 80, 90, 100, 110, and 120.

$$T = + .20Y$$

$$G = 30$$

If the full employment level of income is 110 and the current equilibrium level of income is 100, is the full employment budget expansionary or contractionary? If the multiplier is 2.5, what type of government action would restore full employment in the absence of negative feedback effects?

6. If the marginal tax rate (t) varies according to the level of income (as it does for a "progressive" tax) instead of being constant, are the automatic stabilizers stronger or weaker? Why?

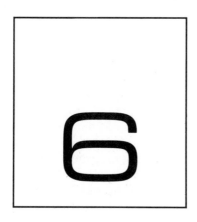

More on Consumption
and Investment

The Keynesian income-expenditure model developed in previous chapters assumed that consumption and investment are functions of the level of income and other factors. These other factors are assumed to be constant. This chapter will deal with some of the more important of these other considerations.

6-1 INCOME REDISTRIBUTION AND AGGREGATE DEMAND

Up to this point we have accepted a consumption function in the form $C = \overline{C} + bY$ as the basis of the Keynesian cross diagram. This form states that consumption expenditures in any time period are related to measured income (Y) in that time period. This consumption function assumes some given distribution of income. Recall from Chapter 4 (Section 4-1) that the consumption function is an aggregate of the decisions of millions of consumers. For any given aggregate level of income, each consumer makes spending decisions based upon his or her expected individual income. If that expected income were to change as a result, for example, of a program that increased taxes on some people while increasing subsidies to others, the aggregate consumption function would change. We can't say how until we specify individual responses to income changes. It is the individual responses that we add together and summarize as the aggregate consumption function. The effect of income redistribution (taxing some people to give to other people) can be seen only by comparing the consumption functions of the group receiving the subsidies and the consumption functions of the group being taxed.

Suppose that there are two groups of individuals with the same marginal propensity to consume (MPC). If money is taken from the first group in taxes and turned over to the other group as a subsidy, there will be no effect on aggregate consumption. Consumption, as we saw in Chapter 4 (Section 4-1), depends on disposable income (the income that a person has to spend after paying taxes and receiving subsidies). Because the first group's disposable income decreases by the same amount as the second group's disposable income increases and both groups have the same MPC, total consumption doesn't change. The first group spends less, but the second group consumes more.

However, suppose that the two groups have unequal MPCs. For example, suppose the group that is taxed has an MPC of 0.5, while the group that is subsidized has an MPC of 0.8. If the tax imposed on the first group and transferred to the second group is 100, aggregate consumption will increase by 30. The first group spends 50 less, but the second group spends 80 more. Such a policy would shift the aggregate consumption function up by 30.

Does this result in a higher equilibrium level of income? Here again the answer depends on what you assume about the nature of saving. Although consumption is 30 higher at each level of income, saving is now lower by 30. The group whose MPC is 0.5 and from whom 100 was taken saves 50 less than before. The group whose MPC is 0.8 and who received 100 saves 20 (0.2×100) more than before. If this saving is used by firms for investment expenditures, the decrease in available funds will lower the level of investment by a corresponding amount leaving aggregate demand unchanged. However, if the saving is achieved through hoarding money, aggregate demand will shift upward by 30. Since saving usually is not in the form of hoarding, the impact of a redistribution of income on aggregate demand is much less than it is often asserted to be. Redistribution policies affect the consumption plans of individuals and therefore aggregate consumption, but they do not necessarily have an effect on aggregate demand. Any redistribution that increases consumption will, most likely, reduce investment. With less acquisition of plant and equipment the ability of the economy to produce real goods and services will not grow as fast as it otherwise would.

6-2 LONG-RUN AND SHORT-RUN CONSUMPTION

Actual aggregate consumption data can be plotted against actual aggregate income data. Such a graph would indicate whether the actual data are consistent with the consumption-income relationship assumed in Keynesian theory. That relationship, you will recall from Chapter 4 (Section 4-1), indicates that consumption rises as income rises, that the MPC is constant, and that aggregate consumption as a percentage of income declines as income increases.

$-Y = -C = $ vopc $C \neq 0$
$- C = .25 (800)$
$= 2.5$
$\times 100$
$+ 75$

There are two apparently conflicting pieces of empirical evidence concerning the relationship between aggregate consumption and aggregate income:

1. Over the long run the ratio C/Y is constant as Y increases. That is, the consumption function suggested by the analysis of a long time series of data on C and Y (say from 1929 to 1979, omitting the World War II years) is a straight line emanating from the origin. $\overline{C}$ is equal to zero.
2. If the long time series is broken up into several shorter periods (say 1929–40, 1947–57, 1958–68, and 1969–79), the statistical analysis of the data on C and Y suggests that within each of the shorter periods C/Y falls as Y increases ($\overline{C} > 0$) and that the slope of the consumption function is smaller than it is over the long run. Similar results are obtained from studies that, for a given year, examine the different consumption expenditures of families with different amounts of disposable income. (Such studies are called "cross section" studies.)

Figure 6-1 illustrates the dilemma. Over the whole period 1929–79 the relationship between C and Y is best represented by a line such as that labeled

$$C = \alpha Y \tag{6-1}$$

The C line, in other words, comes out of the origin instead of starting from higher on the vertical axis. The slope of the C line is constant and equals α. Every time there is a change in Y, the resulting change in C is equal to α times the change in Y. Since the line comes out of the origin, the ratio of C to Y is constant.

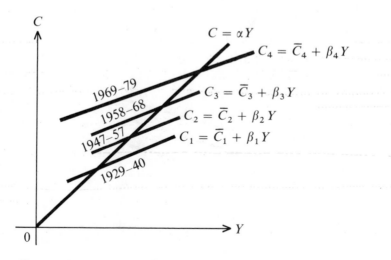

Figure 6-1 Long- and short-run consumption functions.

No matter what the level of income, consumption is the same percentage of income. If I made $100 a year or $1000 a year, I would spend α percent of my income on consumption.

For the period 1929–40 the C, Y relationship is best represented by a line such as $C_1 = \overline{C}_1 + \beta_1 Y$. The three 10-year periods 1947–57, 1958–68, and 1969–79 also are best summarized by consumption functions of the form

$$C = \overline{C} + \beta Y \qquad (6\text{-}2)$$

As we have seen, consumption functions of this form indicate a declining ratio of C to Y as Y increases.

Why is this the case? Can these results be reconciled? Which relationship, a constant C/Y or a declining C/Y, is the "true" relationship? We will consider three hypotheses advanced to answer these questions: the absolute income hypothesis, the permanent hypothesis, and the life cycle hypothesis.[1]

ABSOLUTE INCOME HYPOTHESIS

This hypothesis asserts that the short-run consumption function is the "true" relationship. The $\overline{C}$ term in such a function indicates that other variables in addition to income determine consumption. If these other variables change over time in a way that makes $\overline{C}$ become bigger and bigger, the consumption function will keep shifting upward. Figure 6-2 illustrates the argument. The long-run data simply trace out points such as A, B, and D, which are really points on

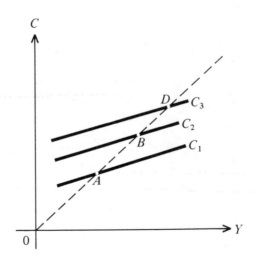

Figure 6-2 Absolute income hypothesis.

different consumption functions. If all of these points are connected we get a line that is described by an equation of the form $C = \alpha Y$. This line is, however, a statistical illusion, and it is not appropriate to call such a line a consumption function.

Arthur Smithies used the following factors to explain why the "true" consumption function shifts upward over time:[2]

1. Wealth increases over time. As people accumulate assets, they will reduce the percentage of their current income that they save because they recognize that their accumulated assets already provide a sufficient hedge against a rainy day. This means that the ratio of consumption to income will increase at each level of income or, in other words, that the consumption function will shift upward.
2. Over time there is a shift in population from rural to urban centers. Urban dwellers typically have a higher consumption-to-income ratio than the rural population does.
3. The percentage of elderly people in the population increases over time. Since elderly people typically live off past savings, their consumption doesn't fall as fast as their income.
4. Over time the set of goods that consumers regard as essential gets larger and larger. Saving is made out of income left over after "essential" consumption expenditures have been made; hence, the ratio of consumption to income increases at each income level.

PERMANENT INCOME HYPOTHESIS

What income measure do people use to make consumption decisions—a week's income? a month's? a year's? a decade's? a lifetime's? The permanent income hypothesis says that *permanent consumption is a proportional function of permanent income.* "Permanent consumption" refers to all consumption expenditures except those made in response to short-run special deals such as particularly attractive sales.

Distinguishing Permanent Income from Transitory Income   Obviously, people do not cut their consumption for one week simply because their income for that week went down. They probably know what their income will be over a whole month and so will set consumption expenditures according to this longer period. For instance, suppose a man's expected income for the month is $100 the first week, $50 the second week, $300 the third week, and $22 the fourth week. His average income per week is $118. Instead of adjusting his consumption expenditures from week to week, he will probably set his weekly expenditures (by the use of a credit card, for instance) at some fixed percentage of $118.

The same kind of reasoning can be applied to longer planning horizons. A woman who is at the peak of her earning capacity recognizes that in the future she will retire and receive less income. She will adjust her current consumption downward so that she won't have to adjust her future consumption levels down to her retirement income level. In other words, she will "iron out" her rate of consumption spending over time according to her average expected income flow. This average expected income flow is called *permanent income.*

Current measured income (Y) has two parts: permanent income (Y_p) and transitory income (Y_T). *Transitory income* is simply the difference between current measured income and permanent income. That is, at any point in time each person has an idea of what his or her average income flow is. A person may be lucky, however, and find that the actual income in a given period is larger than normal. In this case the person's transitory income is positive. A negative Y_T indicates that the current income is below what the person considers normal. People regard their permanent income as having gone up if their transitory income remains positive for a sufficiently long time. If a worker is laid off, his transitory income is negative; but if he expects, after search, to find a job that pays as well as the previous one, his permanent income stream is unchanged. On the other hand, if his skills are specialized and no longer in demand at his previous wage, he will have to lower his supply price and his permanent income will decrease.

The Permanent Income Consumption Function   The equation of the consumption function is

$$C = \alpha Y_p \tag{6-3}$$

where α is the slope of the (proportional) consumption function. The theory states that α depends on two variables, the interest rate and the ratio of nonhuman wealth to total wealth. In symbols

$$\alpha = \alpha\left(r, \frac{W_{nh}}{W}\right) \tag{6-4}$$

where r is the interest rate and W_{nh}/W is the ratio of nonhuman wealth to total wealth.[3] Total wealth is the sum of the market values of all assets, human and nonhuman, owned by an individual. Nonhuman assets are physical items such as houses, cars, and clothes and financial assets such as stocks, bonds, and money. Human assets are merely people's mental and physical abilities. One way to think of permanent income is that it is the maximum amount that can be consumed per year without selling off any assets. It is the average yearly income flow generated by a person's total wealth.

We would expect that as the interest rate goes up, α would go down because saving would become relatively more attractive. (We will take a more careful look at this idea in Section 6-4.) As W_{nh}/W goes up, we would expect α to go up because nonhuman assets are easier to convert into cash than are human assets. The higher a person's ratio of nonhuman wealth to total wealth, the greater the amount of his permanent income stream the person will be willing to spend on consumption, because he recognizes that if he gets in a financial bind, he can sell some of his nonhuman assets to raise the desired cash. If most of his assets were in the form of human wealth, it would be much more difficult to raise the desired cash (slavery, even voluntarily entered into, is after all illegal).

To test the permanent income hypothesis, its creator, Milton Friedman of the University of Chicago, had to find a way to estimate permanent income from the data available on measured income. Young people's permanent incomes will generally be larger than their current incomes. Those who are retired will also have a permanent income stream that is higher than current income. Those at the peak of their earning power will have a permanent income stream less than current income. For the economy as a whole, however, it seems reasonable to assume that average expected permanent income is a weighted average of past measured incomes. That is, the average individual forms his expectations about his permanent income stream from his recent past experience.

It also seems reasonable to assume that these weights are declining; income received 10 years ago is less significant in determining current permanent income than last year's income, but the sum of all of these past weights is greater than the weight attached to current income. Friedman proposed the following equation:

$$Y_{pt} = \beta Y_t + (1 - \beta)Y_{pt-1} \qquad (6\text{-}5)$$

Current permanent income, Y_{pt}, is equal to a weighted average of current income, Y_t, and last year's permanent income, Y_{pt-1}. The weight, β, equals 0.33. That value for β was indicated by Friedman's statistical analysis. If current income equals last year's permanent income, so too does this year's permanent income. For example, if $Y_{pt-1} = 1000$ and $Y_t = 1000$, then

$$Y_{pt} = 0.33(1000) + 0.67(1000) = 1000$$

If current income increases to 1200, then

$$Y_{pt} = 0.33(1200) + 0.67(1000) = 1066$$

Note that permanent income does not rise as much as current income. This is a very important point in the analysis. Current income is more variable than permanent income. In our example, since current income was 1200 and permanent income was 1066, transitory income was 134.

During an upswing in business activity, when current income increases, transitory income is positive. During a downswing with current income decreasing, transitory income is negative. (Try it.) Consumers spend a higher percentage of permanent income than of current income. This can be demonstrated mathematically. Since

$$C_t = \alpha Y_{pt} \tag{6-6}$$

a dollar increase in Y_{pt} will cause consumption to increase by α.

By substitution of Equation 6-5 into Equation 6-6 we see that

$$C_t = \alpha \beta Y_t + \alpha(1 - \beta)Y_{pt-1} \tag{6-7}$$

If Y_t increases by one dollar, consumption will rise not by α, but only by $\alpha\beta$. (Since $\beta < 1$, α must be greater than $\alpha\beta$.) Increases in spending out of current income must be less than increases in spending out of permanent income. The reverse is also true. If current income falls, consumption will fall but not by as much as it would if permanent income fell.

When $Y_{pt} = Y_{pt-1} = 1000$, if we assume that $\alpha = 0.8$, consumption would be $800(0.8 \times 1000)$. An increase in current income to 1200 increases permanent income to 1066; consumption would increase to $852.8(0.8 \times 1066)$. The ratio of additional consumption to additional current income would be 52.8/200 or 0.264. If the rise in current income had been viewed as permanent, consumption would have risen to $960(0.8 \times 1200)$. The slope of the consumption function with respect to current measured income is $\alpha\beta$ or (0.8×33) or 0.264; the slope of the consumption function with respect to permanent income is α (which is 0.8).

Equation 6-7 can be considered a short-run consumption function with a vertical intercept of $\alpha(1 - \beta)Y_{pt-1}$. Equation 6-6 can be considered a long-run consumption function. Figure 6-3 illustrates both consumption functions.

Suppose that in Figure 6-3 both measured income (Y) and permanent income (Y_p) equal $0A$ and then Y increases to $0B$. This change in Y increases Y_p only to $0D$. Although the increase in Y appears to have caused the increase in consumption of C_2, actually the increased consumption was caused by the increase in Y_p. (With reference to our numerical example, $0A = 1000, 0B = 1200$, $0D = 1066$, $C_1 = 800$, and $C_2 = 852.8$.)

The short-run consumption function is an illusion. The illusion arises because *any increase (decrease) in current measured income causes permanent income to increase (decrease) by a smaller amount.* The observed consumption increase appears to be associated with the increase in measured income, but it is actually associated with the smaller increase in permanent income caused by the increase in measured income. If measured income remained at $0B$ for period after period, permanent income would grow until permanent and measured income equaled each other at $0B$. At this time the short-run consumption function would intersect the long-run consumption function immediately above income level $0B$. The intercept term of the short-run consumption function is $\alpha(1 - \beta)Y_{pt-1}$. If

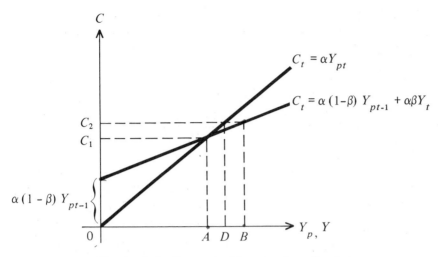

Figure 6-3 Permanent income hypothesis.

current measured income remained at $0B$ for period after period, permanent income would grow, period after period; hence the short-run consumption function would shift up, period after period, until permanent income stopped growing. Permanent income stops growing when measured income and permanent income become equal.

THE LIFE CYCLE HYPOTHESIS

Smithies and Friedman developed different theories of the consumption function, and both can be understood in the framework of the traditional income-expenditure model (as Figures 6-2 and 6-3 illustrate). Smithies argued that the long-run consumption function is an illusion, while Friedman argued that the short-run consumption function is an illusion. The life cycle hypothesis, put forward by Albert Ando and Franco Modigliani, reconciles the two. It can be viewed as an extension of the permanent income hypothesis. An individual's consumption is taken to be a function of current income, expected future income, wealth, expected remaining years of work, and expected remaining years of life.

Wealth is different from the income derived from that wealth. This is an important distinction. A person's (nonhuman) wealth is the total market value of all the assets (houses, stocks, bonds, personal property, savings accounts, checking accounts, and so on) the person owns. Nonlabor income is the flow (so much per unit of time) of payments received from such assets. Interest on savings accounts and bonds, dividends on stocks, and rentals from houses are examples of nonlabor income payments. Labor income can be similarly thought of as a flow of payments arising from the sale of the services of human wealth. The sum of these income flows in the current year constitute current income, while current perceptions of future flows constitute expected future income.

In the long run an individual's consumption is related to his or her total resources, R_t, which include current wealth (W_t), current income (Y_t), and expected future income (Y_t^e). This relationship is written as

$$C_t = \alpha R_t \tag{6-8}$$

where

$$R_t = W_t + Y_t + Y_t^e \tag{6-9}$$

If all components of R_t increased at the same rate, consumption would increase proportionately. The ratio of C_t to Y_t and Y_t^e would be constant because Y_t and Y_t^e would be increasing at the same rate as R_t. Thus the aggregate consumption function would come out of the origin, as does the permanent income consumption function.

Short-run fluctuations in one of the three components of total resources would not cause a proportionate change in consumption. For example, if a woman receives a year-end bonus from her company and does not anticipate receiving it in future years, her total resources will rise slightly. When this increase is spread over the remaining years of life, the impact on consumption will be quite small. As current and expected income and wealth rise, consumption will rise by α times that change. If current income alone rises, consumption will rise but by less than α. The short-run consumption function is flatter than the long-run consumption function.

Current income over a lifetime follows a typical pattern: low at the start of a career, rising to a peak in a person's fifties, declining to retirement, and then steady but relatively low during retirement. What remains of this expected profile at a given point in time makes up expected future income (Y_t^e). One implication is that age affects consumption. A man at the peak of his earning powers consumes a smaller percentage of his current income than does either a younger or an older man. At the peak of earnings a person pays off debts accumulated in earlier years and saves for retirement. Young workers consume a high percentage of their income by buying on credit and postponing saving until their high-income years. People in retirement live off their accumulated savings.

Another implication of the typical time profile of income is that more will be saved by a person whose income comes mainly from wages than by a person with the same income that comes mainly from stocks and bonds. The reason is that labor income falls with retirement, while interest and dividend income continues as long as the financial assets are owned.

6-3 TAX REBATES AND THE CONSUMPTION FUNCTION—
A CASE STUDY

For a theory to be useful, it must make useful predictions. Each theory must be able not only to explain past data, but also to predict future behavior. It is much easier to explain the past than to predict the future. Fiscal policy prescriptions, if they are to work, depend upon the latter; the impact of fiscal policy should be known in advance so that it does not produce undesirable results.

The three views of the consumption function we have considered give different predictions about the effects of a tax rebate. The conclusions drawn from the permanent income hypothesis and the life cycle hypothesis depend upon the type of rebate proposed: Is it a one-time only rebate or a permanent reduction in taxes? Consider Figure 6-4. If the former is the case, current income would rise, and consumption would move from the initial level of C_1 to $C_2 (Y_2 - Y_1$ is the size of the rebate). If this rebate were permanent, consumption would rise to C_2'. The absolute income hypothesis does not distinguish between a permanent change and a temporary one; it would simply predict a shift to C_2. If consumption increased to C_2', Smithies would argue that some factor caused the consumption function to shift upward from C_{SR} (short-run consumption) to C_{SR}'.

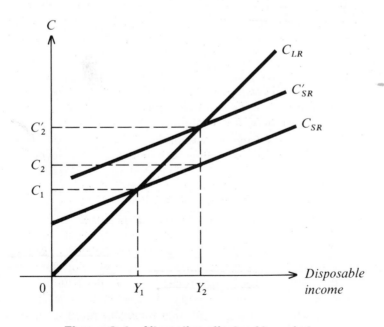

Figure 6-4 Alternative effects of tax rebate.

The tax rebate caused consumption to increase from C_1 to C_2, and some other factor or factors caused consumption to rise from C_2 to C_2'.

6-4 CONSUMPTION AND THE RATE OF INTEREST

One of the factors affecting consumption in both the permanent income hypothesis and the life cycle hypothesis is the rate of interest. A change in the rate of interest will affect the individual's desire to save because it changes the relative prices of current consumption compared to future consumption. Assume that a woman with an income of $100 decides to spend $90 and save $10. If the interest rate is 10 percent, she will receive $1 in interest and so will have $11 to use for consumption to augment next year's income. She currently sacrifices $10 in consumption in order to be able to consume $11 next year. If the rate of interest were to rise to 20 percent, the same $10 saved will result in $12 of increased consumption opportunity next year. At this higher rate, the cost of consumption in the current year is higher in terms of the foregone future consumption than it was before. In the absence of inflation (which would reduce the purchasing power of future income) any rise in the price of current consumption relative to future consumption will decrease current consumption. This is merely an example of the *first law of demand. There is an inverse relationship between the amount of something bought and the relative price of that thing.*

The consumption function can be written in general terms as

$$C = f(Y, r) \tag{6-10}$$

Any increase in Y by itself, either permanent or current, will increase C, while an increase in r by itself will decrease C. Figure 6-5 illustrates these relationships. Instead of one consumption function, we have a different consumption function for each rate of interest. $C(r_1)$ is the appropriate consumption function if the rate of interest is r_1, while $C(r_2)$ is appropriate if the interest rate is r_2, where $r_2 > r_1$. The level of planned consumption expenditures, at any level of Y, varies inversely with the rate of interest.

6-5 PRESENT VALUE INVESTMENT DECISION RULE

How do the decision makers in a firm decide whether to undertake a given investment project? They estimate the impact of the project on the firm's profit and compare this with the cost of the project. But how do they make this comparison? It may seem that all they have to do is to estimate, for each year of the expected life of the project, the amount that the firm's profit is higher than it otherwise would be, add all of these bits of additional profit together, and com-

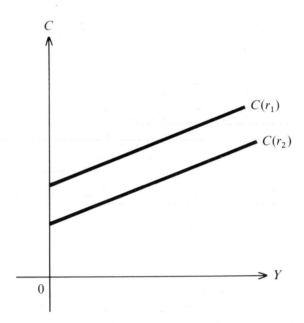

Figure 6-5 **The relationship between consumption
and the rate of interest.**

pare this sum with the project's price tag. But this will not suffice, because one cannot add together profit received in 1978 and profit received in 1980. This would be like adding three rulers to two pens and coming up with five what-chamacallits. We must find a common denominator to use when adding dollar amounts for different dates.

Suppose that you offer to pay me $1.10 one year from today, and that today I can buy for $1.00 a one-year bond that pays an annual rate of interest of 10 percent. How much would I be willing to pay you today for your promise to pay me $1.10 next year? Clearly, I would not pay you any amount over $1.00 because I can get $1.10 next year by buying a bond for $1.00 today. We say that the "present value" of $1.10 received a year from now, if the rate of interest one can earn by buying bonds is 10 percent, is $1.00.

THE EXAMPLE OF A MORTGAGE

Suppose you purchase a house for $80,000 by obtaining from a savings and loan association a loan that you agree to pay back, with interest, in 30 annual install-ments. After signing the mortgage contract, you calculate the total amount of money you will give to the savings and loan association over the 30 years. You are shocked to discover that your 30 annual payments total $253,000. Is it correct to say that the house cost you $253,000? The answer is no.

Assume for the moment that the yield on bonds is equal to the rate of interest you must pay on the mortgage. Suppose you had $80,000 in cash but you decided to borrow the money for the house anyway. You could take your own $80,000 and buy bonds today. At the end of every year you would receive an interest payment and you could sell a portion of the bonds. With this money you could make the payment due the savings and loan. If you did this each year, at the end of the 30 years you would have no more bonds, and you would have no more mortgage. The cost you incurred to pay off the mortgage was the $80,000 you used to buy the bonds. The amount you have to tie up today to generate the exact amount of money you need to make your series of payments is called the *present value* of that series of payments.

If you didn't have the $80,000 you needed to buy the bonds, the house still costs you only $80,000. If you used the money you borrowed to buy bonds instead of a house, the bonds could be used to make the series of payments to the savings and loan association. The loan would cost you nothing. You don't buy bonds; you buy a house instead. The cost of the house is the dollar value of the bonds you could buy with the same money—$80,000.

If the interest rate you can earn on bonds is less than the rate you must pay on the mortgage, the cost of the house will be greater than $80,000. You could use the returns from the $80,000 bond purchase to meet the largest portion of the payments you must make to the savings and loan association, but you would have to add an extra amount from other sources.

If the rate of interest on bonds is higher than the mortgage rate, the house would cost less than $80,000. Only a portion of the returns from the bonds would have to be turned over to the savings and loan association. You could use the rest to give an annual party in the new house.

Again, this is true even if you do not have a spare $80,000 you can use to purchase bonds. Any time you borrowed money you could conceivably use it to buy bonds. When you use borrowed money to buy a house or a car or anything else, the cost of the thing you have purchased is the value of the bonds you could have bought instead of the house or the car. When I go to a grocery store, the cost of purchasing a jar of roasted soybeans that has a price of $1.50 is the half-gallon of ice cream that I could have purchased with the $1.50. In other words, the real cost of any good X is the amount of some other good Z that I must give up in order to get X.

EQUATIONS FOR DETERMINING PRESENT VALUE

If I start out with A dollars and invest them at an annual rate of return of ($r \times 100$) percent, at the end of one year I will have $A + rA = A(1 + r)$ dollars. If I take the full amount and reinvest it for a second year, at the end of the second year I will have $(1 + r)A + r(1 + r)A = A(1 + r)^2$ dollars. For example, if I start with $2.00 and the interest rate is 5 percent, at the end of the first year I will have $2.10 ($2.00 + 0.05 of $2.00). I start the second year with $2.10 and end the second year with $2.205 (or $2.10 + 0.05 of $2.10). At the end of i years I will have accumulated $A(1 + r)^i$ dollars $= 2(1 + 0.05)^i$.

Now let's turn this idea around. How much money must I *start* with so that at the end of i years I will have accumulated $A(1 + r)^i$ dollars, where $(r \times 100)$ percent is the annual rate of return on the initial investment? Clearly, I must start with A dollars today to meet my goal. The *present value* of the $A(1 + r)^i$ dollars achieved i years from today is A dollars.

The present value of any specified sum of money, S_i, received i years in the future with a rate of return on bonds of r, is

$$V_0 = \frac{S_i}{(1 + r)^i} \tag{6-11}$$

This means that the amount of money you must take out of your pocket today to buy enough bonds so that you have S_i dollars i years from now is V_0 dollars. For example, suppose the interest rate is 6 percent ($r = 0.06$), and you are offered $10, which you will receive two years from today. The present value of this $10 is

$$V_0 = \frac{10}{(1 + 0.06)^2} = \$8.90$$

This means that you can buy $8.90 worth of bonds today and when the bonds mature in two years you will have $10. At the end of one year you will have $8.90 + 0.06($8.90), which equals $8.90(1 + 0.06)$. At the end of two years you will have $8.90(1 + 0.06) + 0.06[\$8.90(1 + 0.06)] = \$8.90(1 + 0.06)^2 = \$10$. (You should check this calculation for yourself.) Thus a dollar received today is worth more than a dollar received in the future (and this has nothing to do with inflation). If you are going to add together dollar amounts of different dates, you must convert each of these dollar amounts into present values.

EVALUATING INVESTMENT PROJECTS

When the decision makers for a firm consider buying a machine, say, they try to estimate, for each year of the life of the machine, the amount that the firm's profits would be higher with the machine than without it. Let π_i be the estimate of the extra profit in the ith year. They will have a list as follows: $\pi_1, \pi_2, \pi_3, \ldots, \pi_n$. This is called the *expected incremental profit stream*. They also know what the price of the machine is. Let's call this C_0. They will compute the present value of the stream of extra profits by computing the present value of each π_i and adding them together:

$$V_0 = \frac{\pi_1}{1 + r} + \frac{\pi_2}{(1 + r)^2} + \cdots + \frac{\pi_n}{(1 + r)^n} \qquad (6\text{-}12)$$

If V_0 is greater than C_0, they will buy the machine; if V_0 is less than C_0, they will not. Suppose $V_0 = \$1800$ and $C_0 = \$1000$. They will buy the machine because it costs them $\$1800$ to get an income stream of $(\pi_1, \ldots, \pi_n)$ by buying bonds and only $\$1000$ to get the same income stream by buying the machine. *The present value of any investment project is equal to the amount of money you have to spend on bonds to get an income stream equal to the income stream you get from the investment project in question.* Ten dollars in profit received i years from now adds less than $\$10$ to the net worth of the firm today, because it costs the firm less than $\$10$ today to assure itself of $\$10$ extra profit i years from now by buying bonds.

If $V_0 = \$1000$ and $C_0 = \$1800$, the machine is a bad buy because the cheaper way to buy the income stream in question is to buy bonds. Why spend $\$1800$ when you can get the same thing for $\$1000$?

Suppose that V_0 is greater than C_0 and C_0 equals $\$1000$. What if the firm doesn't have $\$1000$ with which to purchase the machine? This doesn't matter. It can simply borrow the money by (say) floating a bond issue. If the going rate of return on bonds is 6 percent, these bonds will also have to pay 6 percent or they won't sell. If they pay 6 percent—the same as the interest rate we used for discounting—the firm will incur the obligation to make a series of payments over the life of the bonds, whose present value is C_0.

In Figure 6-6 we plot the relationship between the discount rate, r, and the net present value of a representative investment project. Net present value is simply the difference between the present value of the project and the cost of the project, or $V_0 - C_0$. It is the amount the investment project adds to the present value of the firm's wealth or net worth. Clearly, as the discount rate increases, $V_0 - C_0$ decreases because as r increases V_0 decreases. In the figure, for any discount rate between 0 and x (such as b) the investment project in question (such as buying a machine) adds to the present value of the firm's wealth. If the interest rate on bonds rises above x, the machine is not worth buying. The firm should be buying bonds instead of the machine because the bonds would give a higher return stream; the firm's net worth would be higher if the bonds are bought than if the machine is bought.

At any point in time a number of investment projects will be under consideration. Each investment project can be represented by a separate line that shows the relationship of $V_0 - C_0$ to the discount rate for that project. Figure 6-7 portrays three investment projects—A, B, and D. For all values of r less than x, all three investment projects could be undertaken profitably. If $x < r < y$, only

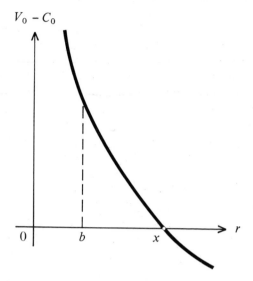

Figure 6-6 Net present value as a function of interest rate.

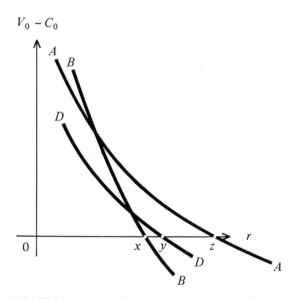

Figure 6-7 Net present values of alternative investment projects.

projects D and A would be profitable. If $y < r < z$, only project A would be profitable. If $r > z$, none of the projects should be undertaken.

In other words, as the interest rate increases, the number of profitable investment projects for any firm decreases. We would therefore expect that an increase (decrease) in the interest rate would decrease (increase) total investment spending in the economy.

6-6 INVESTMENT AS A FUNCTION OF RATE OF INTEREST AND LEVEL OF INCOME

In the last section we saw that the evaluation of investment projects by a firm depends upon the rate of interest. Each firm evaluates projects according to the net present value criteria. Turning back to Figure 6-7, assume that each of these investments—A, B, and D—is available to the firm and that each represents an initial outlay of 100. If the interest rate is less than x, all three projects will be undertaken and the level of investment by the firm will be 300. At any rate greater than x but less than y, only A and D will be undertaken. At a rate equal to or greater than y but less than z, only A (for 100) will be pursued. If the inter-

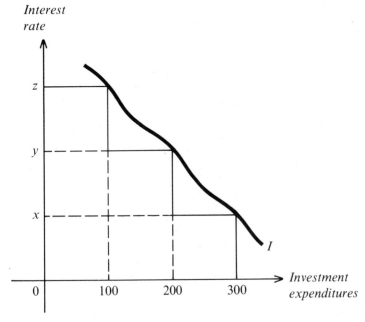

Figure 6-8 The relationship between investment and the rate of interest.

est rate is at or above z, no investment will be undertaken. Thus we see that as the rate of interest rises, more and more projects become unprofitable; hence the rate of investment falls as the rate of interest rises.

Figure 6-8 shows this relationship for this firm. With only three projects, the relationship between investment and the rate of interest would be a step function. For example, at any rate between 0 percent and x percent, investment would be 300; between x and y, investment would be 200; and between y and z, it would be 100. If the firm had many projects, the steps would get smaller and smaller. If we were to sum up the investments of the millions of firms in the economy, each with different investment opportunities, investment could be represented by a continuous line such as I in the figure. The negative slope of that line depicts the inverse relationship between aggregate investment and the rate of interest.

The income-expenditure model considered investment as a function of the level of income. I was determined by other factors. The analysis above suggests that one of those factors is the rate of interest. At a given level of income, investment will be higher at a low rate of interest than at a high rate of interest. Again, as we did for the consumption function, we can depict that relationship by showing different lines of relationship between investment and income. Figure 6-9 illustrates how. At income level Y_1, if the rate of interest is r_1, investment

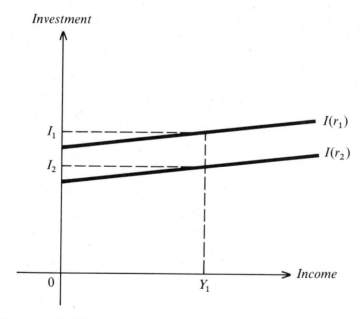

Figure 6-9   The investment function at alternative interest rates.

will be I_1. If the rate of interest increases to r_2, the investment function shifts to $I(r_2)$; at income Y_1, investment will have fallen to I_2.

SUMMARY

In this chapter we have examined some extensions of the Keynesian model. Aggregate consumption depends upon the distribution of income. Changes in this distribution will have an impact on aggregate consumption as long as the marginal propensity to consume (MPC) of the individuals being taxed is different from that of the individuals receiving subsidies. The effects on aggregate demand are smaller than many believed because of the individual negative impact on saving and investment.

Reconciliation of Keynes' consumption function with the observed proportional relationship was undertaken by Smithies, Friedman, and Ando and Modigliani. The latter three stress the difference between current income and normal or expected income. Changes in current income have less effect on consumption than changes in expected or normal income.

Finally, the relationship between the rate of interest and consumption and investment was examined. Both consumption and investment are inversely related to the rate of interest. This implies that the Keynesian aggregate demand line, $C + I + G$, shifts when the rate of interest changes.

In the next chapter we turn our attention to the labor market of macroeconomic theory.

=========================== **APPENDIX** ===========================

INTERNAL RATE OF RETURN RULE

Look back at Figure 6-6. If the discount rate is x,

$$V_0 - C_0 = 0 \qquad \text{(6A-1)}$$

For every potential investment project there is a discount rate that makes $V_0 - C_0 = 0$. The discount rate that does that is called the *internal rate of return* on the project in question. It is the rate of return that, if applied to C_0 dollars, would generate an income stream equal to the income stream in question.

If it costs me A dollars today to get a certain claim on S_1 dollars one year from now and if

$$S_1 = A + \rho A \qquad \text{(6A-2)}$$

the internal rate of return is ρ. In the expression

$$A = \frac{S_1}{(1 + \rho)} \tag{6A-3}$$

both A and S_1 are fixed numbers. The variable ρ must assume the value that makes

$$A(1 + \rho) = S_1 \tag{6A-4}$$

Clearly, if the rate one must pay to borrow money (or the rate one gives up when one ties up the money) is smaller than this internal rate of return, the project is worthwhile and should be undertaken. This is simply another way of stating the rule that it is profitable to undertake all projects for which V_0 is greater than C_0. In Figure 6-6, suppose the borrowing rate or the rate of return on bonds is b. At b, $V_0 - C_0$ is greater than 0 and x is greater than b. Both rules state that the project is desirable.

A problem arises, however, when choices must be made among a set of po-tential projects, all of which have $V_0 - C_0$ greater than 0. Under these circum-stances the projects that would maximize the present value of the net worth of the firm have the largest spread between V_0 and C_0. Projects should be ranked according to this difference. To maximize the present value of net worth, the firm should undertake first the project at the top of the list, then the second, and so on until the funds for investment expenditures are depleted.

6A-1 SUPERIORITY OF THE PRESENT VALUE RULE

Suppose a firm ranks several potential projects according to their internal rates of return and follows this listing in deciding which projects to undertake. Won't this necessarily give the same answer as the present value rule, which involves ranking according to the difference between V_0 and C_0? The answer is no, for two reasons:

1. The time paths of the receipts streams of two projects may be dissimilar.
2. The sizes of any projects that are being ranked (i.e., the amounts of money that must be tied up in the projects) may be dissimilar.

Time Paths

Consider two projects, A and B, with receipts streams as pictured in Figure 6A-1. Project B pays a little at first and then pays a lot, while project A pays a fairly constant amount over the life of the investment. At high interest rates present payments will dominate future payments. Thus at high interest rates project B

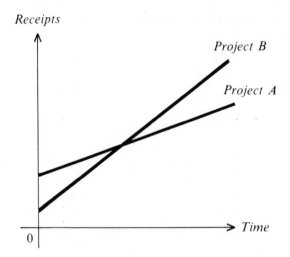

Receipts

Project B

Project A

Time

0

Figure 6A-1   Time profiles of receipts from alternative projects.

will have a low $V_0 - C_0$ relative to project A. At low interest rates, future pay-ments are not discounted as heavily; hence project B will have a high $V_0 - C_0$ relative to project A.

From Figure 6A-2 it is clear that the internal rate of $B(\rho_B)$ is less than that for project $A(\rho_A)$. However, if the interest rate is less than c, project B should be chosen over project A (if such a choice must be made) because project B would maximize the present value of the net worth of the firm for interest rates less than c. If no choice need be made, both projects should be chosen at any interest rate less than ρ_B.

Project Size

Suppose a firm has $100 and faces the following possibilities:

1. Invest $100 for one year at 10 percent.
2. Invest $30 for one year at 15 percent; use the remaining $70 to buy a 7 percent bond.
3. Use the entire amount to buy a 7 percent bond.

A correct analysis of these three choices must consider the effects of these alternatives on the net worth of the firm. Choosing the investment with the highest rate of return (15 percent) would be incorrect. We can easily calculate the incremental net worth of the firm from each of these alternatives:

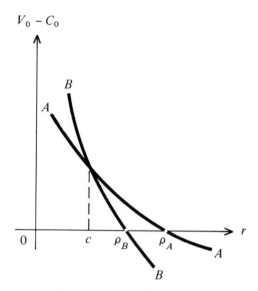

Figure 6A-2   Effects of different time profiles.

- Alternative 1 yields $10 (10% of $100).
- Alternative 2 yields $9.30 (15% of $30 + 7% of $70).
- Alternative 3 yields $7 (7% of $100).

Project size is important because the project yielding the highest rate of return in our example does not use up the entire amount of the available funds. Using a decision rule that ranks the desirability of projects according to their internal rate of return would result first in the $30 project, then the $100 project, and finally the bond. This rule will not maximize the net worth of the firm.

QUESTIONS

1. It is frequently asserted that (ignoring exemptions) sales taxes are regressive. That is, the tax paid as a percentage of income falls as income increases. The absolute income hypothesis supports this contention, and the permanent income hypothesis and the life cycle hypothesis deny it. Can you see why?

2. Suppose a temporary tax is imposed on incomes in order to reduce total spending. If the tax is announced as a temporary tax, and if the permanent income hypothesis is valid, what effect would you expect the tax to have on total spending?

3. Construct an aggregate consumption function for two families with the following individual consumption functions.

$$C_1 = 20 + .5Y_d \qquad \text{(Family 1)}$$

$$C_2 = 70 + .8Y_d \qquad \text{(Family 2)}$$

What assumptions are necessary to construct this aggregate function?

4. The national income accountant's definition of consumption expenditures includes all expenditures by households on final products (except new houses) in a given period. When I purchase a car, a refrigerator, or any consumer durable good (a good that lasts more than one year), do I consume (use up) my wealth or am I really saving? What is a good definition of consumption? What is a good definition of saving? What is a good definition of wealth? What is a good definition of income?

5. In trying to assess the impact of a new tax policy, should a consumer-oriented firm be more concerned with the short-run effects or the long-run effects? Why?

6. Current consumption and the current rate of interest are inversely related. How are current consumption and the expected rate of inflation related? Why?

7. Current investment and the current rate of interest are inversely related. How are current investment and the expected rate of inflation related? Why?

8. Many foreign investments have higher expected incremental net present value than domestic investments. Does this suggest that foreign investments are necessarily superior to domestic investments? If not, what other factors are important in making investment decisions?

9. Some owners of business firms are said to base their investment decisions on payback periods. That is, they estimate the period of time it takes for added profit to equal the cost of an investment project; when they must pick between mutually exclusive projects, they pick the one that has the shortest payback period. Show that owners who behave this way are not maximizing their wealth.

10. You decide to purchase a car that costs $3000. The saleperson says you can pay $3000 today or $3150 a year from now. The rate of interest on bonds is 10 percent. Which is the cheaper way to pay for the car? At what interest rate are the two payments identical?

11. In the April 1972 issue of *Consumer Reports*, home buyers were given the following advice: purchase a dishwasher from a department store that charges $675 plus 15 percent interest each year for two years, rather than having the builder put a dishwasher in the house. The builder, it was argued, could get the dishwasher for $450, but he would add this amount on to the mortgage. If the mortgage matured in 27 years, and if the mortgage rate of interest were 7.75 percent, the dishwasher would cost a total of $1075. The total cost of the dishwasher purchased at the department store on a two-year contract would be $785. What do you think of this advice?

12. All three theories of the consumption function discussed in Section 6-2 imply that the marginal propensity to consume, measured as the change in income in two adjoining years divided into the change in consumption in the same two adjoining years, would be unstable. For each theory explain why this is so. What implications does this have for the stability of the multiplier? Why?

13. To decide between alternative investment strategies, most firms calculate both the internal rate of return and the incremental net present value. If you had to convince a decision maker of the superiority of one method or the other, how would you do it (without using graphs)?

NOTES

1. Arthur Smithies, in "Forecasting Postwar Demand," *Econometrica* (January 1945), advanced the absolute income hypothesis; Milton Friedman, in *A Theory of the Consumption Function* (Princeton: Princeton University Press, 1957), set forth the permanent income hypothesis; and Albert K. Ando and Franco Modigliani, in "The 'Life-Cycle' Hypothesis of Saving," *American Economic Review* (March 1963), developed the life cycle hypothesis.

2. Smithies, "Forecasting Postwar Demand."

3. The usual way to write a function is to place the variable that depends on other variables on the left-hand side and a list of the variables upon which the first one depends, separated by commas, within parentheses on the right-hand side of the equation. The letter on the outside of the parentheses is merely the name of the function. Thus Equation 6-4 merely says that α depends on the interest rate and the ratio of nonhuman to total wealth.

PART

3

THE LABOR MARKET

Employment, Unemployment, and Search

In macroeconomic theory all of the diverse kinds of labor (e.g., computer programmers, plumbers, secretaries) are lumped together and treated as a homogeneous entity called "labor." The market for this aggregated labor is analyzed using the traditional tools of supply and demand.

In the absence of labor unions, the wage that would be paid to any particular kind of labor would be determined by the interaction of the demand and supply for that kind of labor. We get the total demand for a particular kind of labor merely by adding together, at each price (wage), the quantity of workers wanted by each employer who hires that kind of labor. The supply of a particular kind of labor depends on the skills and training people have and/or choose to acquire. In general, the higher the wage that people see they can earn by providing a particular type of labor, the larger the number of people who will want to be employed selling such labor, and the larger the amount of labor time each individual will want to sell.

In this chapter we will look particularly at unemployment. One type of unemployment ("frictional unemployment") can be understood only by looking at the demand for labor on the part of individual employers. Another kind is best understood in terms of the demand for labor in the aggregate. The demand for aggregate labor is the demand for labor that results when all of the individual demands are added together.

7-1 BASIC CONCEPTS

Past chapters have made reference to the labor market, full employment, and inflationary and deflationary gaps. This chapter will deal specifically with the labor market. For this purpose we need to define some key concepts.

1. Every person 16 years or over in the civilian noninstitutional population (N) can be classified as employed (E), unemployed (U), or not in the labor force (O). That is,

$$N = E + U + O$$

2. An individual is unemployed, according to the Bureau of Labor Statistics (BLS), if that individual has tried to find a job within the past four weeks and is currently available for work. This category includes both full-time and part-time job searchers.
3. An individual is employed if that individual did any work at all as a paid employee, worked in a family business for 15 or more hours, or worked independently in a business or profession.
4. All other individuals 16 or over, civilian (not in the armed services) and not institutionalized (e.g., not in jail), are not counted in the labor force. Full-time college students not seeking employment and full-time housewives would not be counted, as would also individuals who have been searching for employment in past months but have given up their search.
5. The unemployment rate, one of the most closely watched statistics, is defined as $U/(U + E)$. Since this rate is usually expressed as a percentage, the equation must be multiplied by 100. An unemployment rate of 5 percent means that 5 out of every 100 persons in the civilian labor force that are available for work are searching for work.
6. The employment rate is defined as E/N, and it, too, is usually expressed as a percentage. Its current value is 60 percent. That is, 60 percent of all the people in the United States who are 16 or over and not in the armed forces or incarcerated in an institution are employed, according to the definition of the BLS. During 1974 and the first quarter of 1975 the unemployment rate increased from around 5 percent to over 9 percent; yet, at the same time, the employment rate increased. More and more people were finding jobs, but the number of people looking for jobs grew even faster. If a student who was not searching for a job suddenly decides to search, U would rise without any corresponding change in E. It is important, when examining unemployment statistics, to determine why they change.
7. Another important statistic is the average duration of unemployment— that is, the average time spent in job search by unemployed people. Many

economists argue that one individual unemployed for 40 weeks is a more serious social problem than 40 individuals each unemployed for one week. Unemployment benefits are intended primarily to ease the financial strain of short-run unemployment, while retraining programs are intended to solve long-run unemployment problems.

The BLS conducts a monthly survey of approximately 50,000 households to gather employment and unemployment statistics. From this sample, population figures are projected. As with all sampling, the results are subject to a sampling error. On a month-to-month basis, this can be about .2 percentage points. Thus a change in the unemployment rate from 5 percent to 5.1 percent would not represent a statistically significant change because the sampling error is larger than the measured change. We must always be careful in interpreting month-to-month changes because of this sampling error, but a trend over a period of months can be correctly interpreted as a statistically significant change.

7-2 DEMAND FOR LABOR IN A PARTICULAR EMPLOYMENT

In any particular employment there is an upper limit to what an employer is willing to pay any particular seller of labor services. That upper limit is based on what difference the presence or absence of the worker makes in terms of revenue earned net of nonlabor costs such as raw materials and energy.

MARGINAL PRODUCT OF LABOR

Suppose that there are 20 people working a standard workday in some job and that the total amount produced of whatever the firm produces is 100 units per day. On the average, each worker produces 5 units per day; however, if any one of the people were to quit, the drop in output per day would be (say) only 3 units.

There is a fixed amount of capital (plant and equipment) for workers to use at any given time in a given job. (Of course, a firm can add to or subtract from the amount of plant and equipment it has, but that takes time. We here are interested in the impact of a change in the number of workers on the output of a firm when the amount of capital available for use is constant.) When there is one worker fewer on site, the remaining workers may have more ready access to equipment and tools, and thus they each can produce a little more than before—though probably not enough to completely make up for the one who quit. (If they could, the one who quit would never have been hired.) Hence, in our example the drop in output would be only 3 instead of the 5 units that the worker who quit used to produce.

Economists call the lost output the *marginal product of labor* (MP_L). The MP_L is merely the change in output that is experienced when there is a 1 unit change in the amount of labor used. It will almost always be less than what each worker produces because the presence or absence of another worker changes the amount of capital available per worker. As the amount of equipment and tools per worker declines (increases), the amount, on average, each worker produces declines (increases). An additional worker adds to total output the amount he or she produces, but also reduces the amount that each of the workers already there produce. Thus the lost output from the workers already there must be subtracted from the extra output produced by the new worker to get the marginal product.

The marginal product of labor is *not* what an additional worker produces; it is the additional output when one more worker is hired. Similarly, if there is one worker less, the ratio of capital to workers increases and so each of the remaining workers can produce slightly more than they could before. The loss of what the missing worker produced must be corrected for the additional output produced by those who remain in order to compute the marginal product.

Clearly, the marginal product of labor depends crucially on the amount of plant and equipment that is on site available for use. With a given amount of workers, the MP_L will increase as the firm adds to the amount of plant and equipment, and it will decrease as the firm decreases the amount of plant and equipment available for the workers to use.

MARGINAL REVENUE PRODUCT OF LABOR

It isn't merely the change in output when there is a 1-unit change in the amount of labor used that determines the value to an employer of the presence or absence of a worker. What the employer really cares about is the revenue gain or loss that results. When 3 units less of output are produced, there are 3 units less that can be sold; and so less revenue will be brought in. If we multiply the change in revenue collected per unit change in output by the change in output per unit change in the amount of labor used, we get the full revenue impact of the presence or absence of any single worker in dollar terms. (Of course, the dollars we are talking about must be corrected for inflation; i.e., they must be real dollars.)

When there is a change in the amount of output produced, there will also be changes in the amounts of such things as raw materials and energy used in production. Thus the change in revenue that is experienced when there is a 1-unit change in the amount of labor used must be adjusted to take into account additions to other costs when output is increased and reductions in other costs when output is reduced. When it is so adjusted, the result is called the *marginal revenue product of labor* (MRP_L). This MRP_L is the upper limit that an employer would be willing to pay any single worker. It is the full value to the employer of the presence or absence of any single worker.

We see that the MRP_L depends on how productive a worker is, what effect the worker's presence or absence has on the physical productivity of other workers because of the change in the ratio of capital to workers, how much the amount of dollars collected changes when the amount of output being sold changes, and how other (nonlabor) variable costs change when the amount being produced changes.

In Figure 7-1 we see a downward sloping line labeled MRP_L. On the horizontal axis we measure the number of people working a standard workday (N). On the vertical axis we measure MRP_L, which, as we have just discussed, is in dollar terms (corrected for inflation). When 20 people are working, MRP_L on an hourly basis is \$4 (point *a*), while when five people are working the MRP_L on an hourly basis is \$13 (point *b*). The latter is more than the former because the significance of the presence or absence of a single worker decreases as more workers are working. (Again, this is because, with a fixed amount of capital, the ratio of capital to labor decreases as more workers are on site.)

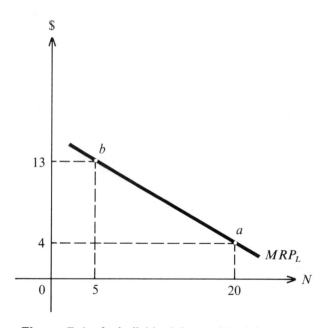

Figure 7-1   An individual demand for labor curve.

The MRP_L line is the demand for labor line for the employer we are talking about. After all, a demand line tells us the quantity of workers that the employer will want to hire at each wage rate. Suppose the wage rate is $4 per hour. If only five workers have been hired, it would clearly be profitable to hire more workers. Starting at five workers, if one more were hired today, today's hourly revenue net of nonlabor variable costs would be more than yesterday's by $13. The cost of hiring the additional worker is only $4 per hour. The employer would hire more and more workers as long as the addition to revenue (net of nonlabor additional costs) exceeds the wage that has to be paid. Thus, if the wage is $4, 20 people would be hired. Suppose we begin with 20 people working at $4 per hour. If, for any reason, the wage should increase to $13, and if nothing happened to shift the MRP_L line (such as an increase in the demand for the product that the employer is hiring the workers to produce), the quantity of workers hired would fall to five. Beginning at point a, if the wage went to $13, the lost revenue if one worker were fired would be only $4 per hour (the MRP_L at point a), while the cost saving would be $13 (the new higher wage). Workers would be fired or laid off as long as the cost saving (the wage) exceeds the revenue loss from having less to sell (the MRP_L).

Were we to draw a line to show the quantity of labor offered for sale at each wage rate, it would slope upward. The wage where the supply line intersects the total demand line for the particular kind of labor we are talking about would be the equilibrium, or market-clearing, wage.

7-3 FRICTIONAL UNEMPLOYMENT

Sometimes particular people in particular jobs decide to leave their jobs and search out other ones. Sometimes they are forced to leave. Whichever way it happens, *frictional unemployment* arises from job switching made necessary when the demand for labor in some employments decreases while the demand for labor in others increases.

AN EXAMPLE

Consider two industries which utilize the same kind of labor inputs. That is, labor employed in industry A could just as easily be employed in industry B, since the skills and training required by both industries are identical. Suppose consumer tastes change away from product A and toward product B so that at the existing wage rate the decrease in the number of labor-hours demanded in industry A is exactly equal to the increase in the number of labor-hours demanded in industry B. Unemployment will result from this situation. To see why, let us consider Figure 7-2.

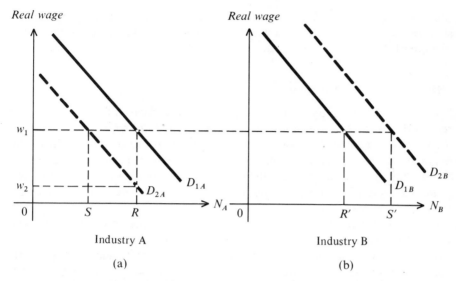

Figure 7-2   Interindustry shifts in demand for labor.

Suppose that initially the wage rate is w_1 (with homogeneous labor it must be the same in the two industries). The lines labeled D are demand for labor curves. The changed purchases of consumers cause the demand lines to shift to D_{2A} and D_{2B}. If an all-wise dictator were running the show, he could simply order RS labor-hours to move from industry A to industry B. The wage rate (w) would not have to change and there would be no unemployment.

Of course, dictators cannot be all-wise. In any actual economy the information about tastes and preferences, resource availabilities, and production possibilities that is relevant to coordinating what some people want and what others plan to make available is highly scattered. Such information is perceived and known only in bits and pieces. Each person perceives those bits that are most relevant to him or her. The information does not exist in any one place. It cannot possibly be comprehended and acted on by any single mind or committee of minds. Instead, the voluntary exchange process gives rise to the multitude of individual prices that permit the plans and actions of the thousands and millions of individual transactors, each acting on their own bits and pieces of information, to become coordinated.

In a world of voluntary exchange the workers in industry A are presented with two alternatives: a wage cut of $w_1 - w_2$ or a layoff equal to RS labor-hours. The affected workers are likely to choose the second alternative, since they have no reason to think that w_2 is now the best wage they can get, and they are likely to expect that normal conditions will soon return and so they will be recalled.

Moreover, the pain of accepting a layoff is greatly eased by unemployment insurance payments. Accepting a wage cut rather than a layoff is likely to seem like utter folly.

THE COSTS OF SEARCH

If the demand shift in our example is permanent, as such shifts often are in the real world, normal conditions do not return and unemployment benefits begin to run out. When the workers adjust their expectations to reality, they must begin to *search* for alternative employment. Alternative opportunities exist, but the workers do not know where they are. *Information* about where the opportunities are and what they pay is not free and can be obtained only by incurring the costs of search.

Employers in industry B in our example will also invest some resources in search, because it doesn't pay for them to hire the first applicants who come along. They will want to be sure that they hire the "best available." Unfortunately, they can never be sure of this without interviewing *every* applicant *forever*. They clearly won't do this, but neither will they spend zero time in search.

What is the optimal time to spend in search? That depends on the costs of search and the benefits derived from it. Assuming that the longer one searches, the higher will be the best offer one receives, the marginal cost (*MC*) of search will rise with respect to time. A worker laid off from industry A, for example, will face an upward sloping marginal cost of search curve, as in Figure 7-3.

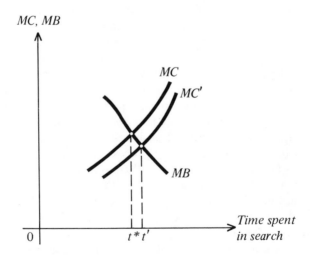

Figure 7-3   Optimal search time.

Marginal cost rises because the major cost of an additional unit of time spent in search is the wage that could have been earned during that time. The relevant wage is the best offer received to date. Moreover, unemployed workers are likely to focus their search at first in nearby areas. As time spent in search increases, workers canvass larger geographical areas and so marginal search costs increase.

The searcher faces a downward sloping marginal expected benefit (MB) curve with respect to time spent in search. The expected benefit from an additional unit of time spent on search is the receipt of an offer better than the offer that was previously best. The longer the time already spent in search, the lower the probability that an additional unit of time will yield a better offer. The optimal search time is the time at which marginal cost and marginal expected benefit are equal (t^* in Figure 7-3). For any t less than t^* the cost of an additional day spent in search is less than the expected gain. The searcher clearly will not spend an additional day in search if the costs of the extra day exceed the benefits of the day *as he perceives them.*

Anything that lowers the marginal cost of search will *increase* the optimal search time. For instance, if unemployment insurance benefits increased, the marginal cost curve in Figure 7-3 would shift to MC' because the marginal cost of search is the best offer received to date less any transfer payments received while searching. In this case the optimal search period would be t'.

In contrast, anything that lowers information costs will *reduce* the optimal search time. Here the student must keep clear the distinction between search costs and information costs. *Search costs* are incurred because a decision has been made to engage in search. *Information costs* determine the expected *benefits* from engaging in search. If information is cheap, individuals already know about the market situation; therefore search activity would not be beneficial because there would be nothing to search for. The higher the cost of information, the less the individual will know without search and hence the greater the expected benefit of search. If someone were to set up a national data bank of job information that anyone could plug into (for a fee), information costs would be reduced, the marginal benefit curve of Figure 7-3 would shift to the left, and the optimal search period would be reduced.

THE NATURAL UNEMPLOYMENT RATE

As long as the time spent in search by employees and employers is greater than zero, demand shifts will result in frictional unemployment. This type of unemployment is unavoidable in a system of voluntary exchange as long as information costs are greater than zero. It is generally agreed that frictional unemployment is responsible for unemployment rates up to 5 percent. This is why a 5 percent unemployment rate is sometimes called the "natural" rate of unemployment. Rates of this magnitude merely indicate that resources are being reallocated toward higher valued uses (i.e., where there is a greater demand for them). On the other side of this market are jobs that are not filled. Employers are engaging in a similar type of search. The existence of unemployed workers and unfilled jobs is a sign that markets are responding to shifts in demand. Only if all buying patterns were frozen could frictional unemployment be avoided in a world where information can only be obtained by search. Furthermore, since information is not free and resource owners must search for the highest valued uses of their resources, we would not want unemployment to drop below its "natural" level. If resource owners spent less than the optimal time in search, the resources would be misallocated.

It is useful to think of frictional unemployment as a pipeline. There are always people who are entering the job search pipeline, and there are always others who are leaving it. The number of people in the pipeline at any one time is normally 5 percent of the labor force, but the names of the people in the pipeline are constantly changing. The average period of job search (length of time in the pipeline) since the end of World War II has been around 12 weeks.

7-4 STRUCTURAL UNEMPLOYMENT AND MINIMUM WAGES

Let us drop the assumption that the workers in industry A are perfect substitutes for workers in industry B. Under these circumstances, when buyers decrease their purchases of product A and increase their purchases of product B, it may be impossible for workers displaced from industry A to find employment at wage rate w_1, no matter how much time they spend in search. Because of the difference in training and skills necessary for industry B, employers in industry B will hire workers from industry A only at a lower wage rate than w_1. Of course, employers in industry A can also be induced to hire the displaced workers, *but only if the wage rate falls.* If the law specifies a minimum wage above that which is necessary to employ all the workers who were previously employed, "structural" unemployment (a mismatch between available jobs and the labor available for employment) will result.

Structural unemployment, like frictional unemployment, results from demand shifts. The difference is that workers in the declining industry do not have the skills necessary to be employed in the growth industry *at the old wage level.* They must accept a lower wage to get employment simply because the market evaluation of their skills has declined. In the absence of a minimum wage law or other impediments to lower wages (e.g., union pay scales), there will be short-run unemployment as workers search for their best (now lower) offers. If the wage rate is not permitted to fall or is not permitted to fall enough, long-run unemployment will result. Programs such as the 1964 Manpower Development Training Act, designed to teach marketable (at more than the minimum wage) skills to displaced workers, are intended to cope with this type of unemployment.

Structural unemployment is, to a lesser extent, also caused by the unwillingness of people to move away from their homes where jobs are declining to areas where jobs are increasing. Programs that offer inducements to unemployed workers to migrate from high unemployment areas to low unemployment areas might partially overcome the reluctance to move.

Another factor contributing to structural unemployment is government-provided incentives not to work. In a recent study Arthur Laffer compared the costs and benefits of working.[1] A Los Angeles inner-city family of four would receive $739.33 per month from various types of federal, state, and local transfer payments if no one in the family worked. If family wages increased to $100 per month, it would acquire only $31.54 in additional disposable income. If wages were $1000 per month, that same family would receive $167.98 in additional spendable income. Since not working has become so inexpensive, it is no surprise that many people are reluctant even to attempt an honest job search. Moreover, many people who are officially unemployed are actually employed in what has been called our underground economy. We will consider this in Section 7-6.

7-5   UNEMPLOYMENT AS A RESULT OF DECLINING AGGREGATE DEMAND

Macroeconomics has traditionally been concerned with another kind of unemployment—that which arises from declining *aggregate demand.* A fall in aggregate demand means that most industries will face declining sales at the same time. Earlier we discussed what happens when the demand for labor falls in one industry and rises in another; now we must investigate what happens when demand for labor in most industries falls simultaneously. The existence of positive information costs will give rise to unemployment under these circumstances just as it did in the case of demand shifts.

THE IMPORTANCE OF MONEY WAGES

A decrease in aggregate demand will cause a corresponding decrease in the demand for workers in many employments at the same time. Individual firms, experiencing a decrease in sales, begin to lay off workers and cut back output. Employees in any particular industry have no information that permits them to distinguish this decline in demand for their services from a simple demand shift. They will not immediately take wage cuts but will, instead, search for better offers. Only after some time is spent in search will they become convinced that their best money wage offer is lower than what it used to be. If, just before they become convinced of this, the level of demand is further depressed, causing the demand for labor to fall still further, still more time and search will be necessary to convince the workers that their best wage is even lower.

After aggregate demand stops decreasing, there will be a gradual movement back to full employment as workers' views of best offers come to coincide with reality. Workers will reduce the money wage levels they hold out for—the jargon is that they will reduce their "reservation price." The longer the period of decreases in the level of aggregate demand, the farther the workers will have to lower their reservation prices; hence *the longer the period of decreases in the level of aggregate demand, the longer the time of recovery to full employment.*

This analysis of the cause of unemployment—the failure of money wages (and, as we will soon see, of money prices for goods and services) to adjust instantaneously to their new equilibrium values—would hold even if every firm in the economy were a perfect competitor and there were absolutely no monopolistic unions. The essential item in the analysis is the fact that when equilibrium prices change, the knowledge about what the new equilibrium prices are is not free. It takes time to discover the new equilibrium price set. Add to this the fact that there are labor unions with considerable monopolistic power that can *temporarily* resist wage reductions in the face of unemployment. Even when the unemployed become willing to offer their services at a lowered wage, they cannot do so if employers are constrained to pay according to union scales. Under these circumstances, workers who cannot be employed in the unionized industries because the wage rate is too high must search for employment in nonunionized industries. (Only 20 percent of the total private sector labor force was unionized in 1978, in contrast to 25 percent in 1953.) This situation will prolong the time required for the average wage to fall to its full employment value. The increased supply of labor in nonunionized industries will lower wage rates in these industries.

As long as aggregate demand in nominal terms remains at its new low level, unemployment will continue until the average wage rate, also in nominal terms, is lowered.

FROM THE VIEWPOINT OF THE COMMODITIES MARKET

In Figure 7-4 the commodities market is in equilibrium with aggregate demand as represented by D_1D_1. (The E on the vertical axis stands for expenditures—both actual and planned.) Equilibrium Y (nominal GNP) is the product of "the price level" (P_1) and real GNP (Q_f). Q_f is the level of real full employment output produced by employing N_f labor-hours (Figure 7-5). Something happens to depress the level of aggregate demand to D_2D_2.

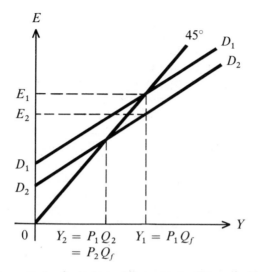

Figure 7-4 Search and the commodities market.

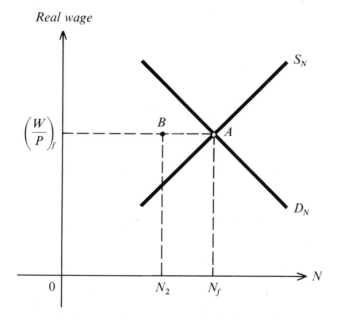

Figure 7-5 The aggregate labor market.

At income level Y_1, planned expenditures have decreased to E_2. Producers find their inventories accumulating $(E_1 - E_2)$ as sales fall below expectations. From the perspective of a single firm, this could, however, be a transitory phenomenon. The sales rate for any firm is not constant but is randomly distributed around some mean. When a firm experiences sales rates below the mean, decision makers don't know whether this is merely an unfortunate sampling from the sales distribution or an actual downward shift of the entire distribution. Since firms lose a lot of goodwill capital when they raise prices, they will not immediately respond to a low sales rate by lowering prices because if the low sales rate is transitory they will have to raise the prices back to the original level. It makes sense for the decision makers of the firm to adopt a wait-and-see policy. Their first response to the unexpected inventory accumulation is to cut back production. Only after they are certain that the lower sales rate is permanent will they respond by cutting prices. As prices are lowered, sales rates will increase and so too will production and employment.

When aggregate demand is depressed to D_2D_2 in Figure 7-4, the initial response is to lower real output to Q_2 and to maintain price level P_1. Thus there is a lower level of equilibrium nominal income $(Y_2 = P_1Q_2)$. Eventually, however, prices will fall to P_2 and real output will return to Q_f. The nominal income level is still Y_2, but this is now the full employment level of nominal income, since now $Y_2 = P_2Q_f$.

The decrease in prices from P_1 to P_2, which restores Q to Q_f, corresponds to the fall in money wages that was a result of workers' lowering their reservation price. Nothing real has changed in the economy. Workers have lower money wages but prices are also lower, and so real wages are unchanged. The output of real goods and services is exactly what it was before (Q_f), and the number of labor-hours employed is unchanged. All that has happened is that the economy has "deflated." The deflation, or the fall in wages and prices, has restored the economy to full employment even though the level of aggregate demand in nominal terms is lower than it used to be.

We are all painfully aware of the fact that *average* money prices and wages have not fallen since World War II. Some individual prices and wages have fallen, but the average money price and wage levels have almost constantly increased. That does not mean, however, that the above discussion is irrelevant. It examines what would happen *if* the level of nominal aggregate demand were permitted to decline and remain at its new lower level for some time. It demonstrates that deflation is a logical possibility. However, since World War II the federal government has actively sought to prevent declines in nominal aggregate demand. It even tries to sustain a steady *growth* in nominal aggregate demand. It does this through the fiscal policy tools we discussed in the last chapter and the monetary policy tools we will discuss in Chapter 9.

If nominal aggregate demand always grew at the same rate as the growth of the ability of the economy to produce real goods and services, the *average* money price and wage levels would not change. Dollar spending would keep up with the quantity of goods and services available to be bought. When, however, as it often does, nominal aggregate demand is made to grow faster than the real productive ability of the economy, the average money price and wage levels are forced up. If nominal aggregate demand grew at a rate less than the rate of growth of real productive ability, the average money price and wage levels would fall. Government policy usually forces nominal aggregate demand to grow too fast. In Chapters 11 and 12 we will explore the pressures on politicians that cause them to behave this way.

FROM THE VIEWPOINT OF THE AGGREGATE LABOR MARKET

In Figure 7-5 the line labeled D_N is the aggregate demand for labor. That is, it shows the quantity of all the diverse kinds of labor lumped together that employers (all employers lumped together) would like to hire at each average real wage rate. The average real wage is the average money wage (W) divided by the average money price level (P). But the quantities of labor indicated for each wage by D_N are the quantities that would be hired if the employers could sell all they plan to sell in the commodities market. In other words, the quantity of labor N_f is the quantity of labor that in the aggregate employers would like to hire when the average real wage is $(W/P)_f$, *assuming that the quantity of output that is produced by that many workers can be sold in the commodities market.*

Look back at Figure 7-4. Initially, nominal aggregate demand is D_1, nominal income is Y_1, the average money price level is P_1, and real output produced and bought is Q_f. This situation corresponds in Figure 7-5 to point A. The real wage is $(W/P)_f$, which is the ratio of the average money wage W_1 and the average price level P_1. The quantity of labor hired is N_f, and that quantity of labor produces Q_f of real output. Aggregate demand falls to D_2. At first, nothing happens to either W or P. The multiplier reduces nominal income to Y_2, and since P hasn't changed, Q has been reduced to Q_2. Since the quantity of output sold is Q_2, only N_2 of labor will be hired even though the real wage hasn't changed. In the labor market the economy has gone to disequilibrium point B. It is not on the aggregate demand for labor line because that line shows the quantity of labor demanded at each real wage, assuming that all the output produced by the labor will be sold.

As the search processes in the labor market and in the commodities market go on, gradually the money wage level (W) and the money price level (P) fall. Although it need not happen, they might fall at the same rate and so the real wage would never be different from $(W/P)_f$. In any case, as wages and prices fall, real output bought and labor employed to produce that output will increase. In the labor market diagram (Figure 7-5) the economy would be seen to move back toward point A; in the commodities market diagram (Figure 7-4) the economy would remain at the intersection of D_2 with the 45° line, but Y_2 would come to be composed of P_2 for prices and Q_f for real output.

Again, this analysis does not depend on any specification of market structure. It holds in the case of perfect competition, pure monopoly, and everything in between. A pure monopolist will charge the price that permits him to sell the quantity for which marginal cost equals marginal revenue. When aggregate demand (in nominal terms) declines, the demand curves faced by monopolists as well as the demand curves in competitive industries will decline. The profit-maximizing price for both the monopolist and the competitor will decline. Prices are not lowered immediately because it takes time for both the pure monopolist and the perfect competitor to *perceive* changes in demand.

There is much confusion about this relatively simple point. It is true that the monopoly price for a commodity is likely to be higher than if that commodity were sold competitively. However, given that there are monopolists, it is nevertheless true that when a monopolist's demand curve shifts to the left, his profit-maximizing price will fall. Nothing in the theory of monopoly says that a monopolist can insulate himself against declining aggregate demand.

GOVERNMENT'S ROLE IN WAGE AND PRICE ADJUSTMENT

Unfortunately, price and wage adjustments take time—frequently much time. Between June 1930 and June 1933, for example, the money supply decreased by 25 percent. This decrease in money supply decreased the level of aggregate demand in nominal terms. During this period, and for this reason, price and wage expectations had to be revised downward if full employment were to be attained. At the same time that a declining nominal aggregate demand dictated lower prices and wages, a sequence of acts by the federal government made these price adjustments very difficult. The Guffey Coal Act, the National Industrial Recovery Act, the agricultural price support program, the National Labor Relations Act, and minimum wage legislation raised prices and wages by fiat, and thus made it practically impossible for the existing low level of nominal aggregate demand to become a full employment level of nominal aggregate demand. Each of these laws was designed to raise some price. The thinking behind the laws was that if prices were high, more money would be in the pockets of everyone, and thus aggregate demand would increase. If the wage rate were raised, for example, workers would have more pay and thus would spend more. The fallacy in this idea rests on a confusion regarding wage rate and income. Aggregate spending depends on the level of income. Labor's income is the product of the wage rate and the number of hours worked. When aggregate demand is depressed, and at the same time the wage rate is increased, there will be a large decrease in the number of labor-hours employed. Aggregate incomes will fall in the face of the rising wage rate.

Any level of prices and wages can be an equilibrium (full employment) level if nominal aggregate demand is changed to "ratify" existing prices and wages (i.e., to make existing prices and wages equilibrium prices and wages). Since adjustments in prices and wages take time even when they are not blocked, we may want to avoid having to go through adjustment periods of high unemployment by manipulating the level of nominal aggregate demand so that existing prices and wages won't have to change.

Fiscal policy in the Keynesian model examines the ways and means of seeing to it that aggregate demand in nominal terms is at whatever level is necessary to maintain full employment at existing prices. Some economists believe that the process of adjustment without governmental intervention can be costly to the economy in terms of lost output and high unemployment. If, in Figure 7-4, the government were to increase expenditures or decrease taxes to restore aggregate demand to D_1 as soon as it had fallen to D_2, the recession that accompanies price and wage adjustment could be avoided. This is what is called *countercyclical policy*: government increases expenditures and/or decreases taxes in economic slowdowns, and does the reverse in expansions.

In 1969 economist Bent Hansen examined the effectiveness of fiscal policy in seven developed countries.[2] For the period 1955–65 he found very mixed results. Countercyclical policy seemed to be successful in Belgium, West Germany, Sweden, and the United States. The best results were obtained by U.S. policymakers, where cycles were 17 percent less severe than they would have been had there been no countercyclical policy. In the other three—France, Italy, and Great Britain—these policies made the cycle more severe. France represented the worst case; cycles were 35 percent more severe than without any explicit governmental intervention. We should reexamine Figure 5-1 in light of this evidence. In some countries discretionary policy dampened economic cycles; in others using the very same fiscal policies, the cycles were more severe.

7-6   HOW FULL IS FULL EMPLOYMENT?

In our discussion of frictional unemployment, we used 5 percent as a benchmark for full employment. If work disincentives and nonmarket opportunities did not exist, this figure would probably be unacceptable to policymakers. Two recent articles, however, question our ability to interpret official unemployment statistics. These articles suggest that the United States has experienced a permanent increase in the number of officially unemployed individuals.

Kenneth Clarkson and Roger Meiners suggest that one of the most important factors affecting the unemployment rate in the 1970s was a 1973 change in the law.[3] Individuals must now officially register as unemployed if they wish to receive transfer payments such as food stamps, AFDC, and general state welfare. Registration was not required earlier. If these individuals were deleted from both the civilian labor force and the list of the officially unemployed (as they were prior to 1973), unemployment rates would decline dramatically. Presenting statistics from the Bureau of Labor Statistics, these economists show that the official rates of unemployment for 1974 through 1976 were 5.6 percent, 8.5 percent, and 7.7 percent. These are high by post–World War II standards. But for most of the post–World War II period the law was different. Correcting these statistics by deleting recipients of food stamps and AFDC (those who earlier were not included in the statistics) lowers the unemployment rate to 3.8 percent, 6.1 percent, and 5.3 percent for the same years. These statistics do not include any other effects on unemployment such as rent subsidies and increased unemployment benefits.

Peter Gutmann, in a subsequent article, includes adjustments for those seeking only part-time work as well as estimates of the "subterranean" work force.[4] He estimates that approximately 11 percent of those officially unemployed were searching for part-time work. An additional 5 percent were working but were not officially employed; these individuals were working in the underground, away from official eyes, avoiding all tax payments while remaining eligible for transfer payments. If we add these to the estimates developed by Clarkson and Meiners, approximately 40 percent of those reported as unemployed in 1978 should not have been so reported.

We can safely conclude that 5 percent is too low an estimate of full employment. If policymakers set 5 percent as a target and pursue economic policies to achieve that level, the results are likely to be inflationary. That is, planned expenditures would be too high relative to the capacity of the economy to expand output without inflationary pressures. Phillip Cagan estimates that an official unemployment rate of 6.6 percent would cause neither a worsening of the inflation rate nor more unemployment.[5]

7-7 INFLATION AND UNEMPLOYMENT

It used to be thought that economic policymakers could reduce the unemployment rate merely by expanding total dollar spending enough so that inflation resulted.[6] The lower the desired rate of unemployment, the higher the amount of inflation that would have to be accepted as the price. Similarly, if the policymakers attempted to reduce inflation, they could do so only at the cost of having to put up with high unemployment rates. It was thought that there was a trade-off between unemployment and inflation. We now know that such a trade-off doesn't exist except very temporarily.

We know that because of frictional unemployment, it is natural or normal to have some unemployment all the time. Even in an economy without any inflation and without any declining aggregate demand, an economy in full macro equilibrium, there will be some unemployment due to resource reallocation (in response to shifts in the patterns of demand in individual sectors of the economy). Such unemployment, as we said before, is usefully thought of as a pipeline. There are always some people entering the pipeline and others leaving it. Normally around 5 percent of the labor force is in the pipeline at any given time.

WHEN ACTUAL INFLATION RISES ABOVE EXPECTED INFLATION

Suppose the rate of inflation that actually exists and the rate of inflation that people expect to exist is zero. Ignoring structural unemployment, the only unemployment that would exist would be the normal frictional sort. In Figure 7-6, the economy would be depicted at point N. The unemployment rate (on the horizontal axis) would be N, and the inflation rate (on the vertical axis) would be

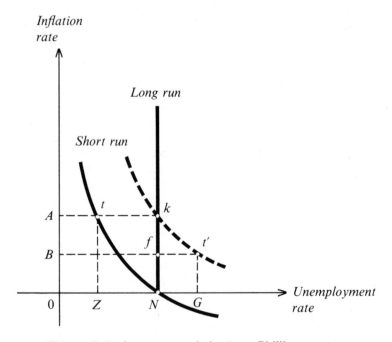

Figure 7-6 Long-run and short-run Phillips curves.

zero. Suppose now that expansionary policies that increase total dollar spending relative to the total amount of real goods and services bought were initiated. The result would be that the money prices of many things would increase at the same time (albeit at different rates). The average money price level would increase at some rate, say the rate represented by distance $0A$ on the vertical axis. Although the actual rate of inflation is now $0A$ instead of zero, both workers and employers still expect the inflation rate to be zero.

Employers have noted an increase in expenditures on their products, but each individual employer sees only his own increased sales. He is not aware that the increase in spending is general. He responds to his perception of his own increase in sales by increasing the price for his product. Workers, having been accustomed to zero inflation, do not translate their perception and expectation of general inflation, and thus do not increase their demands for money wages. This is true of workers searching for a job as well as workers who are employed.

Thus employers see unchanged money wage demands but increases in the prices they *individually* receive for what they sell. They are thus willing to increase their hiring. Moreover, in order to successfully recruit additional workers, they offer somewhat higher wages.

Workers searching for a job still expect zero inflation, but they find somewhat increased money wage offers as their search continues. These wage offers look high relative to the zero expected inflation, and thus many in the job search pipeline are induced to cut short their search and accept employment even though the wage offer they accept is below what their reservation price would be if they correctly perceived that inflation is occurring.

Employers are induced to hire more workers because each one thinks he is the only one able to charge higher prices while not having to raise commensurately the money wages offered. Workers looking for a job are induced by attractive money wage offers (which are *not* attractive in real terms—that is, relative to the inflation that is underway but unperceived as yet) to cut short their search. The unemployment rate falls from $0N$ to $0Z$. The economy is at point t in Figure 7-6. The (*unanticipated*) inflation has caused a reduction in the unemployment rate.

But that reduction is only *temporary*. If inflation continues at the rate $0A$, both employers and workers will come to expect it. Workers who were looking for jobs will return to normal search times, and employers will find that the money wages they now have to pay to obtain and keep workers are no longer low relative to the prices they can charge for the products being produced. Employers' abnormal intensity of demand for workers will disappear, and the unemployment rate will return to normal—to $0N$. The economy will be at point k in Figure 7-6. There is inflation of $0A$, but because it is fully anticipated, the normal amount of unemployment will exist along with the inflation.

In order permanently to reduce the unemployment rate to $0Z$, the actual rate of inflation would have to constantly exceed the expected rate of inflation. Since both employers and workers eventually catch on to any existing inflation, the inflation rate would have to constantly increase. But employers would also soon catch on to the acceleration of inflation. People form expectations about the rate of change of inflation as well as the rate of inflation itself. Because of these "rational expectations" we must conclude that inflation can never permanently reduce the rate of unemployment.

WHEN ACTUAL INFLATION GOES BELOW EXPECTED INFLATION

Suppose in Figure 7-6 that the economy is at point k. If the actual rate of inflation is reduced from $0A$ to $0B$, the expected rate of inflation will temporarily remain at $0A$. Individual employers will think their demands are declining and they will reduce their hiring and the wages they offer to workers. Workers in the job search pipeline will respond to the lower money wage offers by *expanding* their time spent in search. Since they still expect the higher inflation rate, they do not perceive that the lower money wage offers are not lower in real terms—that is, relative to the actual inflation rate. Less hiring and extended search periods make the unemployment rate increase to $0G$. The economy would be at point t'. But that, too, is temporary (just like point t). As employers come to perceive that their demand has not fallen relative to others' demands, and as workers come to expect lower inflation and hence accept lower wage offers than before, unemployment will return to $0N$. The economy would then be at point f.

PHILLIPS CURVES

In Figure 7-6, the lines on which points t and t' are located are short-run Phillips curves.[7] They show the temporary effects of changes in the inflation rate on the unemployment rate. The short-run curve that the economy is on at any point in time depends on the expected rate of inflation. When the expected rate of inflation is zero, the short-run curve is the line through points t and N; while if the expected rate of inflation is $0A$, the short-run curve is the dashed line through points k and t'. In the long run, however, the economy always ends up on the vertical line. That is, when the expected inflation rate equals the rate that actually exists, no matter how high or how low, the rate of unemployment is the normal rate.

SUMMARY

This chapter discusses some important aspects of the labor market. Factors influencing the commodities market—whether through shifts in demand for individual products or through increases or decreases in aggregate demand— have important effects on the labor market. Three types of unemployment were examined: frictional unemployment, structural unemployment, and declining aggregate demand unemployment. Full employment was defined as the rate of unemployment that would exist if there were only frictional unemployment and no unanticipated inflation or deflation. This rate is not zero; the efficient flow of resources in the presence of positive search costs necessitates some positive rate of frictional unemployment.

Official unemployment statistics were examined in light of actual changes in the labor market. Inducements to withhold labor services, growth of nonmarket opportunities, part-time job searchers, and changes in the law requiring transfer payment recipients to register as unemployed have all boosted the unemployment rate. These factors suggest that a 5 percent target rate of unemployment would be inflationary. Finally, we saw that there is only a very short-run tradeoff between inflation and unemployment. In the long-run, no such trade-off (Phillips curve) exists.

QUESTIONS

1. Unemployment is wasteful and should be avoided at all costs. Do you agree? Should anything be avoided at all costs? Is unemployment wasteful?
2. What is natural about the so-called natural rate of unemployment?
3. Construct a rigorous definition of involuntary unemployment. If Mr. A is looking for a job as a teacher at a pay rate of $1000 per day, and he cannot find such a job, is he involuntarily unemployed?
4. What is the difference between search costs and information costs?
5. The longer it takes to lower wages and prices in the face of a decrease in aggregate demand, the more severe will be the ensuing recession. Comment.
6. One way to solve the poverty problem is to raise the minimum wage rate and extend its coverage. Do you agree?
7. Should armed forces personnel who have volunteered for service be excluded from the employment statistics? Are the services performed by military personnel included in GNP? Are their wages included in GNP? Should draftees be treated differently?
8. Investment should be discouraged because by making each worker more efficient, fewer workers are needed to produce a given level of output. This will cause unemployment to rise. Comment.
9. Would progressive taxation of earned income affect reservation wages during an inflation? Why or why not?
10. From an elected policymaker's point of view, which is more significant: the short-run Phillips curve or the long-run Phillips curve? Why?

NOTES

1. "The Disincentive Factor," *Time Magazine* (October 2, 1978), p. 55.
2. Bent Hansen, *Fiscal Policy in Seven Countries, 1955–1965,* Organization for Economic Cooperation and Development (Paris, 1969).
3. Kenneth W. Clarkson and Roger E. Meiners, *Inflated Unemployment Statistics: The Effects of Welfare Work Registration Requirements,* Law and Economics Center, University of Miami (March 1977).
4. Peter M. Gutmann, "Are the Unemployed, Unemployed?" *Financial Analysts Journal* (September-October 1978), pp. 26–29.
5. Phillip Cagan, "The Reduction in Inflation and the Magnitude of Unemployment," in *Contemporary Economic Problems,* W. Fellner (ed.) (American Enterprise Institute, 1977).
6. The exposition of the theories in Section 7-7 follows Milton Friedman, *Price Theory* (Chicago: Aldine Publishing Co., 1976), pp. 213–28.
7. The name "Phillips curve" comes from an article written by the English economist A. W. Phillips: "The Relation between Unemployment and the Rate of Change of Money Wage Rates in the United Kingdom, 1861–1957," *Economica* (November 1958), pp. 283–99. In the article Phillips tried empirically to demonstrate such trade-offs for the economy of the United Kingdom.

PART

4

THE MONEY MARKET

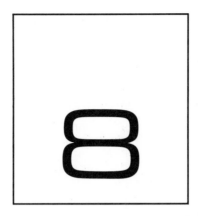

The Quantity Equation of
Exchange and the
Demand for Money

One of the closest relationships in macroeconomics is that between the amount of money in circulation in a country and that country's nominal GNP. This relationship is illustrated in Figure 8-1, which plots, for each of the eight countries indicated, the average annual rate of growth of the money supply (horizontal axis) against the average annual rate of growth of nominal GNP (vertical axis) for the period 1973–78. Figure 8-1 clearly suggests a strong positive association between the two variables, one that grows stronger as the two variables increase.

It is important to note that the association emerges using 5-year averages of the data. Short-term (quarter-to-quarter) changes in the money supply are not as closely related to short-term changes in nominal GNP. The reasons for this will become clear in Section 8-7.

In Chapter 3 we saw that interaction between markets is necessarily a vital part of economic analysis. In Chapters 4 through 6, we discussed the commodities market with only an occasional reference to any other market. In the last chapter we saw how the commodities and labor markets affect each other. Figure 8-1 indicates that changes in the money market are associated with changes in the commodities market. We must, therefore, turn our attention to developing the theory of the demand for and supply of money. This chapter focuses on the demand for money, and the next chapter considers the supply of money.

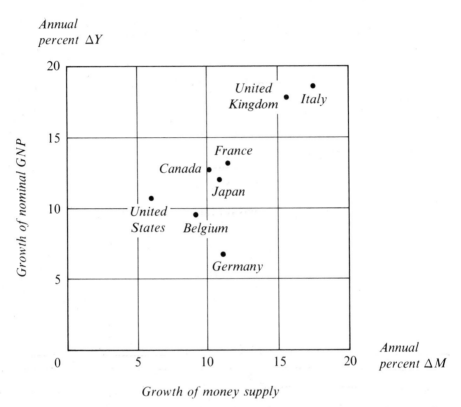

*Annual
percent ΔY*

Growth of nominal GNP

*Annual
percent ΔM*

Growth of money supply

Figure 8-1 The historical relationship (1973–78) between monetary
growth rates and income growth rates.

8-1 MONEY AND TRANSACTION COSTS

From microeconomic theory we know that whenever two people have different evaluations of the same two goods, both can be made better off by exchange.[1] Furthermore, one need not always trade for the commodity one hopes to end up with. Suppose Mr. A has some of commodity X_1, Mr. B has some X_2, and Mr. C has some X_3. Suppose Mr. A wants less X_1 and more X_3 but cannot find anyone who will make the trade at a satisfactory rate (price). However, he sees that Mr. B is willing to give up some X_2 to acquire X_1, and he likes Mr. B's suggested price because he knows he can use the X_2 to buy enough X_3 from Mr. C to make the loss of X_1 worthwhile. After Mr. A has acquired the X_3, he has his preferred bundle, which he has acquired through the use of an *intermediary good.*

There are costs associated with this exchange process. Mr. A had to physically transport X_1, X_2, and X_3; he had to inspect X_2 to make sure of its quality so that he could be sure of the rate at which he could exchange it for X_3; and he had to search out the sequence of trades, since not everybody will accept X_2 for X_3. The logical question that emerges is, what are the attributes of an intermediary good that minimize these transaction costs?

1. First, the intermediary good must have a low recognition cost—that is, it must not require too much time and effort for the traders to inspect and identify. Suppose I have 100 apples, which I trade for 100 peaches, which I then trade for 100 bananas. If, instead of using peaches as my intermediary good, I used 100 packages of No. 4 staples, I could get (say) 103 bananas. In this case the person I purchase the bananas from must spend less time and effort discovering the quality of the staples than that of the peaches. In other words, the cost of recognizing staples is less than the recognition cost for peaches.

2. The intermediary good must also have a low transport cost—the cost of moving the thing itself and of transferring rights to it. It is unlikely that a car would be used as an intermediary good even though it is mobile, because title to the car can be transferred only after much paper work and correspondence with a state department of motor vehicles. On the other hand, title to deposits in a demand deposit account is transferred at a fairly low cost—one simply writes a check.

3. In addition, the cost of dividing up the intermediary good and reassembling it must be low, since one is likely to use the asset to purchase many different things and the exchange rates of these things are likely to be diverse.

4. Finally, the cost of maintaining the asset itself and of maintaining the rights to it must be low. The asset must be either durable or cheap to replace, since it is likely to change hands many times. An asset that is easily stolen or difficult to protect will be a very expensive asset to carry to the marketplace.

The asset that best combines all of these features will emerge as the commonly used medium of exchange precisely because it will minimize the costs of engaging in exchange. Such an asset will be more generally acceptable when the cost of predicting its exchange value in relation to the set of all other goods and services is low.

8-2   QUANTITY EQUATION OF EXCHANGE

Every purchase is a sale. Suppose we wish to add together the dollar value of the sales of all the goods and services that are counted in GNP. That sum would be

PQ, where Q is real output of goods and services (goods and services evaluated in base year prices) and P is a weighted average of individual prices such as the GNP deflator. All of these sales are made using money as the medium of exchange. When purchases are made, money changes hands. Money is on one side of each transaction, whether the transaction is viewed as a purchase or a sale. If you buy a record for $8, you exchange money for the record (you have made a purchase), and the record seller exchanges a record for money (he has made a sale).

If we multiply the existing money stock, M, by the number of times that an average dollar changes hands, V (the velocity of circulation of money), in the exchange of the goods and services included in GNP, we get MV. Thus

$$MV \equiv PQ \qquad (8\text{-}1)$$

The definition of *money stock* used in this book is the sum of currency held by the public outside of banks and demand deposit credits (deposits in checking accounts) in commercial banks. This definition is called M1A in newspapers, magazines, and journals. A broader definition, which adds savings account deposits in commercial banks to M1A, is often referred to and used in statistical studies. This broader definition is called M_2. Its chief advantage is that the statistical relationship between M_2 and nominal GNP is closer than the statistical relationship between M1A and nominal GNP. Its chief disadvantage is that savings account credits do not in fact serve as a medium of exchange. Savings account credits must be converted into checking account credits or cash before they can be used to purchase things. Since the main function of money is to serve as a medium of exchange, M1A is a conceptually superior definition of money. In this book the symbol M will mean the money stock as defined by M1A. In the United States about 80 percent of the money stock is in the form of demand deposits, while cash makes up only 20 percent of the total.

If nominal GNP in 1979 was $1 trillion, and if the average size of the money stock in 1979 was $200 billion, then the number of times each dollar changed hands in transactions involving GNP was five. $MV = PQ$ is an identity and must always hold. V, therefore, is calculated as PQ/M.

In Chapter 5 we discussed the increase in nominal income, $Y(= PQ)$, that is brought about by an upward shift in the $C + I + G$ aggregate demand line. We said that if government spending were increased and taxes were not increased sufficiently to offset this increase, aggregate demand would shift upward and cause an increase in nominal income. No mention was made of whether this fiscal policy changes the money stock. Let's assume that it does not. (In Section 3 of Chapter 10 we will see that this means the Treasury's deficit is financed by selling bonds to the private sector.) If M does not change while PQ increases, V must have increased to accommodate the increase in PQ. The Keynesian income-expenditure model assumes that velocity will automatically assume whatever value it must to allow the Keynesian multiplier process to work. In this model velocity is determined residually. That is, once nominal income is established, it is simply divided by the money stock to determine the velocity. No attention is paid to whether velocity can change—it is simply assumed to change.

8-3 THE OLD QUANTITY THEORY

Given that $MV \equiv PQ$, if V is constant and if Q is maintained at the full employment level, any change in M will cause an equal percentage change in P. This is the classical (pre-1935) version of the quantity theory of money. Velocity was considered to be determined by institutional factors such as credit practices, communications systems, and frequency of income payments, which are invariant with respect to changes in the money stock. For instance, velocity would be higher in an economy where wages were paid weekly than in one where they were paid monthly. The average amount of money balances held in a checking account would be higher in the latter case because the deposit must finance transactions occurring over a longer time. Changing the stock of money would not change the frequency of wage payments and hence would not change velocity.

In a world of perfectly flexible prices (i.e., where information costs are zero), real output would always be at the full employment level. Since changes in the money supply would not affect the supply of labor or capital, and since technology is fixed in the short run, changes in the money stock would not affect the full employment level of real output.

The classical quantity theory therefore concluded that changes in the money stock would cause equiproportionate changes, in the same direction, in the price level. The link between the supply of money and the price level was considered to be direct and mechanical. No analysis of individual behavior was thought to be necessary. Notice that in this analysis the price level is the variable to be determined.

In 1936, when Keynes' *General Theory* appeared, the quantity theory fell into disrepute. Early Keynesian analysis stated that velocity would move to offset changes in the money stock. An increase in the money stock, even if it lowered interest rates just a little, would cause velocity to fall substantially. Since $MV \equiv PQ$, if nominal aggregate demand (and therefore nominal income) is to change, the product MV must change. If, whenever M increases, V falls to offset this increase, money can exert no direct effects on the level of aggregate demand.

It was therefore thought that policymakers should keep money in plentiful supply to make the financing of government debt as easy as possible. Since aggregate demand wouldn't be affected, inflation would not result. But after World War II many countries followed this advice, and in each case inflation resulted. This phenomenon indicated that money *does* make a difference and provided the impetus for a rehabilitation of the quantity theory.

8-4 THE NEW QUANTITY THEORY

 The new quantity theory is really a theory of the demand for money balances.

MONEY BALANCES AND INDIVIDUAL BEHAVIOR

As we noted in Section 8-2 money is defined as deposits by the public in checking accounts plus currency held by the public. At any time, no matter what the existing stock of money is, it is held by someone; each person has an average balance in his or her checking account and possesses some amount of currency. At any time, a person may or may not be satisfied with the amount of money he or she holds, relative to his or her income or wealth. If you wanted to hold more of your wealth in the form of money, you could refrain from spending as much of your income as before, or you could sell some other assets (such as bonds) to build up your money balances. If you wanted to hold less of your wealth in the form of money, you could simply spend your income at a faster rate than before until your money balances reached the desired level.

Of course, not everyone can diminish his or her money balances at the same time, because the money stock will physically exist in someone's hands. However, it is the *purchasing power* of these money balances that really matters to the individual. If I double the average amount of dollars I keep on deposit in my checking account when the price level doubles, I am keeping the same proportion of my real wealth in the form of (real) money balances as before. All people can simultaneously reduce the stock of real money balances (or purchasing power) they hold by increasing their spending until the price level rises enough to reduce the ratio of the money stock to the price level to its desired level.

In equilibrium, the amount of money each person holds must equal the amount he or she wants to hold. In other words, the quantity of money supplied must equal the quantity of money demanded, or $M = M_D$. From $MV = PQ$, we can conclude that *in equilibrium* $M_D V = PQ$, or that

$$M_D = kPQ \tag{8-2}$$

where $k = 1/V$. Dividing both sides of Equation 8-2 by P we get

$$\frac{M_D}{P} = kQ \qquad (8\text{-}3)$$

Equation 8-3 states that, in equilibrium, desired (and actual) real money balances will be some fraction (k) of real income. What determines the value of k? We will answer this question in the next three sections.

EQUILIBRIUM AND CHANGES IN THE MONEY STOCK

If the money stock, M, is increased, actual real money balances, M/P, will be larger than desired real money balances, M_D/P. Individuals who have received some increase in M (those who sold bonds to a Federal Reserve bank, for instance) will find that they have too large a proportion of their wealth in the form of real money balances. Each will reshuffle his or her portfolio of assets by buying assets other than money balances. The price level will rise until $M/P = M_D/P$. If the increase in M does not change the level of desired real money balances, P must increase by the same percentage that M has increased in order to restore equilibrium. The money stock and the average price level must increase proportionately.

This increase is the same result as that predicted by the old quantity theory, but there is an important difference. The focus of the new quantity theory is on the behavior of individuals in response to changes in the money stock. An increase in the money stock will mean that actual real money balances (the money stock divided by the price level) are larger than desired real money balances, and so there is an excess supply of real money balances. People will reduce their holdings of money balances by spending the money on other things. This spending will increase the price level until actual and desired real money balances again equal each other. Increases in the money stock cause people to react in a manner that will increase aggregate demand in nominal terms.

If, when the money stock is increased, the desired stock of real money balances decreases (we will see in Section 8-7 what could cause this), the price level must increase by a larger percentage than the percentage increase in the money stock. This increase presents no problems as long as we can predict the fall in desired real money balances. For example, suppose we know that a 10 percent increase in the money stock causes a decrease of 2 percent in the stock of desired real money balances. The initial money stock is $100, the price index is 2, and the initial stock of desired real money balances is $50. People wish to hold $50 worth of constant purchasing power in the form of money balances. Thus the actual and the desired levels of real money balances are equal. Now the money stock is increased 10 percent, to $110, and the desired level of real money balances falls

2 percent, to \$49. The actual stock of real money balances is \$110/2, or \$55. There is thus an excess supply of real money balances. People are induced to spend the excess balances, and these expenditures cause the price level to rise. The price level must rise to 2.24 in order to reduce actual real money balances to the desired level of \$49. So we can see that the 10 percent increase in the money stock caused a 12 percent increase in the price level.

Consider again the quantity equation of exchange, $MV \equiv PQ$. Our discussion concerns *moving from one equilibrium point to another.* In equilibrium, Q (real output of goods and services) has the value that makes the unemployment rate equal its natural level. In other words, Q is the full employment Q. It is also true that, in equilibrium, the quantity of real money balances supplied equals the quantity of real money balances demanded. (In Chapter 11 we will see that full equilibrium requires that the money market, the bond market, the labor market, and the commodities market are each in equilibrium. In other words, in each market the quantity supplied must equal the quantity demanded. If any one of these markets is out of equilibrium, something will happen in at least one of the other markets to bring about full equilibrium. Say's Principle, explained in Chapter 3, indicates that this is the case.)

In the case above in which an increase in the money stock did not change desired real money balances, the increase in the money stock caused an equal percentage change in PQ, but Q did not change at all. The full employment rate of real income, as we saw in Chapter 6, does not change when nominal aggregate demand changes. Since the percentage change in the money stock equals the percentage change in nominal income, velocity did not change from the initial equilibrium to the new equilibrium. In the second case cited above, where the increase in the money stock was accompanied by a *decrease* in desired real money balances, the percentage increase in nominal income was greater than the percentage increase in the money stock. Therefore, velocity increased.

Even though velocity changes, there is still a direct link between changes in the money stock and changes in nominal income. When the money stock changes, we can predict the resulting changes in nominal income *if we can predict the accompanying changes in velocity.* Changes in velocity, as we have just seen, are caused by changes in the level of desired real money balances. Changes in velocity are predictable if changes in desired real money balances are predictable. The predictability, or stability, of the demand function for real money balances is therefore extremely important.

IMPLICATIONS FOR POLICYMAKING

The new quantity theory suggests that policymakers need to consider the relationship between actual and desired levels of real cash balances and actual and

desired levels of velocity. Examining only actual levels may well result in erroneous policies. If the Federal Reserve System (the Fed) were to increase the stock of money (we will see how this is done in the next chapter), the actual (measured) level of velocity would immediately fall. That is simply because $V = Y/M$, and Y doesn't change immediately. Individuals cannot react immediately to an unexpected increase in their cash balances. Although velocity falls initially, there is no reason to think that equilibrium velocity will change. Ultimately, individuals will reduce their cash balances by spending. This increases Y and therefore moves velocity back toward its initial value. If the Fed were to interpret the initial decline in measured velocity as an increase in the demand for real cash balances, it may well be tempted to increase the money stock again. This would only lead to further price increases. Most of you probably think that policymakers know better and that this wouldn't happen; however, one of our most outspoken and powerful senators, Senator William Proxmire, Chairman of the Senate Committee on Banking, Housing and Urban Affairs, has frequently confused actual with desired levels of real cash balances and advocated more expansionary monetary policies in the face of increasing rates of inflation.

8-5 KEYNES' DEMAND FOR MONEY

In *The General Theory,* Keynes proposed two major reasons for holding money— as a medium of exchange and to provide some protection against losses that could result from holding assets such as bonds and stocks. Following Keynes, we will suppose that the only financial asset other than money is bonds, which are claims to perpetual nominal income streams.

MONEY AS A MEDIUM OF EXCHANGE

The aggregate demand for money that arises because of its role as a medium of exchange would logically depend on how many transactions are being carried out via its use. If we confine ourselves to transactions that involve only the items that are included in GNP, we can say that the transactions demand for money (M_t) is positively related to nominal GNP. In equation form:

$$M_t = f(P \cdot Q) \tag{8-4}$$

A simplifying assumption that is often made is that this relationship is linear, and so

$$M_t = \alpha PQ \tag{8-5}$$

where α is a positive constant less than one. We would expect that $0 < \alpha < 1$ because a dollar can be used in more than one transaction during the accounting

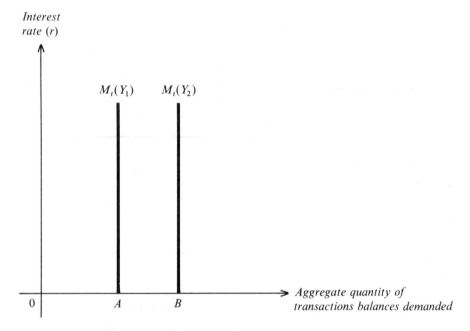

Figure 8-2 The transactions demand for money.

period. It is vital at this point to recognize that α is *not* the reciprocal of velocity. M_t is not equal to the aggregate supply of money—it is only *one portion* of the aggregate *demand* for money.

Figure 8-2 illustrates this relationship. The vertical relationship between transactions demand for money (transactions balances demanded) and the rate of interest indicates that M_t is not a function of r, but only of the level of income. If income increases from Y_1 to Y_2, transactions demand will increase from $0A$ to $0B$.

MONEY AS PROTECTION AGAINST LOSSES FROM BONDS

The other role that money plays is to guard against the losses that are possible if one holds bonds. Holding money is an alternative to holding bonds; hence when it seems likely that the price of a bond is going to fall, people will try to sell the bond before the price falls. They plan to hold on to the money they get when they sell the bond until bonds again seem to be an attractive way to hold wealth.

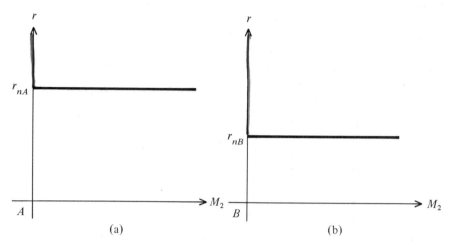

Figure 8-3 Individual speculative demand curves.

The price of a bond depends upon the fixed interest payments paid by the bond issuer relative to the market rate of interest. Roughly, if a bond yields $100 per year and the market rate of interest is 5 percent, the value of the bond is $100/.05, or $2000. In other words, at a price of $2000, the $100 represents a 5 percent rate of return. If the market rate of interest becomes 10 percent, the same bond would fall in price to $100/0.1, or $1000.

Assume, with Keynes, that each individual has his own idea of what constitutes the normal rate of interest on bonds. If the actual rate were greater than this normal rate, the individual would expect the rate to fall, which is the same as saying he would expect bond prices to rise. If he were certain of this, he would hold all his accumulated savings in the form of bonds in the anticipation of capital gains—he would hold zero "speculative" money balances. In Figure 8-3, we see that Mr. A's demand for money balances as protection against losses from bonds is zero at any interest rate above r_{nA} (what to him is the normal rate). If the actual rate were less than r_{nA}, he would expect the rate to rise and would expect to suffer capital losses if he held bonds; hence he would hold only money balances. His demand for money from this second motive (M_2) is L-shaped. If r_{nA} were 10 percent and the actual rate were 5 percent, Mr. A would expect the interest rate to increase. If it increased to 10 percent, the price of the bond would fall to $1000 and he would suffer a $1000 capital loss. By holding money instead of bonds, Mr. A expects to avoid such a loss.

People are likely to differ about what they think the normal rate is. For instance, Mr. B. thinks it is r_{nB}. His L-shaped speculative demand for money (M_2)

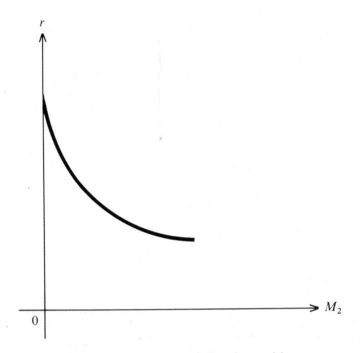

Figure 8-4 **Aggregate speculative demand for money.**

line has its kink at a lower level than Mr. A's. If all individual M_2 lines are added horizontally and there are many individuals, we will get a smooth aggregate M_2 line as in Figure 8-4. The negative slope of the M_2 line reflects the likelihood that, as we consider lower rates of interest, we include more and more people in the set of people who consider that rate or one above it to be the normal rate.

TRANSACTIONS DEMAND PLUS SPECULATIVE DEMAND

The Keynesian total demand for money function, then, has two parts—transactions demand (αPQ) and speculative demand $[L_s(r)]$, which must be added together:

$$M_D = \alpha PQ + L_s(r) \qquad (8\text{-}6)$$

As the interest rate rises, some people will come to think that the actual rate is above the normal rate and they will reduce the quantity of money demanded in favor of bonds.

8-6 TWO DEVELOPMENTS OF THE KEYNESIAN APPROACH

The problem with the approach proposed by Keynes is that there is a clear dichotomy between the motives for holding money. Transactions demand is only a function of the level of income and the speculative demand only a function of the rate of interest. A change in the rate of interest would not affect the transactions demand, while a change in income would not affect the speculative demand for cash balances. The analysis also leads to an either-or decision for speculative balances—either money or bonds, but never both for any one individual.

In order to make the Keynesian analysis of the demand for money more realistic, a second approach was developed by two economists working independently—W. J. Baumol and James Tobin. Both have developed an inventory-theoretic approach to the transactions demand for money, which recognizes that people don't have to keep all their transactions balances idle in their checking accounts. They could, for instance, use a portion of these balances to buy short-term securities and earn some interest. Because short-term securities are highly liquid, they can be readily sold as transactions needs arise. People carry an inventory of cash that they use up as they make transactions, and this cash inventory is replenished by selling off an inventory of short-term securities. This approach indicates that the transactions demand for money depends on short-term rates of interest and brokerage fees (the exchange costs of buying and selling bonds) as well as income.

BAUMOL'S TRANSACTIONS DEMAND FOR CASH BALANCES

Assuming that the individual has short-term alternatives to holding cash, Baumol's model concludes that the transactions demand for cash balances is directly related to the level of transactions (following Keynes), inversely related to the rate of interest that could be earned on short-term securities, and directly related to brokerage fees involved in the purchase or sale of the short-term securities.[2]

If money is held instead of short-term securities that can be readily sold for money as the need arises, the interest that could be earned on the securities would be sacrificed. Thus the higher the rate of interest that can be earned on such securities, the less willing people will be to hold on to money rather than the securities. Similarly, the purchase and sale of these short-term securities involves costs such as brokers' fees. The higher these costs, the less attractive the securities will be and the more attractive money balances become.

Baumol also found that an increase in income would not necessarily increase M_t proportionately. When a firm's average sales of a commodity increase by 10 percent, it typically increases its inventories of the commodity to handle the larger transitory changes in sales that go along with the higher average. But the increase in inventories is less than 10 percent. Transitory changes in sales do not increase to the same extent that average sales increase. (From statistics we know that the standard deviation does not grow in proportion to increases in the average.) Similarly, an increase in the average dollar amount of real transactions to be carried out (which is proportional to real income) won't increase transactions demand proportionately. If nominal transactions increase because of an increase in the average money price level, nominal transactions demand will increase proportionately. If the average money price level increases by 10 percent, for example, it is necessary to have 10 percent more money to carry out whatever real transactions one has planned.

The implications of this theory are very important. Holding all other factors constant (brokerage fees, interest rates, and the speculative demand for cash balances), if M (the quantity of money supplied) increases proportionately with an increase in income, velocity will rise because individuals do not want to hold the same percentage of their income in the form of cash balances. Baumol's analysis would then predict rising velocity through time as income increases.

TOBIN'S ANALYSIS OF THE SPECULATIVE DEMAND FOR MONEY

Tobin's analysis does not depend on the notion of a normal rate of interest, but concentrates on the trade-off between risk and return.[3] Bonds yield an explicit return in the form of interest, but they also carry risk of capital loss (as well as the possibility of capital gain). Return is desirable, risk is not. An individual chooses his portfolio by balancing risk against return. Although some individuals hold only bonds (those who love risk) and others only money (those who are very risk averse), the typical individual holds both bonds and money for speculative purposes. If the return from holding bonds increases while the risk perceived to exist with each bond remains unchanged, more bonds will be demanded. With a fixed dollar value of a portfolio, an increase in the demand for bonds results in a corresponding decrease in the demand for money. Thus return, as measured by the market rate of interest, and the demand for speculative balances are inversely related.

This conclusion is the same as that of the Keynesian treatment of the speculative demand, but in Tobin's analysis an individual will normally hold both bonds and money for speculative purposes, not just bonds or just money as in the Keynesian analysis.

IN CONCLUSION

The work of these two economists extended the original Keynesian analysis, leaving the general conclusions intact. The transactions demand for cash balances is a function of income, interest rate, and brokerage fees; the speculative demand for money is a function of interest rates. An increase in income increases the demand for money (but not proportionately), while an increase in interest rates decreases *both* M_t and the speculative demand for cash balances.

8-7 THE MONETARIST APPROACH

The monetarists, as exemplified by Milton Friedman, have developed an alternative approach.[4] Rather than focusing on the motives for holding money, Friedman suggests that the demand for money should be analyzed as we would the demand for any other good such as houses or apples. Money yields a stream of services such as convenience, security, and liquidity. As with any good, a decision to hold or buy more of it involves the sacrifice of streams of services of some other goods. For convenience, these competing goods can be lumped into three categories: bonds, common stock, and physical assets such as a house.

MONEY VS. BONDS, COMMON STOCKS, AND PHYSICAL ASSETS

If an individual holds money rather than bonds, the alternative sacrificed is the interest that would be received on the bond as well as any change in the capital value (market price) of the bond that may occur during the holding period. The capital value, of course, could increase or decrease. The combination of these two components can be measured as a yield r_b. An individual making portfolio decisions will have some expectation about what r_b will be; he doesn't know what it *actually* will be. We shall call that expected yield on bonds r_b^e.

Similarly, if the individual holds money rather than common stock, the perceived alternative sacrificed is the expected dividends from the stock and the expected change in the capital value of the stock. We will represent this expected yield by r_s^e.

Finally, an individual may hold physical assets. These assets yield a flow of services through time rather than an interest payment or a dividend. If I decide to hold money rather than a car, I sacrifice the stream of transportation services the car yields. The service streams of physical assets are fixed, in real terms. The transportation services a car can offer do not change when the price level increases. However, the attractiveness of physical assets relative to money as a form of holding wealth increases as the *expected* inflation rate increases. Let $\Delta P^e/P$ stand for the *expected* rate of inflation. As this rate increases, people will want to hold less of their wealth in the form of money and more in the form of physical assets, because physical assets provide protection against the expected inflation. As inflation proceeds, the price of the physical assets an individual owns increases. The stream of services is completely unaffected by the inflation.

In real terms, a holder of physical assets cannot lose from inflation. On the other hand, the holder of money balances *can* lose, because the purchasing power of his money balances will diminish. If the expected inflation rate decreases, money becomes a more attractive way to hold wealth, relative to physical assets. If I expect that prices will be lower next year than they are now, I will hold on to money balances now while I wait for the purchasing power of those balances to increase.

THE COMPLETE DEMAND FOR MONEY EQUATION

An individual's demand for any good logically depends upon the level of wealth or income the individual has. For most goods, an increase in wealth causes an increase in demand. Such goods are called normal goods. Money is no exception—an increase in one's wealth will increase one's demand for money. This is merely the formal way economists state the obvious proposition that the richer you are, the larger the average amount of money you keep in your checking account and carry around as cash.

Friedman considers the form of a person's wealth as well as the actual level of wealth to be important. It is more difficult to exchange human wealth (W_h) for money than to exchange nonhuman wealth (W_{nh}) for money. I cannot sell you my future earnings for a lump sum today because slavery (even voluntarily entered into) is illegal and because I would probably not work very hard in the future if I had to turn over my earnings to you. Recognizing this, you will be willing to pay a sum less than the present value of the earnings stream I expect to make working for myself. This indicates that for a given level of total wealth, the higher the ratio of W_h/W_{nh}, the larger the demand for money balances. The liquidity of money balances makes up for the lack of liquidity of human wealth.

Finally, we note that as the price level, P, increases, the amount of nominal money balances needed to carry out an individual's plans will increase by an equal percentage amount. (This, of course, is consistent with both Keynes' and Baumol's analysis.) Suppose, for example, that at some given average price level I decide to hold $100 of my wealth in the form of money. Thus my $M_D = \$100$. Let's suppose this amounts to 1 percent of my wealth. If the price level doubles, the average of the prices of all my assets except money will also double. I would be able to sell my bonds, my common stock, and my house at higher prices than before. (Remember that the average price level is the average of the prices of all assets.) If I am going to continue to hold 1 percent of my nominal wealth in the form of money, I must now increase my M_D to $200.

We can summarize our conclusions in the following way:

$$M_D = L\left(W, \frac{W_h}{W_{nh}}, r_b^e, r_s^e, \frac{\Delta P^e}{P}, z\right) \cdot P \qquad (8\text{-}7)$$

where M_D stands for the quantity of money demanded, W for wealth, z for "tastes," and P for the average price level. Tastes must be included because institutional factors may well change the demand for money. The average price level (P) is placed outside the parentheses because we know for sure that when the price level changes by some percentage amount, the amount of money needed to carry out whatever plans the individual may have will change in the same direction by the same percentage amount. The letter L to the left of the parentheses merely means "is a function of." It is traditional for the demand for money to use L instead of F.

If we divide both sides of Equation 8-7 by P, we get

$$\frac{M_D}{P} = L\left(W, \frac{W_h}{W_{nh}}, r_b^e, r_s^e, \frac{\Delta P^e}{P}, z \right) \tag{8-8}$$

This equation emphasizes that what is being demanded is money balances made up of constant purchasing power, or *real* money balances.

SIMPLIFYING THE EQUATION

If people are free to exchange assets, the rate of return on bonds and the rate of return on stocks will move together. If the rate of return on bonds rises above its usual relationship to the rate of return on stocks, people will sell stocks and buy bonds. This pattern will increase the price of bonds, thus lowering the rate of return on bonds, and decrease the price of stocks, thus raising the rate of return on stocks. Since these rates of return move together, we can simplify things if we pick one representative rate to stand for both. We will represent the rate of return on financial assets other than money (including expected capital gains and losses) by the symbol r. This symbol will be called "the interest rate."

Permanent income, Y_p, is an individual's expected annual flow of income over his or her lifetime. The ultimate source of one's income stream is one's stock of human and nonhuman wealth. We can write $Y_p = r_p W$, where r_p is the average rate of return on all the assets that make up wealth, and Y_p is the amount the individual could consume or use up every year without reducing his or her wealth. As wealth increases, so too does permanent income. In fact, permanent income is simply another way of looking at wealth—the statement that my wealth has increased and the statement that my permanent income has increased are identical. We can therefore substitute permanent income for wealth in the demand function for real money balances. If we also use the interest rate (r) to stand for a composite rate of return on bonds and stocks, Equation 8-8 becomes

$$\frac{M_D}{P} = L\left(Y_p, \frac{W_h}{W_{nh}}, r, \frac{\Delta P^e}{P}, z \right) \tag{8-9}$$

In other words, the demand for real money balances depends on (is a function of) permanent income, the composition of wealth, the rate of return on financial assets other than money, the expected inflation rate, and tastes.

THE EFFECT OF VARIOUS CHANGES

As permanent income increases, the quantity of real money balances demanded will also increase. If I hold 1 percent of my wealth in the form of real money balances and my wealth (and therefore my permanent income) increases, I must add to my real money balances if I am to continue to hold 1 percent of my wealth in real money balances. I will continue to want to hold 1 percent of my wealth in the form of real money balances as long as there is no change in any of the other variables upon which the demand for real money balances depends. If, for example, the ratio of human to nonhuman wealth increased, I might decide to hold, say, 1.2 percent of my wealth in the form of real money balances in order to compensate myself for the relative lack of liquidity of human wealth.

As the interest rate increases, I will want to hold a smaller portion of my wealth in the form of real money balances, because interest payments are sacrificed when wealth is held in the form of money rather than other financial assets. They are the cost of holding money. As this cost increases, smaller real money balances will be demanded.

As the *expected* inflation rate increases, there will also be a decrease in real money balances demanded. People will want to hold a smaller portion of their wealth in the form of money so that they can buy other assets before the prices of those assets rise.

EQUILIBRIUM

From the quantity equation of exchange (Equation 8-1) we can deduce that in equilibrium $M_D/P = kQ$ (Equation 8-3). We now know what M_D/P depends on. Once we know Y_p, W_h/W_{nh}, r, and $\Delta P^e/P$ we will know M_D/P. For any specified value of Q (the usual specified value is its equilibrium value, the value Q takes when unemployment is at its natural rate), we can say that k depends on the same variables as those that enter the demand for money function.

Remember that Equation 8-3 is *not* an expression of the demand function for money. It merely states a relationship that will be observed in equilibrium. Indeed, we must know M_D/P before we can determine k.

8-8 INTEREST RATES: NOMINAL AND REAL

Up to now we have referred to "the interest rate," and we have used the symbol r to stand for the interest rate. We have just seen that the expected rate of inflation plays a role in the demand for money, and we will see in Section 10 of Chapter 11 that the expected rate of inflation affects other macroeconomic magnitudes as well.

The rate of interest and the expected inflation rate are not independent. The expected rate of inflation affects nominal rates of interest that are paid in the real world. A nominal interest rate is merely the annual percentage that is applied, for example, to the dollar amount of a loan to determine the number of dollars that the borrower must pay to the lender in addition to the amount borrowed. If you lend $100 to someone on the condition that in one year she must pay you back $105, the nominal rate of interest you receive is 5 percent. Suppose, however, that over the year the average money price level increases by 8 percent. When you receive the $105 at the end of the year, you will have received a negative *real* rate of interest. You received 5 percent more money, but each of the dollars you loaned out has 8 percent less purchasing power. You have not even received the amount of spending power you loaned out. You have 3 percent less purchasing power than you started with; thus the real rate of return you have made is a negative 3 percent.

If, with the expectation of zero inflation, lenders and borrowers would agree on a nominal rate of interest of 5 percent, they will agree on a nominal rate of 13 percent when they expect an 8 percent inflation. The lender insists on the extra 8 percent to compensate for the declining purchasing power of money over the life of the loan, and the borrower is willing to pay it. The addition of the 8 percent doesn't change the loan agreement in real terms from what it would be in the absence of inflation. If the borrower was willing in the absence of inflation to pay 5 percent more purchasing power than the amount borrowed, there is no reason to think that that willingness would change with inflation.

In Chapters 11 through 14 we will pay careful attention to the difference between the nominal rate of interest and the real rate of interest. We will use the symbol r to stand for the nominal rate, and we will use the symbol ρ to stand for the real rate. The nominal rate of interest is the sum of the real rate and the expected rate of inflation. If the expected rate of inflation is zero, the nominal rate will equal the real rate.

Until we get well into Chapter 11, however, we will continue to do what we have been doing all along—assume that the nominal interest rate is the real interest rate. Until then the symbol r will mean both the real and the nominal rate of interest.

SUMMARY

In this chapter we have seen why money exists—to minimize the costs of exchange. The very important quantity equation of exchange was introduced. This equation says that total spending can be viewed either as the product of the money stock and the number of times an average dollar changes hands (velocity) within an accounting period, or as the product of the average price level and the total of real output of goods and services. The modern quantity theory attempts to explain the connection between changes in the money stock and changes in aggregate nominal demand (total spending in current prices).

We then considered the demand for money. Two approaches were used, both suggesting the same results. The quantity of money demanded and some measure of income (wealth) are positively related, while the quantity of money demanded and yields on alternative financial assets are negatively related. When these relationships are combined with the money supply analysis that will be developed in the next chapter, a money market equilibrium can be defined.

QUESTIONS

1. Should the total credit available to credit card holders be included in our definition of money? Of wealth? Of permanent income? Why or why not?
2. Suppose that when the money supply is increased, desired real money balances stay constant. Would an increase in the money supply of 10 percent lead to a 10 percent increase in the average price level if, when the money supply was increased, there was a 10 percent unemployment rate? Why?
3. The answer to Question 2 must be yes or else the new quantity theory cannot be true. Do you agree or not? Why?
4. What observable variable do you think would be a good measure of the riskiness of a bond? Defend your answer.
5. Real cash balances declined during most of the 1973–75 recession. Could you construct an argument that the recession was prolonged by a real cash shortage? What data would you examine to justify this position? Could you also construct an argument that there was a cash surplus during that period? What data would you examine to justify this position?
6. What would happen to the speculative demand for cash balances if all individuals' views about the normal rate of interest increased? What would then happen to V? P? Q?
7. What are the substantive differences between the old quantity theory, the Keynesian, and the monetarist approaches to the demand for money?
8. Would the rate at which income is taxed have any effect on the demand for money? Why?
9. Would seashells be a good medium of exchange in an island economy? Why?

10. Would the advent of discount brokerage houses (firms that reduce the commissions they charge their customers who buy financial securities below established customary rates) have any effect on the demand for money? Why?

NOTES

1. Suppose, for example, that I have 3 units of commodity X and 4 of commodity Z and that, in order to get 1 more X, I would pay as many as 3 Z's. My evaluation of X is 3 Z's. If your evaluation of X is 1 Z, our evaluations differ and we can both be made better off by trade. If I pay you 2 Z's for 1 X, I pay you less than my maximum and so I am better off, and you receive more than your minimum and so you are also better off.
2. W. J. Baumol, "The Transactions Demand for Cash—An Inventory Theoretic Approach," *Quarterly Journal of Economics* (November 1952).
3. James Tobin, "Liquidity Preference as Behavior Towards Risk," *Review of Economic Studies* (February 1958).
4. Milton Friedman, "The Quantity Theory of Money—a Restatement," in *Studies in the Quantity Theory of Money* (Chicago: University of Chicago Press, 1956).

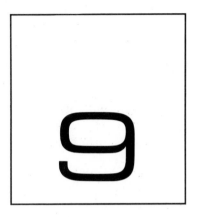

The Supply of Money

In the last chapter we considered the major determinants of people's willingness to hold some of their wealth in the form of money balances—i.e., the determinants of the quantity of money demanded. The demand for money determines what the velocity of circulation (V in the quantity equation of exchange) will be; the Federal Reserve System together with the economy's private commercial banks determines what the quantity of money in circulation (M in the quantity equation of exchange) will be. In this chapter we will discuss how the Fed and commercial banks interact to determine the supply of money.

9-1 COMMERCIAL BANKS AND THE DEPOSIT EXPANSION PROCESS

A *commercial bank* is a financial institution that carries checking accounts. Other financial institutions, such as savings and loan associations and credit unions, are forbidden by federal law to allow their customers to set up checking accounts with them. Like all business firms, a commercial bank summarizes its financial status in an accounting statement called a *balance sheet*. A balance sheet lists the money value of all of the assets that a firm has at its disposal, and divides that total amount into two parts. The portion of the total dollar value of *assets* that is owed to someone else is called *liabilities*, while the remainder is called *net worth*.

In the case of a commercial bank the most significant assets are cash, bonds, loans the bank has extended to borrowers, and such physical assets as the building the bank occupies and the equipment the bank uses. The most significant liabilities (dollar amounts owed to others) are deposits in checking accounts, deposits in savings accounts, borrowings from other commercial banks, borrowings from branches in foreign countries (so-called Eurodollars), and borrowings from the Federal Reserve. The latter is known by its nickname—the Fed—and it is the central banking system of the United States, with 12 district banks located in major U.S. cities. Both the U.S. Treasury and private commercial banks carry accounts at the Fed.

RESERVES

The bulk of a commercial bank's assets are in the form of *earning assets*—assets that generate interest income for the bank. These include loans to individuals and firms; municipal, state, and corporation bonds; U.S. Treasury securities; and loans to other banks. Nonearning assets are called *reserves*, and they include cash held on the premises (vault cash) and deposits made at a Federal Reserve bank.

Commercial banks are required by law to have no less than some specific percentage of their total deposits in the form of reserves. These are called *required reserves*, and the percentage of required reserves differs from bank to bank depending on the size of the bank. The percentage reserve requirement for demand deposits (i.e., deposits to checking accounts) ranges from a low of 7 percent to a high of 22 percent. Small banks have the lowest percentage requirement while large banks are subject to the highest percentage requirement. Savings deposits require minimum reserves of 3 percent and maximum reserves of 10 percent.

AN EXAMPLE OF THE DEPOSIT EXPANSION PROCESS

We can now examine the behavior of the banking system when one commercial bank receives a demand deposit that did not come from another bank but rather from outside the commercial banking system such as a home safe or a Federal Reserve bank. Let's assume that there are no time deposits (savings account deposits) and no cash withdrawals of any type from the banking system during the process. Furthermore, let's assume that commercial banks desire to hold only as many reserves as the law requires.

If a commercial bank receives a checking account deposit of $100, it could simply decide to keep the entire deposit as reserves. As a first step, however, we will assume that the bank will use some of those funds to purchase some interest-earning asset. If the bank is required to keep 20 percent of this deposit as reserves, it can use the remaining $80 to acquire another asset. For example, the $80 could be loaned to a customer. The individual borrowing the $80 has it credited to his checking account. When he spends the money and the bank honors the check, the borrower's checking account is reduced by $80 and the bank loses the $80. The bank is left in the following position:

- Demand deposits + $100 (original deposit)
- Reserves + $ 20
- Loans + $ 80

Both the bank's assets (reserves plus loans) and its liabilities (deposits) have increased by $100.

Some other bank, however, will receive the $80 check written on the original bank by the borrower. When it receives the $80 from the first bank, its deposits and reserves will increase by $80. The second bank will also seek to expand its earnings assets. If it keeps 20 percent in reserves, it can make a new loan of $64. This process can continue as long as no cash is withdrawn from the banking system. A third bank could make a new loan of $51.20 (80 percent of $64) and a fourth, $40.96 (80 percent of $51.20), and so on.

There are two aspects of this process of particular significance:

1. The original deposit of $100 provides the means whereby additional deposits and loans at other banks are made. This is called the *deposit expansion process*: one bank's loan becomes a deposit at another bank, thus permitting this other bank to make loans itself, and so the process continues.
2. Each expansion is smaller than the one preceding it. This is because only (say) 80 percent of a deposit when received can be loaned.

If we followed this process to the end, through each bank's creating new loans that become new deposits, we would find that the deposits created would equal $500 (including the original $100 deposit). This is equal to 5 times $100. The 5 is 1/the percentage reserve requirement, and the $100 is the initial deposit that set the change in motion.

What has happened to the money stock? Has it also increased by $500? The astute reader will realize that it has not. The $500 increase in deposits was initiated by a currency deposit of $100; since we have defined the money stock as currency plus demand deposits, the increase in the money stock was $400.

Moreover, notice that with demand deposits $500 higher than they were to begin with, required reserves are $100 higher than they were to begin with (0.2 of $500). The multiple expansion of deposits continues, causing deposits to get bigger and bigger until all of the $100 that was deposited originally from outside the banking system becomes required reserves. When all reserves are required, it is no longer possible for deposits to continue to expand.

THE DEPOSIT MULTIPLIER

In equation form we write:

$$\Delta D = \frac{1}{\rho_D} \cdot \Delta R \qquad (9\text{-}1)$$

where ΔD denotes the total new demand deposits created, ΔR denotes the new reserves that came into the first bank in the form of a deposit not taken out of any other bank, and ρ_D is the percentage reserve requirement. $1/\rho_D$ is called the *deposit multiplier*. It is the amount by which the initial deposit from outside is multiplied to get the resulting change in demand deposits. It is based on our initial assumptions—that there is no leakage during the process into cash, savings accounts, or excess reserves.

9-2 LEAKAGES AND THE DEPOSIT MULTIPLIER

The deposit expansion process outlined above would occur only if our original assumptions held. Realistically, individuals do withdraw currency from the process by cashing checks, and they also make deposits in savings accounts at commercial banks as well as in checking accounts. While these transactions will cause a change in the deposit multiplier, they do not in any way affect the deposit expansion process. The withdrawal of cash and the diversion of deposits into time deposits are called *leakages* because the final change in demand deposits (and the money stock) will be smaller with them than without them. We will consider each leakage individually to see its effects.

CASH AS A LEAKAGE

Let's assume that individuals desire to have $1 in cash for every $3 in their checking accounts. (The jargon is that the desired currency-to-demand-deposit ratio is $1/3$.) The initial deposit of $100 in our previous example resulted in a loan of $80. Now when $100 is deposited and $80 is loaned, the recipient of the $80 when it is spent will deposit only two-thirds of it ($53.33) and keep the remainder ($26.67) as cash. Thus the second bank will only be able to lend 80 percent of $53.33, which equals $42.66. When this sum is spent, the person who receives it will deposit two-thirds of it ($28.44) and take the rest of it ($14.22) as cash. The deposit expansion process goes on, but less intensively because of the loss ("leak") of cash at each stage.

If we let k be the desired ratio of currency to demand deposits, the new deposit multiplier will be $1/(\rho_D + k)$, which in our example is $1/(.2 + .33)$ or $1/.53$, which equals 1.8867. The initial deposit of $100 under these circumstances will cause demand deposits to be $188.67 higher than they were before the deposit of $100.

On those new deposits of $188.67, banks keep reserves of about $37.73 (20 percent of $188.67). What happened to the remaining $62.27 that was originally deposited? The answer is that currency held by the public increased by that amount. We can check our mathematics by considering k. The currency-to-deposit ratio of $62.27/$188.67 equals 1/3, which is the value that we assumed.

SAVINGS ACCOUNTS AS A LEAKAGE

A second leakage results when people divert some of their deposits into savings accounts. Here the analysis gets complicated. If the original depositor wanted to hold some of his deposits in the form of time deposits, the deposit expansion process would decrease still more. Let's assume that individuals wish to hold $.50 in time deposits for every $1 in demand deposits. The time-deposit-to-demand-deposit ratio, t, would be 1/2. Reserves must also be held against time deposits. We will call the percentage reserve requirement for time deposits ρ_t and assume it is 10 percent. Now $66.67 of the original deposit will go into a demand deposit, while $33.33 will go into a time deposit. (However, all of the $100 does get into the bank.) In the first step, as well as all subsequent steps, demand deposits will expand more slowly than before.

The (demand) deposit multiplier is always 1 divided by the sum of the amount of the leakages out of demand deposits for each dollar deposited in the bank (whether in checking accounts or savings accounts). The new leakage we presently are examining per dollar of deposit is $\rho_t t$, where ρ_t is the amount leaked or "tied up" as reserves against time deposits, and t is the increase in the amount lost to time deposits for every additional dollar of demand deposits. Thus the demand deposit multiplier is now:

$$\frac{1}{\rho_D + k + \rho_t t} \tag{9-2}$$

In our continuing arithmetic example this equals

$$\frac{1}{.2 + .33 + .1\,(.5)}$$

which is 1/.58 or 1.7241. Now demand deposits would be $172.41 higher as the result of the initial $100 deposit than they would be if that initial deposit did not take place. Not surprisingly, as we add more and more leakages, the addition to demand deposits gets less and less.

EXCESS RESERVES AS A LEAKAGE

The final leakage of any importance is the result of conscious commercial bank policy. Commercial banks may well desire to keep some assets as reserves against total deposits even though these reserves are not required. Some banks, such as state banks in Illinois, are not required to hold any reserves whatsoever. Prudent banking, however, induces those banks to hold some reserves as contingencies against deposit withdrawals.

Banks may also hold reserves because they feel that creating new loans may involve undue risk without adequate return. In 1936, for example, banks held 13 percent of their deposits as reserves that were not required. That is an unusually high percentage of deposits as unrequired reserves. It was so high then because between 1929 and 1933 there had been many, many bank failures; in 1936 decision makers in banks were unusually cautious.

We call these reserves *excess reserves*. If we let e be the amount of desired excess reserves per dollar of demand deposits, the deposit expansion multiplier becomes

$$\frac{1}{\rho_D + k + \rho_t t + e} \tag{9-3}$$

If $e = .07$, $t = 1/2$, $\rho_t = .1$, $\rho_D = .2$ and $k = .33$, the deposit multiplier would equal $1/.65$, which equals 1.5384. A \$100 initial deposit from outside the banking system would result in \$153.84 of additional demand deposits.

9-3 THE RELATIONSHIP BETWEEN THE DEPOSIT MULTIPLIER AND THE MONEY MULTIPLIER

In the previous two sections we focused attention on choices of commercial banks (through e) and individuals (through t and k). The deposit expansion process depends in part on these two decision-making groups. The Federal Reserve also has a role since changes in reserve requirements affect the size of the deposit multiplier. A change in any of the determinants of the deposit multiplier will cause a change in the level of both demand deposits (D) and the money stock (M).

The relationship between changes in demand deposits and changes in the money supply can be developed quite simply. We defined k as the ratio of currency held by the public (C) to demand deposits (D). For any given value of k any change in D is accompanied by a change in C. Specifically,

$$\Delta C = k\Delta D \tag{9-4}$$

and since

$$\Delta M = \Delta C + \Delta D \tag{9-5}$$

we can substitute Equation 9-4 into Equation 9-5:

$$\Delta M = k\,\Delta D + \Delta D$$

or

$$\Delta M = (k + 1)(\Delta D) \tag{9-6}$$

Since

$$\Delta m = (k+1) \cdot \frac{1}{\rho_D + k + \rho_t \bar{t} + e}$$

$$\Delta D = [1/(\rho_D + k + t\rho_t + e)](\Delta R) \tag{9-7}$$

then

$$\Delta M = [(k + 1)/(\rho_D + k + t\rho_t + e)](\Delta R) \tag{9-8}$$

The relationship between ΔM and ΔR is called the *money multiplier*. The difference between the money multiplier and the deposit multiplier reflects the fact that currency changes must be included in calculating the former but not in calculating the latter. *1.33*

9-4 EFFECTS OF RATE OF INTEREST ON MONEY MULTIPLIER

Changes in the rate of interest, r, induce changes in e and t, two of the variables that determine the value of the money multiplier. As the market rate of interest goes up, the opportunity cost to a bank of holding excess reserves increases, and so we would expect e to fall. A decrease in r would mean that banks would be giving up less if they held excess reserves rather than converting them into earning assets, and so e would increase.

An increase in r, for a given level of interest paid on time deposits, would tend to decrease t because depositors would be attracted by the rate of return on (say) bonds and would save by buying bonds rather than time deposits at commercial banks. Here again the same kind of reasoning would lead one to expect that a decrease in r would cause an increase in t.

If r increases, e and t tend to decrease. The formula for μ, the money multiplier, is

$$\frac{k + 1}{\rho_D + k + t\rho_t + e} \tag{9-9}$$

As t and e decrease, other things being equal, μ increases. If r decreases, t and e will increase, and so μ will decrease. Thus changes in the rate of interest cause the money multiplier to change in the same direction.

9-5 THE FEDERAL RESERVE SYSTEM AND THE MONEY SUPPLY

The Federal Reserve System plays two important roles in economic activity: it is the bankers' bank (comprised of 12 district banks) and it conducts monetary policy. Let us look at the assets and liabilities of the Fed that are most important in its two functions.

ASSETS AND LIABILITIES OF THE FED

A bank that borrows from a Federal Reserve bank can use the funds as reserves. From the point of view of the Fed, the lender, the loan is an asset. When the Fed buys Treasury securities from banks or the banks' customers, the securities become assets of the Fed. Since the Fed pays for the securities with checks drawn on itself, the checks end up as additional commercial bank reserves.

If the Fed buys a Treasury bond from a corporation, for example, it pays the corporation with a check. The corporation deposits the check in its commercial bank, and its commercial bank presents the check to the Fed for payment. The Fed pays the commercial bank merely by crediting the bank's account by the amount of the check. The check is canceled, but *it is not deducted from any account*. The Fed has merely written a check on itself, which it honors by crediting a commercial bank's account. The credit comes out of the air, but it represents real reserves to the commercial bank.

Thus whenever the Fed increases its loans to commercial banks (such loans are called *discounts*), and whenever the Fed acquires Treasury securities either directly from the banks or from the customers of the banks, it increases its assets; in so doing, it increases the amount of reserves commercial banks have available for lending. The more reserves there are available for the commercial banks to lend, and the more reserves the commercial banks in fact lend, the larger will be the money supply.

When commercial banks pay off their loans from the Fed, they reduce the amount of reserves in the commercial banking system. This is because the commercial banks carry checking accounts of their own with the Fed, and when a commercial bank pays off a loan, the Fed merely "crosses out" or "extinguishes" the amount involved from the bank's account. The payment doesn't go to any other bank, or person, or institution. It merely ceases to exist. The Fed has fewer assets (the outstanding loan is gone), and it has fewer liabilities (deposits of the commercial bank).

Similarly, when the Fed sells a Treasury security to a corporation (or individual), the corporation pays for the security with a check drawn on its commercial bank. The Fed presents the check to the commercial bank for payment. The commercial bank deducts the amount of the check from the corporation's account, and the Fed deducts the amount of the check from the bank's account. The amount is again "extinguished." It does not go into any other account. The Fed has reduced its assets (it sold the securities) and it reduced its liabilities (it reduced the bank's deposit).

THREE INSTRUMENTS OF MONETARY POLICY

Monetary policy is the attempt by the Fed to affect total spending in the economy by causing changes in the amount of money in circulation. An *expansionary monetary policy* is an attempt to increase total spending by increasing the money supply, and a *restrictive monetary policy* is an attempt to reduce the amount of total spending by decreasing the amount of money in circulation.

Open Market Operations   The buying and selling of Treasury securities on the open market is the main technique the Fed uses to affect the amount of bank reserves and therefore the amount of money in circulation. Such buying and selling of securities by the Fed is called *open market operations*. When the Fed wants the money supply to increase, it buys securities; when it wants the money supply to decrease, it sells securities.

Banks keep reserves in the form of vault cash and deposits with the Fed. We have already called this R. The public holds currency and demand deposits, which we have called C and D. We define the monetary base, B, as

$$B = C + R \tag{9-10}$$

By varying R the Fed affects B. The result of a change in B is, by the deposit expansion process, a much larger change in the money supply.

Loans to Commercial Banks   The second type of monetary policy involves the granting of loans to commercial banks by the Fed. If the Fed lends to banks, banks not only gain an asset (increased reserves at the Fed) but also have an offsetting liability (borrowings from the Fed). Until these reserves are repaid, banks can use them to make loans. Again, a change in the base will result in a change in the money stock.

Banks borrow money not only from the Fed, but also from each other. The *federal funds market* is the name given to the interbank lending of reserves. A bank that has deficient reserves may borrow from another that has excess reserves. Such loans are always very short-term, in many cases merely overnight. The interest rate that is paid on these interbank loans is called the *federal funds rate*. At the end of this chapter we will see that for many years the Fed has tried to manipulate the federal funds rate and as a result has introduced more instability into the economy than it otherwise would have.

When one bank borrows from another, total bank reserves are not affected. The bank that borrows the funds has additional reserves, while the lending bank has fewer reserves. When a bank borrows from the Fed, however, that bank has additional reserves and no other bank has fewer reserves, and so total bank reserves increase. To increase bank reserves by lending to banks, the Fed makes the discount rate (the interest rate it charges when it lends to banks) lower than the federal funds rate. To reduce reserves in banks, it makes borrowing from the Fed unattractive by making the discount rate exceed the federal funds rate.

For most of the first three quarters of 1979 the federal funds rate averaged half a percentage point above the discount rate. On October 6, 1979, the Chairman of the Federal Reserve Board of Governors, Paul Volker, announced that the Fed would no longer try to control the federal funds rate. In the following two weeks the federal funds rate increased from 12 percent to $15\frac{1}{2}$ percent, which was $2\frac{1}{2}$ points above the existing discount rate. As a result, in the same two weeks, bank borrowing from the Fed increased by $2 billion.

Changes in Reserve Requirements The Federal Reserve has a third instrument of monetary policy: changes in reserve requirements on time deposits and demand deposits. You will recall from Equation 9-9 (the equation for μ, the money multiplier) that required reserve ratios, ρ_D and ρ_t, appear only in the denominator. An increase in either of these two reserve requirement ratios will decrease the money multiplier. The Fed would increase reserve requirements if it felt that monetary restraint was necessary for the stability of the economy.

9-6 MONETARY POLICY LINKAGES

Monetary policy is most effective when it causes predictable effects on real income. By now you should see the sequence:

$$\Delta B \rightarrow \Delta M \rightarrow \Delta Y \rightarrow \Delta Q \qquad (9\text{-}11)$$

Each of the arrows represents the linkage between the variables. The linkages are between

- B and M: the money multiplier
- M and Y: velocity of circulation of money
- Y and Q: price changes

The first linkage, between the monetary base (B) and the money stock (M), is the money multiplier (μ). The Fed controls B (mainly through open market operations); and changes in B, through the multiple deposit expansion process, generate larger changes in M. The money multiplier is not controlled by the Fed. It depends significantly on the behavior of commercial bankers and their customers. Although μ is not constant and cannot be controlled by the Fed, it is highly stable. Figure 9-1 shows the value of μ over the period 1977–79. Since μ is so stable, it is possible for the Fed to control M with relative precision by controlling B.

The second linkage, between the money stock and nominal GNP (Y), depends on the stability of the demand for money. If people's attitudes toward money as a way of holding wealth were such that in the aggregate the ratio of nominal income to the money stock were constant, any percentage change in M caused by the Fed would induce changed spending until Y changed by an equal percentage amount. The ratio of Y to M is, of course, velocity; and velocity is not constant. Its value depends on the actions of people. It is not controlled by any government agency. Although velocity is not constant, it too is relatively stable. Figure 9-2 shows the value of velocity over the period 1970–78.

The third linkage, between nominal GNP and real GNP (Q), is not as predictable as the first two. Any change in nominal income could be a change in real income, but it could also be a change in the average money price level. It almost always is a combination of the two, and it is very difficult to predict what the combination will be. The Keynesian model simply assumes that the average money price level is constant and that all changes in nominal GNP are real. This assumption requires another assumption: there are always so many unemployed resources that all increased dollar spending can show up as increased real output and employment. These assumptions imply a direct link between nominal aggregate demand and employment, and they lead economists to ignore questions of incentives to work and produce as well as other supply-side issues. We will have more to say about this in Chapter 11.

9-7 THE MONEY SUPPLY FUNCTION

We are now able to develop the money supply function. The money stock (the quantity of money in circulation) is a function of the size of the monetary base and the size of the money multiplier. The whole relationship between the money stock, the money base, and the money multiplier is called the *money supply* or the *money supply function*. The money multiplier is determined by the public's desire for cash, demand deposits, and time deposits; the banks' desire to hold excess reserves; and the required reserve ratios. As interest rates rise, the money multiplier increases (through the effects on t and e). Figure 9-3 illustrates these relationships for one money supply relationship. Given a monetary base of B_1,

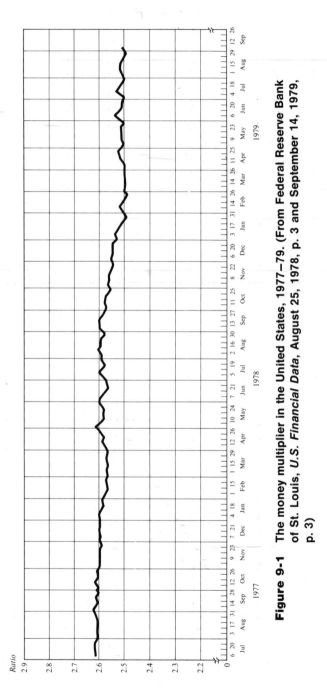

Figure 9-1 The money multiplier in the United States, 1977–79. (From Federal Reserve Bank of St. Louis, *U.S. Financial Data*, August 25, 1978, p. 3 and September 14, 1979, p. 3)

Velocity

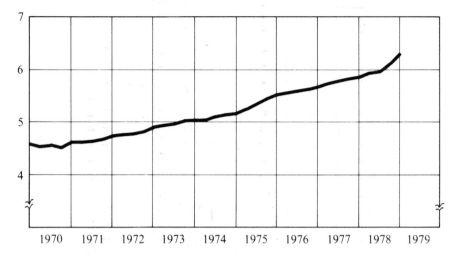

Figure 9-2 Velocity in the United States, 1970–79 (quarterly).

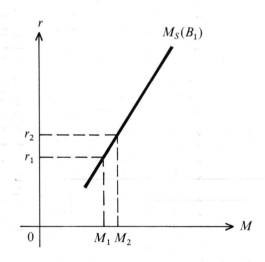

Figure 9-3 The relationship between the money stock
and the rate of interest.

Table 9-1   Impact of various changes in the monetary sector

Change	Effect on	Money Supply Function
Open market operation—Fed sells bonds to public	$B-$	Shifts to the left
Open market operation—Fed buys bonds	$B+$	Shifts to the right
Banks increase borrowings from Fed	$B+$	Shifts to the right
Banks decrease borrowings from Fed	$B-$	Shifts to the left
Fed increases reserve requirements	ρ_D+, ρ_t+	Shifts to the left
Fed decreases reserve requirements	ρ_D-, ρ_t-	Shifts to the right
Banks demand more excess reserves	$e+$	Shifts to the left
Banks demand less excess reserves	$e-$	Shifts to the right
Public increases its demand for time deposits	$t+$	Shifts to the left
Public decreases its demand for time deposits	$t-$	Shifts to the right

the money stock increases from M_1 to M_2 as the interest rate increases from r_1 to r_2.

Table 9-1 summarizes the impact of various changes in the monetary sector. The Fed can control the money stock through its control over the money base, but the public can affect the money stock by changing the ratio between time deposits and demand deposits, and commercial banks can affect the money stock by changing the ratio of excess reserves to demand deposits. This means that there will be some "slippage" when the Fed tries to change the money stock. In Figure 9-4, we start with a money stock equal to M_1 and an interest rate equal to r_1. The Fed increases the money base to B_2. If the interest rate (and therefore the money multiplier) did not change, the money stock would become M^*. If the interest rate fell to r_2, however, the money multiplier would fall and the money stock would increase to only M_2 instead of M^*.

Notice that the shift in the money supply function will equal $\mu\Delta B$ at any rate of interest. Since μ rises as the interest rate rises, the slope of the money supply function will get flatter as the function shifts to the right due to a rise in the base. We can see this in an example. Suppose that μ is 2.5 at r_1 and 2.4 at r_2. If $B_1 = 100$ and $B_2 = 200$, the shift in the money supply function is 250 at r_1 and 240 at r_2. Since the shift is greater at higher interest rates, the function is becoming flatter as it shifts to the right. The reader should also be able to verify that the slope of the money supply function becomes slightly flatter when either ρ_D, e, or t decreases.

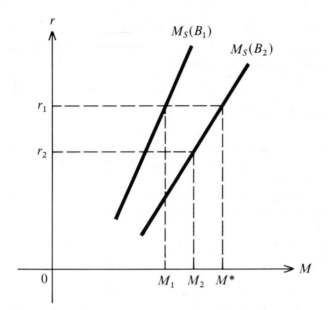

Figure 9-4 The effect, on the money supply, of an increase in the money base.

9-8 MONETARY POLICY TARGETS

The Fed affects the monetary base primarily by engaging in open market operations—buying and selling securities ("bonds"). When the Fed increases its purchase of bonds, it thereby increases the demand for bonds on the market relative to the supply and causes the price of bonds to increase. A higher price of bonds means lower interest rates. When the Fed sells bonds, the supply of bonds on the market increases relative to the demand, bond prices fall, and interest rates increase. Thus the Fed's monetary policy decisions affect interest rates as well as the quantity of money.

The Fed has been criticized for worrying too much about interest rates and not enough about the money supply. As we will see in Chapter 11, the effects of open market operations on interest rates outlined above are only temporary. In fact, open market purchases of bonds lead ultimately to *higher*, not lower, rates of interest. The Fed can *temporarily* cause interest rates to fall by expanding the monetary base, and it can *temporarily* cause interest rates to rise by decreasing the monetary base. Changing the monetary base, however, has more lasting and significant effects on the amount of spending people do.

Suppose that the Fed desires to implement a restrictive monetary policy in order to combat an inflation. It reduces the Fed's rate of purchases in the bond market (or actually sells in the bond market) in an attempt to cut down the rate of increase in the monetary base (or actually decrease the monetary base). This reduction in buying increases the supply of bonds relative to the demand for bonds, bond prices fall, and interest rates rise. Interest rates are important to many people. They affect home mortgages, automobile time payment contracts, and the like. Political pressure is brought to bear on the Fed through senators and representatives who think that the sole job of the Fed is to make interest rates as low as possible. The Fed is then in a dilemma: does it stick to its intent to fight inflation, or does it give in to the pressure to expand the money stock and keep interest rates low?

Of course, it could point out that the higher interest rates are only temporary and that if the fight against inflation is effective, interest rates will soon fall; but apparently many people in government and at large are impatient. They realize that the Fed could *immediately* lower interest rates, so why wait? They either don't understand or don't care that the very increases in the monetary base that would lower interest rates immediately will make them higher later on.

The mass media, both printed and broadcast, pay a lot of attention to interest rates. Whenever interest rates rise, they assert that the Fed is "tightening up on credit," and when interest rates fall, they assert that the Fed is "loosening up on credit." It is credit and interest rates that people hear about, not the money supply. What they don't hear is that "tight credit" now means lower interest rates in the future, and "loose credit" now means higher interest rates in the future. (This will be fully explained in Chapter 11.)

Figure 9-5 demonstrates that the Fed seems to pay more attention to the immediate effects of its policy on interest rates than on the money supply. Panel a shows actual money supply growth rates (the black line) and target money supply growth rates announced by the Fed (indicated by the shaded blocks). Often the actual growth rates were outside the target ranges the Fed itself announced. Panel b shows the actual federal funds rate (the rate of interest commercial banks charge when they loan some of their excess reserves to commercial banks that have reserve deficiencies) and the federal funds rate targets the Fed announced it would try to achieve. The Fed kept the federal funds rate within its announced limits even when, in order to do so, it had to deviate from the limits it announced for money supply growth. In Chapter 11 we will see the utter folly of this behavior. On October 6, 1979 the chairman of the Fed announced that thereafter monetary targets would be given priority.

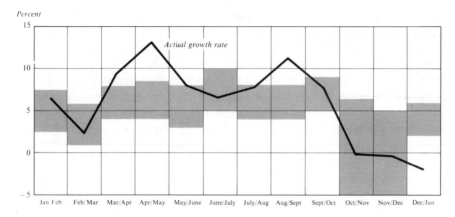

(a) 1978 Target ranges for monetary growth

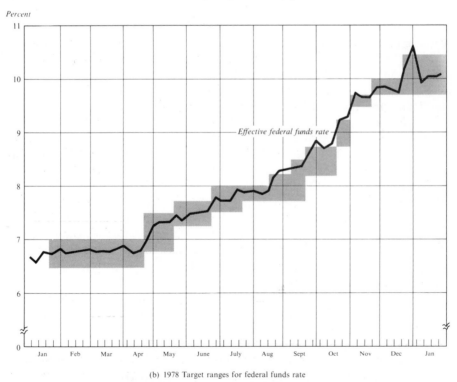

(b) 1978 Target ranges for federal funds rate

Figure 9-5   The 1978 target ranges for monetary growth (a) conflict with the 1978 target ranges for the federal funds rate (b). (From *Federal Reserve Bank of St. Louis Review*, March 1979, pp. 10–11)

SUMMARY

The money supply process in the United States involves the nonbank public, commercial banks, and the Federal Reserve System. The Fed controls the monetary base (mainly through open market operations), and changes in the base imply changes in commercial bank reserves. Since commercial banks can lend most of their reserves, and since one bank's loan becomes a deposit in another bank, any change in the base generates a larger change in the money supply. The relationship between the money base and the money stock is called the money multiplier. The value of the money multiplier is affected by legal reserve requirements on bank deposits, by the ratio of time deposits (savings account deposits) to demand deposits (checking account deposits), and by the ratio of excess reserves to demand deposits. The Fed controls the legal reserve ratios, the public determines the ratio of time to demand deposits, and commercial bankers determine the ratio of excess reserves to demand deposits.

The link between changes in the money base and changes in the money stock is strong and direct because of the stability of the money multiplier. The link between changes in the money stock and changes in total spending is strong and direct because of the stability of velocity. The division of changes in nominal GNP between real changes and price changes is very uncertain because it depends on supply considerations in the commodities market that have been ignored in traditional macroeconomic analysis.

The Federal Reserve faces a policy dilemma when it must choose whether to pay more attention to its monetary growth targets or its interest rate targets. It seems to have paid more attention to the latter than to the former, to the detriment of its ability to cope with inflation.

QUESTIONS

1. Commercial banks have recently been authorized to allow customers to transfer funds automatically from savings accounts to checking accounts. What effect will this have on the money multiplier? Why?
2. Under which circumstances would the money multiplier be larger: when all checks must be microfilmed and made available to the Internal Revenue Service or when all checking account activity is kept confidential? Why?
3. What is the effect of credit cards on the money multiplier? Why? Should credit limits on bank credit cards be included as part of the money supply? Why or why not?

4. When the ratio of time deposits to demand deposits increases, the banks' ratio of desired excess reserves to demand deposits will be lower than it otherwise would be. Why?

5. What would happen to the extent to which the money multiplier changes when the interest rate changes if Regulation Q (the ceiling on interest rates banks can pay on their savings accounts) were repealed? Why?

6. How would the legalization of marijuana, heroin, gambling, and prostitution affect the money multiplier? Would this be a continuous or a once-and-for-all change?

7. If an increase in the monetary base of 20 percent is accompanied by an increase in the money multiplier of 5 percent, what will be the percentage change of the money stock? How is this related to Figure 9-4?

8.

	$r = 5\%$	$r = 10\%$	$r = 5\%$	$r = 10\%$
t	3	2	3	2
ρ_t	.05	.05	.05	.05
k	2	2	2	2
e	.05	.01	.05	.01
ρ_D	.20	.20	.15	.15
B	100	100	100	100

Using the above data, calculate the money multiplier and the money stock at the two given interest rates when average reserve requirements on demand deposits are 20 percent. Do the same for a ρ_D of 15 percent. What has happened to the slope of the money supply function? Why?

 stop

PART

5

INTERACTION OF
THE MARKETS

The Constant Price
IS-LM Model

In this chapter we begin the process of bringing together in one theoretical model all of the building blocks we have up to now developed. Specifically, we will construct a model that shows the interactions of the commodities market, the money market, and the bond market. We will do so under the assumption of a fixed average money price level. In the next chapter we will drop that assumption and add the labor market to our analysis.

10-1 CONSTRUCTION OF THE MODEL

There are two main parts to the model that is usually used to analyze the interaction of the commodities market, the money market, and the bond market. The *IS* curve represents events in the commodities market and, because the rate of interest is part of the analysis, the bond market. The *LM* curve represents events in the money market and, for the same reason, the bond market. When the *IS* and *LM* curves are put together, the analysis of the three markets is complete.

Our derivations of the *IS* and *LM* curves assume a constant price level. In the next chapter we will relax this assumption. In this chapter, however, any change in Y along either the *IS* or the *LM* curve is actually a change in Q, the level of real income.

THE *IS* CURVE

As we learned in Chapter 4, equilibrium in the commodities market is achieved at all levels of income when planned expenditures equal actual expenditures or (saying the same thing in different words) when planned expenditures equal aggregate supply. Planned expenditures, $C + I + G$, are determined by the level of income and the rate of interest.

Graphing Interest Rates and Income   In Chapter 6 (Sections 4 and 6) we saw that both consumption and planned investment depend on the interest rate as well as the level of income. At any given interest rate, as income increases, both of these components of planned expenditure increase. When the (real) rate of interest increases, both the consumption line and the planned investment line shift downward, and so the aggregate planned expenditure line shifts downward.

Figure 10-1a shows these relationships for two different interest rates where $r_2 > r_1$; the planned expenditure function shifts downward whenever the interest rate increases. Income level Y_1 is the equilibrium level of income if the rate of interest is r_1. At that level of income, the planned expenditure line intersects the 45° line, indicating equilibrium in the commodities market. At income level Y_2 and interest rate r_1, the level of planned expenditures is indicated by point D, which lies above the 45° line, indicating an excess demand (ED) in the commodities market. This ED could be removed by an increase in the interest rate to r_2, which would shift the aggregate demand line downward so that it intersected the 45° line at point B.

Since when $r = r_1$, equilibrium income is Y_1, and when $r = r_2$, equilibrium income is Y_2, the points (Y_1, r_1) and (Y_2, r_2) in Figure 10-1b both indicate equilibrium in the commodities market. In this figure the rate of interest is indicated on the vertical axis while income is measured on the horizontal axis. As the interest rate rises from r_1 to r_2, the equilibrium level of income falls from Y_1 to Y_2. Thus the market-clearing curve in the commodities market has a *negative slope*. Points A and B in Figure 10-1b refer to the corresponding points in Figure 10-1a.

We call this market-clearing curve the *IS curve*. Each point along the curve represents a unique pair of income and interest rate that clears the commodities market. Any pair of points not on the curve represents disequilibrium in this market. Point D, for example, indicates income of Y_2 and interest rate of r_1. In Figure 10-1a, interest rate r_1 indicates planned expenditures of $C(r_1) + I(r_1) + G$. Income level Y_2, with this planned expenditure line, generates expenditures represented by point D, which we have already determined to be a point of ED. In fact, *all points below the IS curve represent excess demand*. The reader should verify that all points above the IS curve represent points of excess supply (ES) in the commodities market. The reader should be able to find (Y_1, r_2) on both diagrams to prove this.

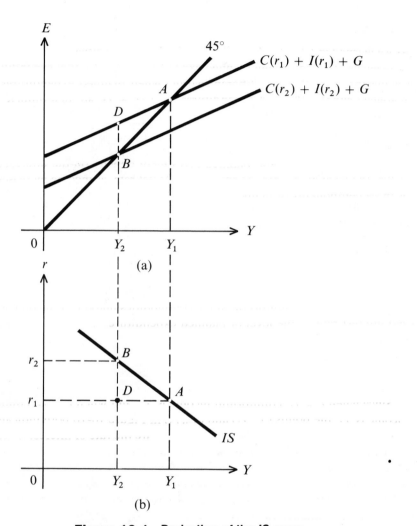

Figure 10-1 Derivation of the *IS* curve.

Equilibrium   The *IS* curve represents all income levels where

$$C + I + G = C + S + T \tag{10-1}$$

(which, as you recall from Section 5 of Chapter 4, is the equilibrium condition in the commodities market). Thus all points where

$$I + G = S + T \tag{10-2}$$

represent points of equilibrium. If injections ($I + G$) into the income stream are not equal to withdrawals ($S + T$), either ES or ED will exist.

In our example, point D represents ED because $I + G > S + T$. From point D in Figure 10-2 (which is the same as point D in Figure 10-1b), if equilibrium is to be achieved, either the interest rate or income or both must increase. These possibilities are indicated by the arrows emanating from point D in Figure 10-2. As we will see in Section 10-2, interest rate changes are generated in the bond market, while income changes are generated in the commodities market. Where will the equilibrium be? The IS curve indicates that there is *no unique equilibrium in the commodities market.* All points on the existing IS curve represent possible points of equilibrium. We have two unknowns (r and Y) and one relationship (the IS curve), and no unique solution is possible. In Chapter 4, when we developed the simple Keynesian model and the multipliers, a unique solution could be derived. We had not yet introduced the rate of interest as a variable influencing planned expenditures. As we add more variables, we will need more relationships in order to find a unique equilibrium.

Shifts in the *IS* Curve   *Any shift in the $C + I + G$ line that is not caused by a change in the interest rate causes a shift in the IS curve.* We have already exam-

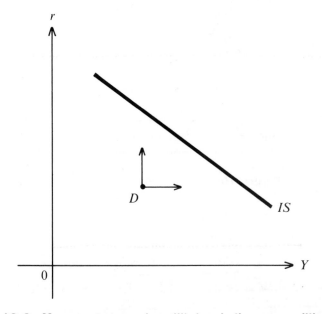

Figure 10-2   Movements toward equilibrium in the commodities market.

ined some of the factors, other than changes in the interest rate, that may cause a shift in planned expenditures. If government expenditures were to increase from G_1 to G_2, the planned expenditure line would shift upward by $G_2 - G_1$. If the interest rate remains unchanged, when this happens the equilibrium level of income will increase by the Keynesian multiplier (m) times the change in government spending. Figure 10-3 shows one planned expenditure line labeled $C_1(r_1) + I_1(r_1) + G_1$ at some rate of $r = r_1$. If government expenditures rise to G_2 and the interest rate remains at r_1, planned expenditures will rise to $C_1(r_1) + I_1(r_1) + G_2$; equilibrium income will rise from Y_1 to Y_2, and $Y_2 - Y_1 = m(G_2 - G_1)$, as shown in Figure 10-3a, the income expenditure diagram. Figure 10-3b shows the same change in the IS curve. The shift in the IS curve at interest rate r_1 would again be $m(G_2 - G_1)$. Other changes in economic conditions would cause corresponding changes in the IS curve. Changes in $\overline{T}$, $\overline{C}$, and $\overline{I}$ will cause corresponding shifts in the IS curve.

Slope of the *IS* Curve   The slope of the IS curve can also change. We can see this by taking an extreme case. If the interest rate had no impact at all on consumption or investment (i.e., if consumption and investment were interest inelastic), rather than having many planned expenditure functions, we would have just one because C and I are not affected by r. This unique planned expenditure line would intersect the 45° line at one point and that would be the only equilibrium level of income. The IS curve would be vertical, indicating there is only one equilibrium level of income regardless of the rate of interest. So we have an important conclusion: the IS curve will be steep if investment and consumption are relatively interest inelastic and flat if I and C are relatively interest elastic.

THE *LM* CURVE

As we learned in Chapter 8, equilibrium in the money market requires that the demand for money (L) equal the supply of money (M). The demand function for money may be written as

$$M_D = L(r, Y) \tag{10-3}$$

All of the other independent variables that enter the demand for money function are assumed to be known and constant. As we shall see in Chapter 12, one of these other variables, the expected inflation rate, has its effect on the demand for money by its effect on the rate of return on bonds. For now, we will assume that the expected inflation rate is zero.

Graphing Interest Rates and Demand for Money   A demand curve for money can be drawn against any of the independent variables, but the most useful one

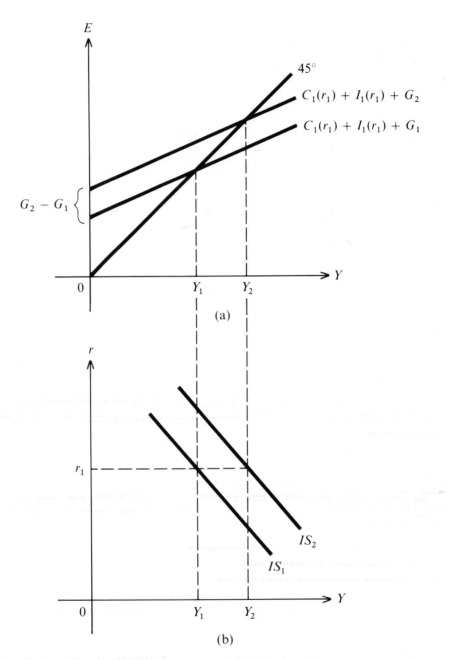

Figure 10-3 Shifts in the *IS* curve.

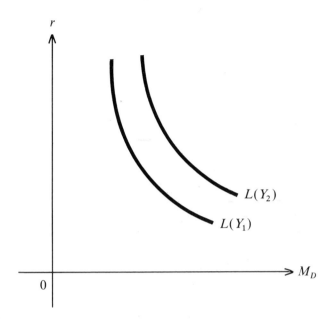

Figure 10-4 Demand for money at different income levels.

is r. In Figure 10-4 such a curve is drawn and labeled $L(Y_1)$. It tells us the quantity of money demanded for various possible values of r, assuming income equals Y_1 and assuming constant values for all the remaining variables. If income increased to Y_2, the demand curve would shift to the right, to $L(Y_2)$, showing an increased quantity of money demanded at each value of r. If income decreased, the demand curve would shift to the left, showing a decrease in the quantity of money demanded at each value of r.

In Figure 10-5a the supply and demand curves for money (M_s and L) are combined. As Y increases from Y_1 to Y_2, the demand curve shifts from $L(Y_1)$ to $L(Y_2)$ and the interest rate rises from r_1 to r_2—just as the price of apples would rise if the demand curve for apples shifted to the right and the supply curve for apples did not shift. If income decreased from Y_1 to Y_3, the demand curve for money would shift to $L(Y_3)$ and the interest rate would drop from r_1 to r_3.

In other words, as income increases (decreases), the interest rate must increase (decrease) if we are to have equilibrium in the money market. A line that represents this relationship is called the *LM curve*. Such a line appears in Figure 10-5b. The positive slope of the line indicates the positive relationship between the income level and the interest rate that would equate the supply and demand for money at that income level. Specifically, if the income level is Y_1, the interest

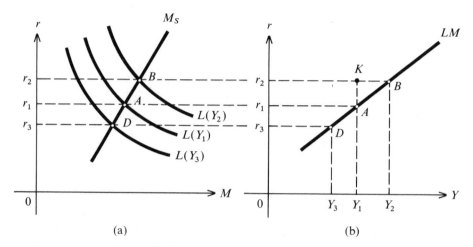

Figure 10-5 The effect of increased income on equilibrium interest rate (a) and the *LM* curve (b).

rate must be r_1 in order to have M, the supply of money, equal to L, the demand for money (hence the name of the line). (Y_2, r_2) and (Y_3, r_3) also clear the money market. We have denoted these points A, B, and D, respectively.

Equilibrium Point K in Figure 10-5b does not lie along the *LM* curve. It represents an interest rate of r_2 and an income level of Y_1. We can go back to Figure 10-5a to find this point. At income level Y_1 the demand for money is indicated by $L(Y_1)$. At interest rate r_2 the demand for money $L(Y_1)$ is less than the supply of money; thus point K is a point of excess supply (ES) in the money market. In fact, all points to the left of the *LM* curve represent points of *ES*. All points to the right represent excess demand (ED). The student should be able to show that (Y_2, r_1) represents ED.

Are there forces in the money market that would induce this market to move from a point such as K to some point on the *LM* curve? If an *ES* for money exists, individuals are holding more cash balances than they desire to hold. One solution would be to increase the purchase of bonds in order to reduce their cash balances. A purchase of bonds bids up the price of bonds and lowers the yield. Thus r would fall. This is shown in Figure 10-6 with a vertical arrow pointing toward the *LM* curve. A second possibility would be for individuals to increase their expenditures on goods and services. This buying would reduce inventories of firms, inducing them to increase production and income. This increase is shown by the horizontal arrow. Some combination of these two alternatives is

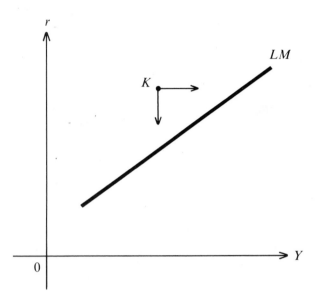

Figure 10-6   Movements toward equilibrium in the money market.

also possible. Again, market forces will ultimately cause the economy to move from a disequilibrium, represented by a point such as K, to an equilibrium somewhere on the LM curve.

Once again there is no unique equilibrium on the LM curve. All points along this curve represent income and interest rate levels that will clear the money market. No unique solution is possible because we have two unknowns, Y and r, and only one relationship, the LM curve.

Shifts in the *LM* Curve   Any change that causes the supply of money curve to shift—specifically any change in the money base—will cause the LM curve to shift. Consider Figure 10-7. Suppose the money supply line is M_s. When income is Y_1, the interest rate must be r_1 if L equals M. With the same money supply line, if income is Y_2, the interest rate must be r_2, Point A in Figure 10-7a corresponds to point A in Figure 10-7b. The two points labeled B also correspond to each other. If the Fed increases the money base, the money supply line will shift to M'_s. Now if the income level is Y_1, the interest rate will be r'_1 and the economy will be at point C in Figure 10-7a and b. If the income level is Y_2, the interest rate must be r'_2 and the economy would be at the points labeled D in both panels of the figure.

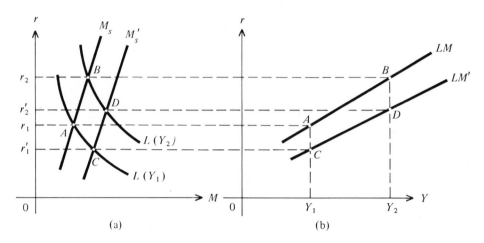

Figure 10-7 The effect of shifts in the money supply line on *LM* curve.

Any factor, other than a change of Y, that causes the demand for money line to shift will cause the *LM* curve to shift. For example, bank regulatory agencies have recently begun to permit banks to transfer deposit credits from a customer's savings account to his or her checking account automatically. Before this change, the customer had to go to the bank to make the transfer. This regulatory change resulted in a decrease in the average size of checking account balances (a shift to the left of the demand for money line). Figure 10-8 shows this effect. In panel a the demand for money curve labeled $L(Y_1)$ becomes that labeled $L'(Y_1)$, and $L(Y_2)$ becomes $L'(Y_2)$. The interest rates that correspond to each income level are now lower ($r_1 > r'_1, r_2 > r'_2$); hence the *LM* curve in panel b has shifted to the right to *LM'*. Again, points A, B, C, and D in the two panels correspond.

We can conclude that a rightward shift of the money supply function shifts the *LM* curve to the right, while an increase in the demand for money (except that caused by a change in Y) causes a shift to the left of the *LM* curve.

Slope of the *LM* Curve   What determines the slope of the *LM* curve? One factor is the slope of the money supply function. If the money stock is perfectly interest inelastic, the money supply function will be vertical. This is shown in Figure 10-9. M_s is interest inelastic, and M'_s is relatively interest elastic. At income Y_2, the vertical M_s line intersects $L(Y_2)$ at r_2, which is a higher interest rate than that which clears the money market with M'_s. Thus the *LM* curve in panel b corresponding to the vertical money supply M_s (LM) is steeper than that associated with M'_s (LM').

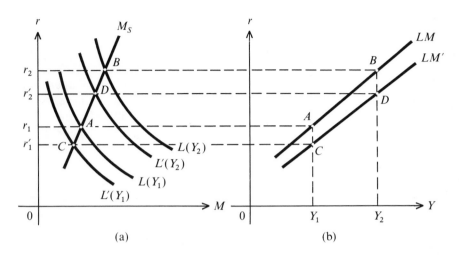

Figure 10-8 The effect of a shift in the money demand line on *LM* curve.

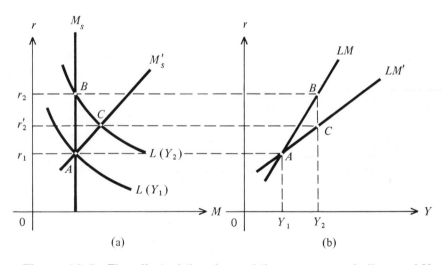

Figure 10-9 The effect of the slope of the money supply line on *LM* curve.

The slope of the *LM* curve is a very important variable. Recall from Chapter 8 (Section 2) the quantity equation of exchange, $MV \equiv PQ$, and that $PQ = Y$. Any change in Y must be accompanied by a change in MV. In other words, as we move from left to right on the horizontal axis of the *LM* curve (as we increase Y), we must be increasing MV. The vertical axis tells us how much of an increase in r is required to get the necessary increases in MV.

10-2 USES OF THE MODEL

The *IS* curve indicates all pairs of Y and r that will clear the commodities market. The *LM* curve indicates all pairs of Y and r that will clear the money market. There is one unique pair of Y and r that will clear both markets simultaneously. Figure 10-10 combines the *IS* and *LM* curves and indicates that the values that r and Y must take to attain simultaneous equilibrium are $\bar{r}$ and $\overline{Y}$, respectively. *No other combination will do.* If $r = r'$ and $Y = \overline{Y}$, neither of the two markets will be in equilibrium. If $r = r'$ and $Y = Y'$, the product or commodities market will be in equilibrium (we would be at a point on the *IS* curve), but the money market would not (we would be at a point off the *LM* curve).

Let us consider point K in greater detail. Since K lies above the *IS* curve, there is an *ES* in the commodities market. It is also above the *LM* curve and so there is an *ES* in the money market. You will recall from Section 1 in Chapter 3 that, by Say's Principle, there must be an accompanying *ED* in other markets. In the constant price *IS-LM* model, the implicit other market is the bond market. Let us examine the full implications of point K with reference to Figure 10-11. Panel a is a reproduction of Figure 10-10. In panel b the *ES* of money would show up as an *ED* for bonds, causing their prices to increase and lowering their yields. As yields (interest rates) fell, the $C + I + G$ line (panel c) would shift upward, eliminating the *ES* in the commodities market. The decline in r would

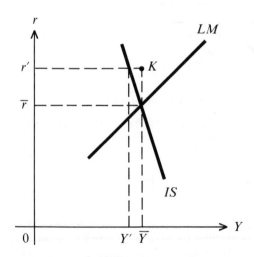

Figure 10-10 The *IS-LM* diagram.

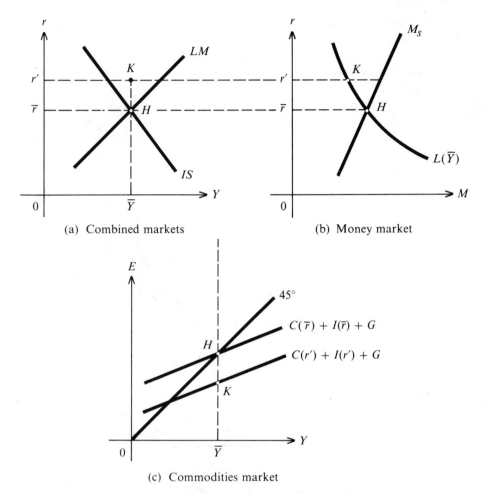

Figure 10-11 **Operation of the *IS-LM* model in combined markets (a),
the money market (b), and the commodities market (c).**

also eliminate the *ES* in the money market. Point *H* in each of the diagrams
would be attained.

What is important here is that as long as markets are not in equilibrium, internal mechanisms cause them to move toward equilibrium. The movement will
not be instantaneous because information must be acquired before correct decisions can be made. Disequilibrium may persist until this information is

acquired, but in the absence of other changes, the economy will move from K to the equilibrium at $\overline{Y}$ and $\overline{r}$.

We can now turn to some of the factors causing either the IS curve or the LM curve to shift. Any shift in these curves will result in a new equilibrium. We will describe these shifts and the reaction in the economy using Say's Principle. While we will show only the IS-LM curves, the reader should remember that these were developed from the corresponding relationships in the commodities and money market. The adjustments we will describe in our examples are idealized representations of what happens in the real world. The changes that we depict happening in orderly sequence actually happen gradually, continuously, and simultaneously. Nevertheless, our analysis brings into focus the essential nature of the interactions between the markets, and that is what any abstract analysis is supposed to do.

WORSENING OF PROFIT EXPECTATIONS

We begin in Figure 10-12 at point 1, with the three relevant markets (commodities, money, and bonds) in equilibrium. This initial equilibrium is also depicted in row 1 of Table 10-1, where zero excess demand is shown in each of the three

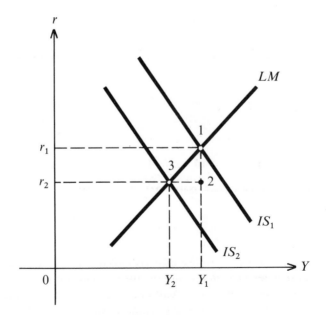

Figure 10-12 Worsening profit expectations.

Table 10-1   Excess demands

Row	Status	Bond Market	Commodities Market	Money Market
1	Equilibrium	0	0	0
2	$\bar{I}$ decreases	ED	ES	0
3	r decreases	0	ES	ED
4	Y decreases	0	0	0

columns. When expectations regarding the future profitability of investment worsen, investment decreases. This decrease causes the *IS* line to shift to IS_2. The economy is still located at point 1, above the new *IS* curve, and so there is an *ES* in the commodities market.

By Say's Principle there must be an accompanying *ED* somewhere, but since the economy is still on the *LM* line, the *ED* is not in the money market. It is in the bond market, since the decreased investment spending causes bond suppliers to decrease the supply of bonds (investors are not borrowing as much as before). The existing situation is depicted in row 2 of Table 10-1. The *ED* in the bond market causes bond prices to rise and the interest rate to fall until equilibrium is restored in the bond market. The decrease in the interest rate puts the economy at point 2 in Figure 10-12 and in row 3 of the table. The decline in the interest rate creates an *ED* in the money market, which is accompanied by some remaining *ES* in the commodities market. (Although the decline in the interest rate causes demand in the commodities market to increase, not all of the *ES* is eliminated.)

Finally, the combination of the excess demand for money (people attempting to build up their holdings of money balances) and the excess supply in the commodities market causes income to fall from Y_1 to Y_2. The economy moves to point 3 in the figure and to row 4 of the table. Full equilibrium is restored at a lower level of income and a lower rate of interest.

UPWARD SHIFT OF THE CONSUMPTION FUNCTION

We begin in Figure 10-13 at point 1 with the three markets in equilibrium. When $\bar{C}$ increases, planned expenditures increase at each level of income and the *IS* curve shifts to the right by m ($\Delta \bar{C}$). Point 1 now represents *ED* in the commodities market because it is below the new *IS* curve, but we are still on the *LM* curve and so there is zero *ED* in the money market. The increase in $\bar{C}$ will reduce saving at each level of income, resulting in an *ES* of bonds (people buy bonds with what they save). We are in row 2 of Table 10-2. The *ES* in the bond market will lower bond prices and raise r to point 2 in Figure 10-13. The bond market is

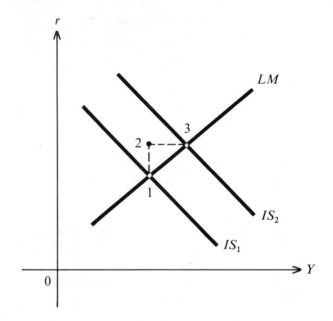

Figure 10-13 Upward shift in the consumption function.

Table 10-2 Excess demands

Row	Status	Bond Market	Commodities Market	Money Market
1	Equilibrium	0	0	0
2	$\overline{C}$ increases	ES	ED	0
3	r increases	0	ED	ES
4	Y increases	0	0	0

cleared. This interest rate increase causes an *ES* of money that will be used to purchase goods and services. We are in row 3 of the table. The *ED* in the commodities market implies an unplanned reduction in inventories that induces firms to expand output, causing *Y* to rise. We move finally to point 3 and row 4, where a new equilibrium is established at a higher level of income and a higher rate of interest.

INCREASE IN RESERVE REQUIREMENTS

An increase in reserve requirements will decrease the value of μ, the money multiplier (as we discussed in Sections 9-2 and 9-3). A decrease in μ will shift

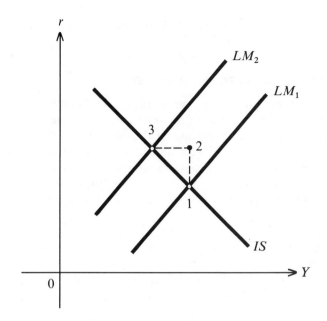

Figure 10-14 Increase in reserve requirements.

Table 10-3 Excess demands

Row	Status	Bond Market	Commodities Market	Money Market
1	Equilibrium	0	0	0
2	Reserve requirements increase	ES	0	ED
3	r increases	0	ES	ED
4	Y decreases	0	0	0

the money supply function to the left at all points. For any given base, B, a smaller μ means a smaller money stock. Thus, the LM curve shifts to the left. We show this in Figure 10-14. At point 1, after the changes in reserve requirements, the commodities market is in equilibrium but the money market is not. Point 1 is below the new LM line, LM_2. ED for money exists, and banks build up reserves by selling some of their assets (bonds). The banks' action creates an ES in bonds. We are in row 2 of Table 10-3. The ES in bonds causes a rise in interest rates to point 2. The bond market clears, but the higher interest rates reduce investment and consumption, creating an ES in commodities. We are in row 3 of the table. The ES in commodities and ED in money cause income to decline until point 3 and row 4 are attained, with income lower and interest higher than before.

CHANGED WILLINGNESS TO HOLD MONEY

If at every rate of interest and income people decided that they wanted to hold more of their assets in the form of money than before, the demand curve for money corresponding to each income level would shift to the right. One thing that could cause this phenomenon is a general belief that the average level of money prices would soon fall. People would want to hold on to money longer (spend it less quickly), hoping to take advantage of the expected lower prices. In any event, we can analyze the results of such a change using Figure 10-15 and Table 10-4.

We begin in row 1 of the table and point 1 of the figure. However, in order to demonstrate how the analysis may be extended, we will change our approach a little. The increase in the demand for money creates an ED for money and shifts the LM curve to LM_2. We remain at point 1, but the ED for money shows up as an ES in both the bond market *and the commodities market* at the same

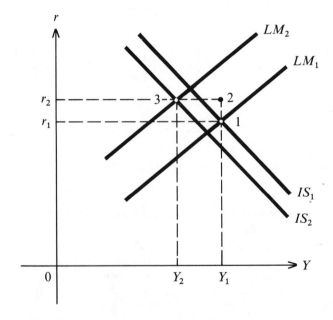

Figure 10-15 Changed willingness to hold money with direct effect on the commodities market.

Table 10-4 Excess demands

Row	Status	Bond Market	Commodities Market	Money Market
1	Equilibrium	0	0	0
2	Demand for money increases	ES	ES	ED
3	r increases	0	ES	ED
4	Y decreases	0	0	0

time. In other words, people are building up their money balances both by selling bonds and by curtailing their expenditure in the commodities market. The latter means that the IS curve shifts to IS_2. We are in row 2 and at point 1. Now the ES of bonds causes bond prices to fall and interest rates to rise to r_2, clearing the bond market. But the higher interest rate increases the ES of commodities, while decreasing the ED for money. (Point 2 is a move away from IS_2 and toward LM_2.) We are now in row 3 and at point 2. The remainder of the ED for money is satisfied by expenditure reductions in the commodities market, which cause Y to decrease until we are in row 4 and at point 3.

In our previous analyses, we assumed that a change in either the commodities market (e.g., worsening of profit expectations) or the money market (e.g., change in reserve requirements) affected the bond market *alone*. It was only after the interest rate changed due to changes in bond prices that the third market was affected. (If the initial shift is on the IS curve, the commodities market is the first‘ market while the money market is the third market. If the initial shift is on the LM curve, the money market is the first market and the commodities market is the third market.) Here we have allowed the initial change to affect the bond market and the third market simultaneously. The third market is affected *directly* by changes in the first market. When there are these direct effects, initial shifts of the LM curve cause shifts of the IS curve and vice versa.

10-3 FISCAL AND MONETARY POLICY IN THE IS-LM MODEL

A common source of shifts in the IS and LM lines is changes in fiscal and monetary policy. We now turn to consider these shifts.

THE MONETARY IMPLICATIONS OF FISCAL POLICY

Fiscal policy involves any change in government spending and/or taxation that is not caused by changes in income. For instance, if the $C + I + G$ line is pushed up, income will start to increase. If taxes depend on income, taxes will increase. This increase in taxes is *not* considered to be a fiscal policy change. A change in the tax rate or in the size of lump sum taxes would be a fiscal policy change. Any change in government expenditures that is unrelated to changes in income implies a change in fiscal policy.[1]

Fiscal policy may or may not cause the money supply curve to shift. If the money supply curve does not shift when fiscal policy changes, the fiscal policy change is said to be *pure*. If the money supply curve does shift when fiscal policy changes, the fiscal policy change is said to be *mixed*. Monetary policy is said to have changed whenever the money supply curve shifts (as it will with a mixed fiscal policy). If the money supply curve shifts for reasons not related to changes in government spending and taxation, the shift represents a pure monetary policy change. We must now consider under what circumstances a fiscal policy change will be pure and under what circumstances it will be mixed.

Suppose the Treasury starts with a balanced budget and then runs a deficit. It must finance the extra spending by borrowing money. It can borrow from the nonbank public, commercial banks, or the Fed. If it borrows the money from (sells bonds to) the nonbank public, demand deposits in commercial banks will decrease. Commercial bank reserves (deposits with the Fed) will fall as the Treasury deposits the proceeds of the bond sales in its account with the Fed. The Treasury, however, will spend these new deposits and the Treasury's sellers will deposit the proceeds of the sales in their banks, thus increasing demand deposits in commercial banks. The Fed will then increase member bank deposits and decrease Treasury deposits. So we are right back where we started—the money supply has not changed.

If the Treasury sells its bonds to commercial banks, the commercial banks must pay for them out of excess reserves. If these excess reserves would have been loaned to other borrowers, there is no change in the money supply. (It makes no difference, as far as the stock of money is concerned, who it is that borrows the excess reserves.) However, if the excess reserves would not have been loaned out to borrowers other than the Treasury, the sale of the bonds to commercial banks will make the money supply bigger than it otherwise would have been. In this case, when the Treasury spends the proceeds of its bond sale, its suppliers will deposit their receipts in the commercial banks and demand deposits will be bigger than they otherwise would have been. But suppose the banks could have loaned the excess reserves to private borrowers instead of to the Treasury. These private borrowers would also spend the money and *their* suppliers could deposit the proceeds in commercial banks. Demand deposits would be the same in both cases.

A sale of bonds by the Treasury to commercial banks may or may not increase the money stock. In the case where the excess reserves would have been loaned to private borrowers if the Treasury didn't sell the bonds, there is no change in the money stock. This is the usual case. In the case where the excess reserves would have been idle if the Treasury didn't sell the bonds, there would be an increase in the money stock.

If the Treasury sells its bonds to the Fed, there is definitely a shift in the money supply curve. Any time the Fed increases its holdings of government bonds, Federal Reserve credit (and therefore the money base) is increased. This type of sale has the same effect as printing money. The Treasury gives bonds to the Fed and the Fed credits the Treasury's account. The Treasury then spends the proceeds. When the Treasury spends the sum borrowed, it does so by writing checks on its account and mailing checks to the individuals and firms who sold goods and services to the government. These checks are then deposited in banks by those individuals and firms. When the checks are cleared, the Fed deducts deposits from the Treasury's account at the Fed and increases the reserve accounts of the banks in which the checks were deposited. Hence the Fed's purchase of bonds from the Treasury leads to an increase in the reserve of commercial banks—and ultimately to a multiple expansion of the money supply. In this case, the Treasury has financed a budget deficit by selling bonds to the Fed—the government has "borrowed" from itself!

In sum, *a fiscal policy change does not affect the money supply curve if it is financed by a sale of bonds to the nonbank public. A sale of bonds to the Fed, on the other hand, shifts the money supply curve to the right.*

Students can test their understanding by considering the case where the Treasury has a *surplus.* What happens when the surplus is used to buy back bonds held by the nonbank public, commercial banks, and the Fed? Also, what happens if the Treasury simply leaves the money on deposit with the Fed?

PURE FISCAL POLICY CHANGE

An expansionary pure fiscal policy (for instance, an increase in G while taxes are held constant) pushes up the $C + I + G$ line. We saw in Section 10-1 that this change causes the IS curve to shift to the right by an amount equal to the change in G times the multiplier. If taxes were decreased and G were held constant, the $C + I + G$ line would shift up by the marginal propensity to consume (MPC) times the change in the tax yield at the initial income level. This shift would cause the IS curve to shift to the right by the MPC times the tax yield times the multiplier. (If the change in taxes were accomplished by a change in tax rates rather than a change in lump sum taxes, the rightward shift of the IS curve would not be a parallel shift. Under these circumstances, the change in the height of the $C + I + G$ line increases as income increases, and so the new IS line is flatter than the old one.)

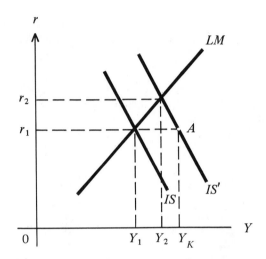

Figure 10-16 Expansionary fiscal policy.

Suppose the economy is initially in equilibrium in Figure 10-16, with $r = r_1$ and $Y = Y_1$. The Treasury increases its deficit because expenditures have increased and taxes have not been raised. This increased deficit shifts the IS curve to IS'. Suppose the Treasury sells bonds to the nonbank public. If the interest rate did not change, Y would increase to Y_K (the level attained in the Keynesian income-expenditure model of Chapters 4 and 5). We must, however, recognize that the Treasury's sale of bonds will lower bond prices and increase the interest rate (the Treasury's actions create an ES of bonds). The increase in the interest rate will decrease consumption and investment spending. This decrease will tend to offset the increase in government spending. However, the increase in the interest rate will also increase velocity and, to a smaller extent, the money stock. Since $MV = PQ = C + I + G$, we know that PQ will end up at some value greater than Y_1 (MV has increased) but smaller than Y_K (C and I have decreased). Final equilibrium will be at the point where $r = r_2$ and $Y = Y_2$.

PURE MONETARY POLICY CHANGE

In a restrictive pure monetary policy government expenditures and taxes are not changed but the (rate of growth of the) money base is decreased. In Figure 10-17 this decrease is shown as a leftward shift of the LM curve to LM'. If the interest rate remained at r_1, income would have to fall to Y'. However, the Fed decreased the money base by selling government bonds, lowering bond prices, and raising

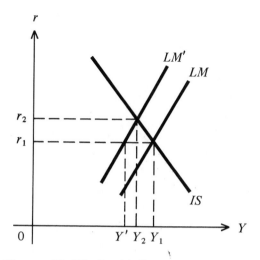

Figure 10-17 Restrictive monetary policy.

interest rates. The increase in the interest rate will increase velocity and will tend to increase M. It will also tend to decrease C and I. In full equilibrium, $MV = PQ = C + I + G$. Initially, M is reduced. If velocity did not change and M remained at its new lower level, PQ would fall to Y'. But the interest rate increases, causing V to increase, and MV will not return to its previous level because the increase in r reduces C and I. Final equilibrium will be at an income level between Y' and Y_1, specifically Y_2. The new equilibrium value of the interest rate is r_2.

MIXED POLICIES

Suppose, in Figure 10-16, that the Fed wanted to maintain a constant interest rate as a complement to expansionary fiscal policy. Since rising interest rates tend to choke off investment and consumption, maintaining the original rate would bring about the full Keynesian multiplier increase in the equilibrium level of income.

By increasing the money base the Fed would cause a rightward shift of the LM curve. As long as the LM curve shifts by the proper amount, income Y_k could be achieved with a constant interest rate r_1. Figure 10-18 shows this mixed policy. Both fiscal and monetary policies are necessary to expand (or contract) income without having any effect on the rate of interest. By how much must the LM curve shift at interest rate r_1? The shift in the IS curve through fiscal policy

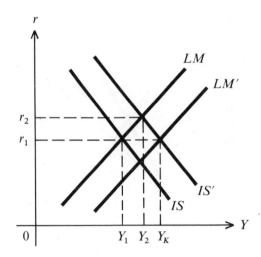

Figure 10-18   **Mixed policies that increase income at a
constant interest rate.**

would, in the absence of shifts of the LM curve, result in an increase of $Y_2 - Y_1$.
The LM curve must shift to LM' to get all the way to Y_K.

In this case monetary policy was accommodating: it accommodated fiscal
policy in its attempt to increase income, by supplying enough bank reserves to
eliminate the upward push on interest rates that results when the Treasury sells
bonds on the open market.

The required amount of accommodation depends upon the relative slopes of
the IS and LM curves. This issue is an important one. Large-scale statistical
models can be developed to estimate the actual slopes of the IS and LM curves.
These slopes will then tell us how effective fiscal policy can be in the absence of
accommodating monetary policy. Of course, these slopes do change through
time as the underlying relationships change.

10-4 THE CROWDING OUT EFFECT

Let's assume that investment and consumption are highly interest elastic. As we
saw in Section 1 of this chapter, such high interest elasticity implies a relatively
flat IS curve. An increase in government expenditures with taxes unchanged
will cause a rightward shift of the IS curve, but income will not rise very much.
Government expenditures have crowded out private expenditures because the

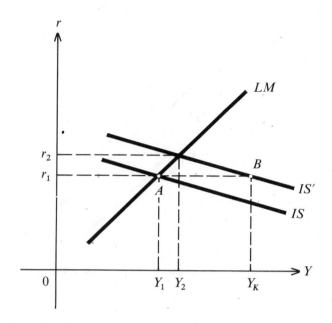

Figure 10-19 Crowding out because of the high interest elasticity of consumption and investment.

increase in the interest rate (along the *LM* curve) has reduced consumption and investment expenditures. Figure 10-19 shows this effect. Beginning at point *A*, in the absence of higher interest rates, income would rise to Y_k; but without accommodating monetary policy, income will increase only slightly to Y_2. The flatter the *IS* curve, the less effective would be any type of fiscal policy in changing the equilibrium level of income.

If monetary policy is accommodating and the *LM* curve shifts to the right, intersecting *IS'* at point *B*, Y_K can be achieved. The shift in income, in reality, was caused primarily by monetary policy, not fiscal policy. Fiscal policy changed income from Y_1 to Y_2, while monetary policy changed income from Y_2 to Y_K.

We can develop the same arguments for a steep *LM* curve. Such a curve would result from a relatively steep demand for money function (M^d is relatively interest inelastic), making monetary policy quite powerful (Y changes, r does not change much) but rendering fiscal policy almost useless. Consider Figure 10-20. A pure expansionary fiscal policy (which shifts the *IS* curve to IS_2) would, in the absence of any increase in the interest rate, cause income to increase to Y_K. However, as the Treasury attempts to raise the money to pay for its deficit by borrowing (selling bonds) on the open market, bond prices fall and

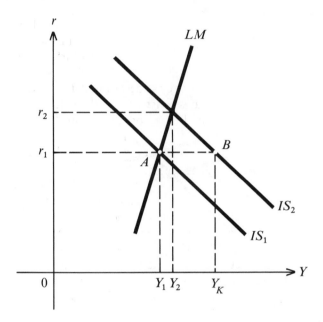

Figure 10-20 Crowding out because of the interest inelasticity of demand for money.

interest rates rise. (The Treasury has created an *ES* in bonds.) Even though consumption and investment do not respond to the increasing interest rate as much as in Figure 10-19, since the demand for money is interest inelastic, velocity will not increase. If *M* doesn't change (this is a *pure* fiscal policy), *MV* cannot change; and if *MV* does not change, *Y* cannot change. The increase in the interest rate will increase *M* some, as a movement along the money supply line, but not very much. The end result is that the interest rate climbs until consumption and investment decline enough to offset almost all of the expansionary fiscal policy. The higher government spending has merely replaced a nearly equal amount of private sector spending. The government spending has "crowded out" the private sector spending. Income increases only to Y_2.

Only actual statistics can tell us which policy is effective and which is not. Philosophical arguments about the relative merits of fiscal and monetary policy are useless. As long as we have a theory about how the *IS* and *LM* curves are developed and why they shift, only statistical analyses can tell us the actual impact of the shifts. The relative slopes of the *IS* and *LM* curves will tell us the magnitude of the crowding out effect in fiscal policy. In a recent article, Brian P.

Sullivan estimates that the *LM* curve is seven times steeper than the *IS* curve.[2] By using Sullivan's example, we can see the relative impact of monetary and fiscal policy. A cut in taxes of $5.2 billion would result in an increase in income of only $1.9 billion and an increase in interest rates of 0.2 percent. The fiscal impact is quite small. If monetary policy is accommodating, the shift in the *LM* curve that would keep interest rates constant would result in a further $15.6 billion increase in income. The total effect of this expansionary mixed policy is $17.5 billion. Only about 11 percent of the added income is the result of the tax change. Accommodating monetary policy was necessary for the rest. There appears to be a *very strong crowding out effect*.

Remember that we are currently employing a fixed-price model. The fixed-price *IS-LM* model is based on the Keynesian assumption that there are always enough unemployed resources available to make any increase in real income possible. No part of any increase in *Y* comes about merely because the average money price level changes. Thus when we say that nominal income increases by $17.5 billion from a tax cut of $5.2 billion accommodated by an expansionary monetary policy, it sounds like a good policy to pursue. As we will see in the next chapter, a good portion of that extra $17.5 billion will actually be the result simply of higher prices.

10-5   THE TRANSMISSION MECHANISM OF MONETARY POLICY

The transmission mechanism in the commodities market has been discussed in great detail in prior chapters. How, then, does monetary policy affect the commodities market? A purchase of bonds by the Fed (an expansionary monetary policy) raises bond prices and lowers the interest rate. The fall in the interest rate increases *C* and *I*. A sale of bonds by the Fed (a restrictive monetary policy) lowers bond prices, increases the interest rate, and thereby decreases *C* and *I*. There are *indirect* effects working through the *ED* or *ES* created in the bond market by the Fed's actions.

As we have already mentioned, there are *direct* effects as well. The changed money supply causes an *ED* or *ES* in commodities directly. The linkage involved is simply the mechanism of the new quantity theory that we discussed in Chapter 8 (Section 4). To start with, actual and desired money balances are equal. When the money supply is reduced, actual money balances are smaller than desired, and individuals will decrease spending (decrease *C* and *I*) in order to restore money balances to the desired level.

You should note that a decreased money supply means that the Fed has sold bonds. The buyers of the bonds have voluntarily exchanged their money balances for bonds, but this exchange does not mean that desired money balances have decreased. The purchase of the bonds was in response to favorable terms (low prices) offered by the Fed. Having taken advantage of these favorable terms, individuals will then set about the task of restoring their portfolios to long-run balance.[3]

Conceptually, each individual and firm can be thought of as managing a portfolio of financial and physical assets. Each asset, including money, yields a flow of services or income, and hence each asset has at least an implicit rate of return. This rate of return can be found for any asset by dividing the dollar value of the annual service or income receipts by the dollar value of the asset itself. People seek to equate these rates of return after allowance for risk. If the rate of return on a common stock is larger than the (implicit) rate of return on a dollar, for example, people will reduce their money holdings and purchase stocks. This buying will tend to raise stock prices and thus will reduce the rate of return on stocks. This process continues until the expected returns from all assets in the portfolio are equal.

When money balances are increased by an expansionary monetary policy, portfolios cease to be balanced. Individuals have more cash balances relative to other assets, and this imbalance causes them to increase expenditures on assets such as houses and cars. In this way consumption and investment spending increases.

Note that this direct link between money and expenditures implies that even if consumption and investment expenditures do not respond to changes in the interest rate, changes in the money supply will still affect aggregate demand.

10-6 THE REVERSE CAUSATION HYPOTHESIS

The analysis in this book is based to a large extent on the existence of direct (difference between desired and actual money balances) and/or indirect (changes in the interest rate) causal links between changes in the money stock and changes in nominal income. Changes in the growth rate of the money stock *cause* changes in the growth rate of nominal income. From the 1930s until the early 1960s many economists doubted this causal relationship. Everyone admitted that the statistics revealed a correlation between changes in the money stock and changes in nominal income, but some argued that the causal relationship ran from nominal income to the money stock rather than the other way around. The size of the existing money stock depends on the extent to which commercial banks extend loans. The multiple deposit expansion process is based on the fact that one bank's loans become another bank's deposits. Since the demand for loans is likely to be higher during periods of increasing nominal income than during periods of less intense economic activity, the money stock is likely to

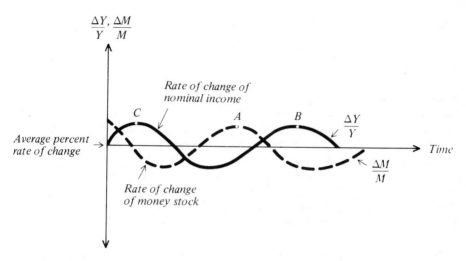

Figure 10-21   **Hypothetical time path for the rate of change in money stock and the rate of change in income.**

grow faster during periods of economic expansion than during periods of declining nominal income.

Ever since the end of the Civil War, peaks in the percentage rate of change of the money stock have always been followed, after an average lag of 18 months, by a peak in the rate of change in nominal income. Troughs in the percentage rate of change in the money stock have been followed by troughs in the percentage rate of change in nominal income after an average lag of 12 months.[4]

Consider Figure 10-21. The broken line represents the percentage rate of change in the money stock and the solid line represents the percentage rate of change in nominal income. The actual data, of course, do not lie along such smooth curves, but this idealized version is satisfactory for our purposes. Those who hold to the reverse causation hypothesis (causation running from nominal income to money stock) claim that peak C causes peak A. Those who claim that the causation runs from money stock to nominal income assert that peak A causes peak B. The issue cannot be settled by simply seeing which peak occurs first. For any peak in either series there exists a previous peak in the other series.

Which is the *dominant* direction of causation—money stock to nominal income, or nominal income to money stock? Can fluctuations in the rate of growth of the money stock account for a substantial portion of the fluctuations in nominal income? Can changes in nominal income account for a substantial portion of the observed monetary changes?

TIMING AND AMPLITUDE OF CHANGES

The analysis in Chapter 9 (Section 9-3) demonstrated a positive relationship between the rate of interest and the money multiplier and therefore between the rate of interest and the money stock. It is true that unless the Fed takes offsetting action on the money base, an increasing (decreasing) interest rate will induce increases (decreases) in the money stock. During periods of expansion of nominal income the demand for loanable funds will expand, and this increased demand will tend to increase interest rates. Conversely, interest rates are likely to fall during periods of declining nominal income. If the magnitude of this feedback mechanism is small compared to the magnitude of the response of nominal income to independent or autonomous changes in the money stock, we can say that money affects economic activity and that this effect is amplified through the feedback mechanism. Autonomous changes in the money stock initiate the process.

If the predominant causal relationship were from nominal income to money stock, we would expect that the timing and the amplitude of the response of the money stock changes would differ for different institutional settings in the money supply process. The United States has been on and off the gold standard. We have had flexible exchange rates and fixed exchange rates for foreign currencies. The U.S. Treasury was the center of control of the money stock until 1913, when the Federal Reserve System was created. Under all of these circumstances the timing and amplitude of the relationship represented in Figure 10-21 have remained unchanged. This lack of change is consistent with the view that no matter what causes changes in the money stock, once those changes are accomplished the effect on nominal income is the same.

HISTORICAL CYCLES

The most conclusive argument offered by those who claim that the predominant direction of influence is from money stock to nominal income is based on the fact that whenever major swings in nominal income have occurred in U.S. history, a large autonomous change in the money stock has always preceded the turning points in nominal income. And it is possible to attribute the observed changes in the money stock to factors entirely unrelated to prior changes in nominal income.[5]

For instance, since the end of the Civil War there have been six major economic contractions: 1875–79, 1892–94, 1907–08, 1920–21, 1929–33, and 1937–38. Preceding each of these downturns there was a decline in the money stock that was caused by autonomous forces clearly unrelated to nominal income. Between 1873 and 1879 the stock of money declined 5 percent as the result of the resumption of gold payments on currency. (Such payments had been suspended during the Civil War.) In the 1890s the contraction was preceded by large reductions in the money base caused by gold outflows due to widespread fears that the United States was about to abandon the gold standard. In 1907 the failure of the New York Knickerbocker Trust Company set off a banking panic that resulted in deposit withdrawals and an increased use of currency to finance transactions. The 1920–21 episode followed drastic increases in the Fed's discount rate and a resultant decrease in the Federal Reserve credit component of the money base. The stock market crash in 1929 resulted in widespread banking failures. Commercial banks had extended numerous loans on the basis of common stock as collateral. When this collateral became worth less than the outstanding loans, banks began to convert their outstanding loans into cash. Between 1929 and 1933, 9000 banks failed—approximately 40 percent of the commercial banks that existed in 1929. The Fed could have averted this wave of failures simply by supplying the private banks with sufficient liquidity, but it didn't. In fact, in 1931 the Fed *increased* the required reserve ratio, which caused additional bank failures. The resulting decrease in the money stock converted a crash in the stock market into a crash in the commodities market. The economy began to recover in 1933 and the recovery proceeded until 1937. In late 1936 and early 1937 the Fed increased reserve requirements until by May of 1937 these requirements had been doubled. The recovery was halted, and a new depression began.

IN CONCLUSION

It seems clear that the evidence does not refute the proposition that monetary changes cause changes in economic activity. In our view, the weight of the evidence is overwhelmingly in favor of that proposition. As we have already seen, we have a theoretical framework within which the connection between the money market and the commodities market may be understood.

10-7 RECENT EXPERIENCE WITH MONETARY AND FISCAL POLICY

In 1964, federal income taxes were cut substantially, for the announced purpose of increasing aggregate demand and reducing unemployment. After the tax cut, the rate of growth of real output increased and unemployment decreased. These results seemed to be proof that "Keynesian economics" in general and fiscal policy in particular were sound and reliable tools. However, although the tax cut was followed by an increase in the rate of growth of real output, the money supply expanded at the same time. Which policy—monetary or fiscal—caused the higher growth rate of income? We cannot answer this question unequivocally, because both policies worked in the same direction. In terms of the *IS-LM* diagram, the *IS* curve shifted to the right because of the tax cut, but the *LM* curve also shifted to the right because the deficit created by the tax cut was financed by selling bonds to the Fed, thus increasing the money base.

Two incidents during the 1960s permit a comparison of the strengths of monetary and fiscal policies. In April 1966 the Fed decreased the rate of growth of the money stock (in fact, the *level* of the money stock declined). At the same time the federal budget moved to a larger and larger deficit. Early in 1967 there was a definite slowdown in the rate of growth of income. (Some have named this the "minirecession" of 1967.)

In mid-1968 a special tax called a *surcharge* was levied on incomes. This levy was 10 percent of the tax that any given individual would have paid before the surcharge. That is, each person would calculate his tax without including the new tax and would then add 10 percent of his tax to the original amount. The total was the amount he actually had to pay. When Congress passed the tax, it was announced that this was a temporary tax designed to combat the inflationary impact of the Vietnam war expenditures, which had been financed by selling bonds to the Fed. As we saw in Chapter 9, when the Treasury sells bonds to the Fed the money supply increases. At the same time that the surcharge went into effect, the money stock continued to grow at an annual rate of 7.6 percent, as it had been doing since January 1967. The rate of inflation continued its upward climb as if the surcharge had never been imposed.

During the 1970s monetary and fiscal policies were never so clearly in opposition to each other. Monetary policy in the United States was almost exclusively expansionary in the 1970s. Fiscal policy, as measured by the budget deficit (see Table 5-1), was also expansionary. The results of monetary and fiscal policy in the 70s can best be seen by referring to Figures 1-1, 1-2, and 2-2, which show prices, unemployment rates, nominal income, and real income from 1971 to 1979.

A serious recession began in the fourth quarter of 1973. At that time inventories of firms rose to levels above those warranted by sales. Firms began to lay off workers and cut prices (automobile company rebates, for example). The unemployment rate rose and real income declined—slowly at first, then rapidly in the last two quarters of 1974 and the first quarter of 1975. The money supply growth rate, which had been averaging over 7 percent for 1972 and the first half of 1973, was just 3.2 percent (annualized rate) for the remainder of the year. Fiscal policy (as measured by the full employment budget) had also become more restrictive. From a deficit of $15.5 billion in 1972 the deficit fell to $4.6 billion in 1973. (Of course, the actual budget was always in deficit.) During the resulting recession the inflation rate fell only from 11 percent in 1973 to 9.1 percent in

1974. The stubbornly high rate of inflation was the result of rapid monetary expansion in 1972–73. The contraction ended in the second quarter of 1975, and the U.S. economy headed for one of its strongest expansions since World War II.

The rate of growth of the money stock averaged about 5.3 percent through 1975–76, up from 3.4 percent in the prior year. At the same time, the full employment budget deficit decreased slightly from $24.3 billion to $18.6 billion. In those years real output (as measured by real GNP) rose by 5.6 percent annually. Nominal GNP was rising by 11.4 percent. At the same time interest rates were rising, causing a corresponding increase in velocity. The difference between nominal and real growth rates in GNP are, of course, price rises. This period represented the initial expansion of economic activity after the recession of 1973–75. Unemployment rates fell and employment growth averaged about 3.6 percent.

In 1977–78, a period of continued expansion of economic activity, a different story was observed. The money stock growth rate accelerated to about 8.5 percent, while the full employment deficit remained relatively constant. Nominal income grew at a rate of about 13 percent, while real income growth declined to 4.6 percent. Thus, inflation rates were increasing. Unemployment rates fell dramatically to levels below the true full employment rate (as discussed in Chapter 7). Interest rates and velocity continued to rise. As the economy approached full employment, monetary and fiscal expansion resulted more in increased prices than in increased real income.

Late in 1978 the Federal Reserve reduced the rate of expansion of the money stock due to widespread fears of inflation. This shift in policy had a dampening effect on real income in 1979. Real income actually declined in the first quarter of that year. Throughout this period policymakers were caught in a dilemma. There was a general desire to follow expansionary policies, but these policies resulted in an increase in inflation and higher interest rates. Moreover, the expansionary policies seemed to have no effect on unemployment. In the next chapter we will expand our *IS-LM* model to include the labor market and flexible prices. This more complete analysis will help us to understand the nature of the dilemma.

SUMMARY

In this chapter we developed and used the fixed price *IS-LM* model. The curves in this model show the relationships between aggregate income and the rate of interest in both the commodities market and the money market. The intersection of these two curves indicates the unique income and interest rate that clears both markets. Any income and interest rate combination not corresponding to this equilibrium represents a disequilibrium in one or both markets. Market forces, reacting to excess demands and/or excess supplies, ultimately adjust these variables to their equilibrium levels.

Shifts of IS or LM curves cause changes in the equilibrium level of income and interest rate. In particular, pure fiscal policy (shifts of the IS curve), pure monetary policy (shifts of the LM curve), and mixed policies (shifts of both curves) were examined for their effects on these variables. We saw that the effectiveness of pure fiscal policy and pure monetary policy depends on the relative slopes of the IS and LM curves. Mixed policies could be divided into fiscal effects and monetary effects. Crowding out was also examined since increasing government expenditures with correspondingly higher interest rates reduce both investment and consumption expenditures.

The logic of our analysis compels us to recognize that changes in the money stock exert direct and powerful effects on total spending as well as indirect effects through changes in the interest rate. This strong relationship is verified by the historical experience of the United States (as well as other countries).

We considered the reverse causation hypothesis—that the causal relationship between changes in the money stock and changes in nominal income runs from the latter to the former. We dismissed this hypothesis for two reasons: (1) the timing and amplitude of the relationship seem to be independent of the particular money supply process that exists and (2) all major economic contractions and expansions in the United States between the Civil War and 1960 were preceded by large autonomous changes in the money stock in the same direction as the subsequent changes in aggregate income. We also saw that experience in the 1960s with the effects of changes in the money stock on economic activity is consistent with the view that changes in the money stock cause changes in economic activity rather than the other way around. Even when monetary policy changes were in a different direction from fiscal policy changes, it was the monetary changes that seemed to determine the direction and magnitude of changes in economic activity. In the 1970s economic activity continued to change in accordance with changes in the (rate of growth of the) money stock. Most notably, the recession that began in late 1973 and did not end until the beginning of 1975 was preceded by a substantial cut in the money stock growth rate.

QUESTIONS

1. Graphically derive the IS curve for the case where consumption and investment are interest inelastic.
2. Demonstrate graphically that points to the right of the LM curve signify an ED in the money market.

3. Graphically derive a market-clearing curve for the bond market in an *IS-LM* diagram. Can such a curve have a positive slope? Can it be horizontal? Can it have a negative slope? What conditions must exist in each case?

4. When the demand for money line shifts to the right, the interest rate increases. Why? Apart from the fact that the supply and demand lines intersect at a higher interest rate, what actually makes the interest rate go up?

5. Suppose that the empirical results found by Brian Sullivan are accurate. It is sometimes suggested that the U.S. Constitution be amended to require a balanced federal budget. What is the significance of the argument often used against such an amendment that it would eliminate fiscal policy?

6. Construct *IS-LM* diagrams and excess demand tables that include both direct and indirect effects for the analysis of:

   a. worsening profit expectations

   b. open market purchase of bonds by the Fed

   c. an increase in the willingness of households to save out of current income

7. What is the significance of the argument about reverse causation?

8. How does the steepness of the demand for money line affect the slope of the *LM* curve? Demonstrate your conclusions graphically.

9. How does the sensitivity of the position of the demand for money line to changes in aggregate income affect the slope of the *LM* curve? Demonstrate your conclusions graphically.

NOTES

1. An example of a change in government expenditures that is related to changes in income is unemployment insurance payments—an automatic stabilizer such as we discussed in Appendix B to Chapter 5. As income and employment decline, unemployment insurance payments increase.

2. Brian P. Sullivan, "Crowding Out Estimated from Large-Scale Econometric Model," Federal Reserve Board of Dallas, *Business Review* (June 1976), pp. 1–7.

3. See Milton Friedman and David Meiselman, "The Relative Stability of Monetary Velocity and the Investment Multiplier in the United States, 1897–1958," in *Stabilization Policies* (Englewood Cliffs, N.J.: Prentice-Hall, 1963), pp. 219–21.

4. Milton Friedman and Anna Schwartz, "Money and Business Cycles," *Review of Economics and Statistics*, Supplement (February 1963), p. 38.

5. For a complete history of the period from the end of the Civil War to 1960, see Milton Friedman and Anna Schwartz, *A Monetary History of the United States, 1867–1960*, National Bureau of Economic Research (Princeton: Princeton University Press, 1963).

11

The Variable Price
IS-LM Model

Up to now we have assumed that the price level is constant, and so any changes in income have been changes in *real* income. The *IS* curve of the previous chapters is based on the relationships between saving and income and investment and income. Whenever income increases, so do saving and investment. Since the price level is held constant, increases in real income cause increases in real saving and real investment expenditures.

Underlying the constant price *LM* curve is the positive relationship between the demand for nominal money balances and nominal income. Here again, however, since prices are assumed constant, any change in nominal income is a change in real income, and any change in nominal money balances demanded is a change in real money balances demanded.

11-1 EFFECTS OF A VARIABLE PRICE LEVEL

At all points on the *IS* curve, $I = S$. Real investment depends on real income and the (real) interest rate, as does also real saving (valued in base year prices). In symbols we write

$$I = I\left(\frac{Y}{P}, r\right) \qquad (11\text{-}1)$$

and

$$S = S\left(\frac{Y}{P}, r\right) \qquad (11\text{-}2)$$

where **I** is real investment, Y/P is real income, and **S** is real saving.[1] The demand for real money balances depends on real income and the (nominal) interest rate (all the other variables in the demand for money functions are held constant) and the supply of real money balances depends on the (nominal) interest rate. In symbols we write

$$\frac{M_D}{P} = \mathbf{L}\left(\frac{Y}{P}, r\right) \tag{11-3}$$

and

$$\frac{M_s}{P} = \mathbf{M}(r) \tag{11-4}$$

At all points on the **LM** curve,

$$\frac{M_D}{P} = \frac{M_s}{P} \tag{11-5}$$

The general forms of the equations for the **IS** and **LM** curves can therefore be written as

$$\mathbf{I}\left(\frac{Y}{P}, r\right) - \mathbf{S}\left(\frac{Y}{P}, r\right) = 0 \tag{11-6}$$

and

$$\mathbf{L}\left(\frac{Y}{P}, r\right) - \mathbf{M}(r) = 0 \tag{11-7}$$

respectively, where **L** is real demand for money, and **M** is real supply of money.

Although the *real* rate of interest is relevant to the **IS** curve and the *nominal* rate of interest is relevant to the **LM** curve, we are at this point continuing to assume that the expected rate of inflation is zero. Therefore, the real rate and the nominal rate are equal, and we can continue to use the symbol r to stand for both of them. The assumption of a zero expected rate of inflation will be dropped starting with Section 11-10 of this chapter.

EFFECTS ON REAL INVESTMENT AND REAL SAVING

Suppose P, the price level, is permitted to change. If $\mathbf{I} = \mathbf{I}(Y/P, r)$, real investment expenditures would be unchanged because Y changes by a proportional amount. Remember, Y equals PQ. A 10 percent increase in P causes a 10 percent increase in Y. If real investment expenditures depend on real income, it makes no difference what the values of Y and P are individually—it is their ratio that counts. If the ratio Y/P is constant, real investment expenditures will not change when P changes. Similar considerations hold for real saving.

EFFECTS ON THE MONEY MARKET

If the demand for real money balances depends on the level of real income, that demand will be the same no matter what the price level is. (We assume for the moment that the *expected* inflation rate is always zero.) An increase in price causes an increase in *nominal* income, but it does not cause an increase in *real* income.

In the case of the money supply, the price level does make a difference. An increase in P does not cause the nominal money stock to change. When the price level increases, unless the Fed increases the nominal money stock by the same percentage amount, the real money stock (M/P) falls. The effect of increasing P while M is held constant is the same as the effect of decreasing M while holding P constant. In both cases the real money stock decreases.

Consider Figure 11-1. We start with equilibrium between the real supply and the real demand for money. Let the price level, P, increase. Since real income, Y/P, is unchanged at $(Y/P)_1$, the demand line does not change position. However, since the nominal money stock is unchanged, the line that represents the real money supply will shift to the left to a position such as that labeled (M_s/P_2) (r). This shift will increase the interest rate to r_2 and decrease equilibrium real money balances to $(M/P)_2$.

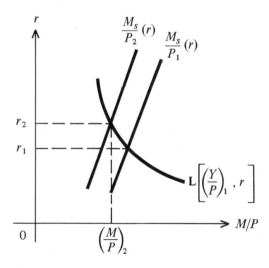

Figure 11-1   The effect of a changing price level on the money market.

EFFECTS ON THE IS-LM DIAGRAM

Let us look at the effects of this price level change on the **LM** curve. Since the new money supply line has moved to the left, the interest rate that will be associated with each level of real income will be higher than before. This means that the **LM** curve has shifted to the left. Actually this result should not be surprising since we have previously seen that a decrease in the supply of money relative to its demand will shift the **LM** curve to the left.

This introduction of a variable price level means that the **IS** and **LM** curves are no longer sufficient to determine the equilibrium values of the interest rate and real income. In Figure 11-2, if the price level is P_1, the **LM** curve is that labeled $\mathbf{LM}(P_1)$. Equilibrium real income is $(Y/P)_1$ and the equilibrium value of the interest rate is r_1. If the price level increases to P_2, $(Y/P)_2$ is the new value of equilibrium real income, and r_2 becomes the equilibrium interest rate. If the price level falls to P_3, yet another pair of values for real income and the interest rate is indicated. Instead of one **LM** curve we have a family of **LM** curves, a different one for each price level.

We have two equations:

$$\mathbf{I}\!\left(\frac{Y}{P}, r\right) - \mathbf{S}\!\left(\frac{Y}{P}, r\right) = 0$$

$$\mathbf{L}\!\left(\frac{Y}{P}, r\right) - \mathbf{M}(r) = 0$$

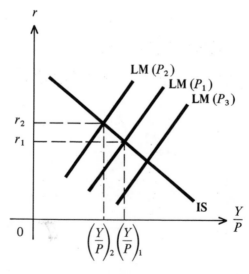

Figure 11-2 The effect of a changing price level on the **IS-LM** diagram.

and *three* unknowns— Y/P, r, and P. If we could discover the equilibrium value of any one of these three variables from some other considerations, the **IS-LM** equations would determine the equilibrium values of the remaining two. Fortunately, this is possible. In particular we can determine the equilibrium value of *real income* by looking at the labor market and the economy's aggregate production function.

11-2 THE LABOR MARKET

Assume that aggregate real output (Q) is a function of two inputs—capital (K) and labor (N). The marginal product of labor (MP_L) is the addition to real output derived from increasing the input of labor by 1 unit while the capital stock is held constant. In Figure 11-3 it is graphed as the slope of the curve in panel a and as the curve labeled D_N in panel b. The "S" curve in panel a describes what happens to Q as N is increased, assuming K is fixed at K_0; at first Q rises sharply, but after some critical amount of N (N_1 in the figure), Q rises more gradually and eventually falls off. The curve labeled D_N in Figure 11-3b shows the rate at which Q increases as N is increased: up to N_1, Q increases at an increasing rate (D_N rises), but after N_1, Q increases at a decreasing rate (D_N falls).

AGGREGATE DEMAND FOR LABOR

How does an employer decide whether to hire one more labor-hour? (Recall the discussion of the hiring decision in Section 2 of Chapter 7.) An employer who is a profit maximizer cares only about what the extra labor-hour will do for him or her and how this return compares to what the extra labor-hour will cost. In real terms, this return is the marginal product of labor. In our aggregate market, since we must add disparate types of real output together, the MP_L is the average value (in base year prices) of the additional output produced when one more labor-hour is employed. (Since this is in dollar units—base year dollars—it corresponds to what we called marginal revenue product of labor in Chapter 7. Since we have aggregated diverse real outputs by using base year dollars, it is also the marginal product of labor.) The cost of an additional labor-hour in real terms is the average wage rate in base year prices, or the wage rate in current prices (W) divided by P—the price index.

Suppose the real wage (W/P) is less than the marginal product of labor, as is the case when $N = N_1$ in Figure 11-3. The real wage is N_1B and the marginal product of labor is N_1A. The cost of hiring one more labor-hour is N_1B and the extra output produced when the additional labor-hour is hired is N_1A. Profits go

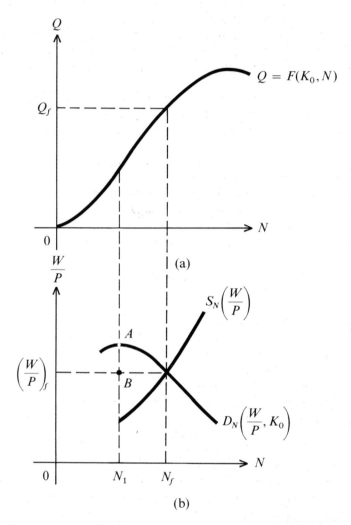

Figure 11-3   The labor market and aggregate production.

up if the additional labor-hour is hired, and so it will be hired. Additional labor-hours will be hired as long as the real wage is less than the marginal product of labor.

Notice in Figure 11-3b that the marginal product of labor decreases as additional labor-hours are hired. The hiring process brings MP_L down to the value of the real wage rate; when the marginal product of labor equals the real wage, profits can no longer be raised by hiring additional labor. For any level of the real wage rate, the quantity of labor that will be hired will be the value of N that makes MP_L equal to the given real wage rate. In other words, the schedule of MP_L is the schedule that tells us the amount of labor demanded at each level of the real wage rate. It is the *aggregate demand curve for labor*. The quantity demanded increases as W/P falls. The position of the demand curve is determined by the fixed amount of capital that labor works with. The aggregate demand curve for labor is drawn in Figure 11-3b and labeled $D_N(W/P,K_0)$.

AGGREGATE SUPPLY OF LABOR

In order to determine the real wage rate that will exist, we must consider the *aggregate supply curve for labor.* Assuming that at a zero real wage people would choose leisure over work, any individual chooses how much labor time to offer for sale on the basis of the real wage that can be obtained. An additional hour of leisure entails the sacrifice of the current real wage rate. If this wage rate increases, the opportunity cost (measured by the real wage rate) of leisure increases, and so less leisure will be consumed; that is, more labor time will be offered for sale than was offered at the lower real wage. However, with the higher real wage, a person who works the same number of hours as before would have more real income. With higher real income his or her demand for all normal goods (e.g., house, food, money, and leisure) would increase. This so-called income effect would tend to reduce the amount of labor time offered for sale.

However, the effect of the higher price of leisure usually is stronger than this income effect; and so we conclude that as the real wage rises, the quantity of labor-hours offered for sale also increases. This aggregate supply of labor curve is drawn in Figure 11-3b and labeled $S_N(W/P)$.

FULL EMPLOYMENT

The interaction of the supply and demand for labor determines the full employment real wage, $(W/P)_f$, and the full employment number of labor-hours, N_f. Once N_f is determined, the full employment real output or real income level, Q_f, is known. This level of real income is the only level consistent with equilibrium in the labor market.

By "full employment" we mean that there is only the normal amount of unemployment that arises from the constant process of job switching because of the constantly changing pattern of relative demands for individual goods, as we discussed in Section 3 of Chapter 7.

11-3 CHANGES IN MONEY STOCK AND PRICE LEVEL

The general equilibrium value of the interest rate and full employment real output are determined without regard to the money market. The labor market, together with the aggregate production function, determines $(Y/P)_f$ (full employment real output). This full employment real output, together with the IS curve, determines the equilibrium value of the interest rate.

The money market determines the price level. Whatever the initial position of the LM curve, changes in prices will shift that position until the LM curve intersects the IS curve at precisely the same point where a vertical line above $(Y/P)_f$ intersects the IS curve. This means that whenever the money stock is increased by X percent, prices will also increase by X percent.

Since changes in M do not affect equilibrium r or Y/P, and since the demand for real money balances depends on r and Y/P, desired real money balances won't change. In equilibrium, desired real money balances must equal actual real money balances, and so M and P must change by equal amounts. (Of course, this statement assumes that the other variables upon which the level of desired real money balances depends, such as the expected inflation rate, do not change when M changes. Starting in Section 10 of this chapter we will drop that assumption.)

Figure 11-4 shows the equilibrium in all three markets simultaneously. The full employment level of real output of Figure 11-3 is labeled $(Y/P)_f$. It is represented by a vertical line indicating it is determined apart from the IS and LM curves. At this level of real output, there will be no pressure on the real wage since the supply of labor and the demand for labor are equal.

To sum up:

1. *The interaction of S_N and D_N determines the equilibrium level of real income.* The labor market is the third relationship that is necessary to determine the equilibrium values of the three unknowns—Y/P, r, and P.
2. *The IS curve, together with $(Y/P)_f$, determines the rate of interest.* The intersection of the IS curve with $(Y/P)_f$ determines the equilibrium rate of interest (r_f) that is consistent with the level of planned expenditures at the real level of $(Y/P)_f$.
3. *The LM curve, together with r_f and $(Y/P)_f$, determines the equilibrium price level.* There is one LM curve that will intersect the IS curve at $(Y/P)_f$ and r_f. Given the nominal money stock, there is one $P(= P_f)$ that is consistent with simultaneous equilibrium in the labor market, the commodities market, and the money market. Of course, by Say's Principle, when these three markets are in equilibrium, the fourth macro market, bonds, must also be in equilibrium.

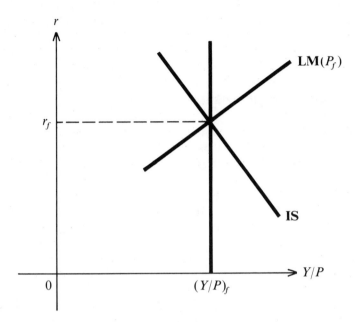

Figure 11-4 Full employment equilibrium.

Figure 11-4 shows the solution to the following set of equations:

$$\mathbf{I}\left(\frac{Y}{P}, r\right) - \mathbf{S}\left(\frac{Y}{P}, r\right) = 0$$

$$\mathbf{L}\left(\frac{Y}{P}, r\right) - \mathbf{M}(r) = 0$$

$$S_N\left(\frac{W}{P}\right) - D_N\left(\frac{W}{P}\right) = 0$$

The solution, $(Y/P)_f$, r_f, P_f, is the only one possible. Any other specification of real income, interest rate, and prices will be inconsistent with full employment equilibrium. Any specification that is inconsistent with full employment equilibrium implies excess demand or excess supply in two or more markets. As long as these markets are permitted freely to adjust to *ED* and *ES the* equilibrium will be achieved through the market process. However, adjustments in the real world do not occur in the twinkling of an eye, or in the time that it takes an instructor to draw a new line on the blackboard. Our analysis is timeless (as are the diagrams representing that analysis): it merely identifies the new equilibrium; it does not consider the time involved in achieving the same. One study of the lengths of actual adjustment processes is discussed in Section 7 of this chapter.

11-4 EQUILIBRIUM AND DISEQUILIBRIUM

In general equilibrium there is simultaneous equilibrium in the commodities market, the money market, the bond market, and the labor market.[2] What happens in these markets if there is a decline in the money stock? How is the equilibrium upset and how can the disequilibrium be remedied?

In Figure 11-5 we start with general equilibrium: $Y/P = (Y/P)_f$, $r = r_f$, and the real wage rate equals $(W/P)_f$. Investment equals saving (we are on the **IS** curve); the supply of and the demand for real money balances are equal (we

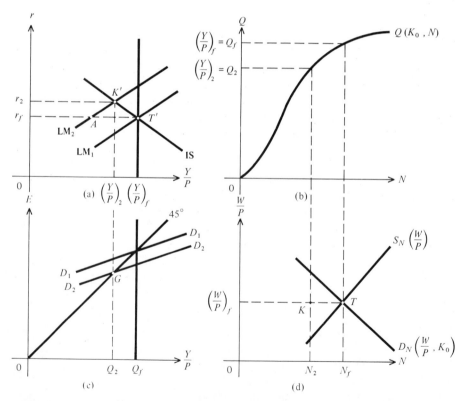

Figure 11-5 Interaction of the commodities, money, and labor markets.

are on the **LM** curve); and the supply of and demand for labor are equal at N_f. The full employment level of output is being produced and purchased.

DISEQUILIBRIUM IN THE COMMODITIES MARKET

Suppose the Fed contracts the money base, causing the **LM** curve to shift to $\mathbf{LM}_2$. The new intersection of the **IS** and **LM** lines indicates a decrease in real income (output) to $(Y/P)_2$. At this intersection we are on the **IS** and **LM** curves. There is an equilibrium in the commodities market in the sense that saving and investment (in real terms) are equal at output level $(Y/P)_2$. However, in another sense there is *disequilibrium* in the commodities market: K' is not the point on the **IS** curve that is consistent with general equilibrium.[3]

Consider Figure 11-5c. (This is the familiar Keynesian cross diagram, but with all variables in real rather than nominal terms. The vertical axis represents real expenditures and the horizontal axis represents real income or real output. The intersection of the solid vertical line above Q_f with the 45° line is the point at which the aggregate demand line (in real terms) must intersect the 45° line if the commodities market is to be in equilibrium at the full employment income level. The vertical line above Q_f is the full employment aggregate (real) supply curve in the commodities market.) The decrease in the money supply has decreased total spending. Since prices do not decrease immediately (because of information costs), the decrease in total spending shows up as a decrease in aggregate (real) demand. The aggregate demand line shifts downward to D_2D_2 in the diagram. Since this line intersects the 45° line at point G, planned investment and saving are equated at income level Q_2. At point G firms are selling all the output they are producing, but they are not producing all the output they would like to, given the real wage rate that exists—$(W/P)_f$. Neither W nor P has changed in response to the decrease in total spending because, as we saw in Section 5 of Chapter 7, information costs prevent the immediate adjustment of prices and wages. Given the labor supply and demand curves, at $(W/P)_f$ firms wish to supply Q_f. In Patinkin's words:

> Even though this point [point G] is not marked by an excess of *output*—firms are selling all they are producing—it is marked by an excess of *supply*. That is, despite the fact that firms have decreased their *actual* output to $[Q_2]$, . . . the fact remains that the *optimum* output they *desire* to supply at the real wage $[(W/P)_f]$ . . . is still $[Q_f]$. . . . In other words, since the real wage rate has . . . remained unchanged, so has the vertical commodity supply curve. Hence at point G there is an excess of desired over actual supply equal to $[Q_f - Q_2]$ . . . units of commodities. This manifests itself as an excess in the productive capacity of firms.[4]

In Figure 11-5b we can see that output level Q_2 is produced, given the fixed capital stock K_0, by using N_2 units of labor. The real wage has not changed, and so the economy must be at point K in Figure 11-5d. Note that this point is off the demand for labor line. This line tells us how much labor will be demanded at each real wage rate, *assuming that the commodities market is in equilibrium*—assuming, in other words, that the average price level that exists is the correct one, given the level of total spending. But total spending has decreased because of the decrease in the supply of money. With the new lower level of total spending, the price level must fall if Q_f—the equilibrium real output rate in the commodities market—is to be produced and bought. The commodities market is not in equilibrium in the sense that producers are not producing desired output levels, given the existing real wage. If the money supply is maintained at its new lower level, we cannot have equilibrium in the commodities market until the price level falls to that value which, when multiplied by Q_f, yields the new lower level of total spending.

The quantity equation of exchange says that $MV \equiv PQ$. M has decreased. The increase in the interest rate has increased velocity (V) but not by enough to offset the decrease in M. (The increase in V is shown as the movement from A to K' in Figure 11-5a.) The product MV is lower; hence the product PQ must become lower. P doesn't fall, and so Q does, to Q_2. When P *does* fall, Q will return to Q_f, and the commodities market will be in equilibrium.

DISEQUILIBRIUM IN THE LABOR MARKET

Until the price level falls, sellers will not be able to sell all they wish in the commodities market; so they will not hire as much labor as they would if they could sell all they wish. Again quoting Patinkin:

> Both firms and workers are being coerced by the same *force majeure* of insufficient demand in the commodity market. Both are thereby being prevented from achieving their optimum mode of behavior. In particular, the involuntary departure of firms from their labor demand curve as revealed by point K . . . is the simple counterpart of their involuntary departure from their commodity supply curve as revealed by point G [in Figure 11-5c]. . . . Not being able to sell all they want, they cannot employ all they want.[5]

The labor demand curve drawn in Figure 11-5d is called the planned demand for labor. In microeconomics we derive demand curves for labor that tell us how much labor will be demanded by a given firm at each real wage level, *assuming the firm can sell all the output it wants to at the prevailing price for its output*. The aggregate demand for labor curve in Figure 11-5d is merely the sum of individual labor demand curves. *Each* of these individual curves assumes that the employer can sell all he or she wishes of the firm's output at the price that exists for that output; hence the aggregate demand for labor curve makes the same assumption. The planned demand for labor curve assumes equilibrium in the commodities market.

To recapitulate beginning from general equilibrium, immediately after a restrictive monetary policy is implemented, the commodities market will not be in equilibrium, because information costs prevent the instantaneous adjustment of prices. Since the commodities market is not in equilibrium, the actual demand for labor will be less than the planned demand for labor, even though the real wage rate hasn't changed. Neither the nominal wage rate nor the average price level has changed; hence their ratio (W/P) has not changed. In Figure 11-5d the actual demand for labor is N_2 labor-hours, while the planned demand for labor (the demand that would exist if the commodities market cleared) is N_f labor-hours.

The situation immediately after the restrictive monetary policy has been implemented as depicted in Figure 11-5 is an excess supply (excess capacity) in the commodities market $(Q_f - Q_2)$ and involuntary unemployment in the labor market. At the existing real wage, $(W/P)_f$, the quantity of labor supplied is N_f labor-hours, while the actual demand for labor is only N_2 labor-hours. Thus $N_f - N_2$ labor-hours will be unemployed because aggregate demand has been depressed while prices and wages have not adjusted. The involuntary unemployment in the labor market will put downward pressure on W (the nominal wage rate), and the excess capacity in the commodities market will put downward pressure on P (the average price level). As P falls, the **LM** curve will shift to the right and will eventually reach $\mathbf{LM_1}$. The counterpart to this shift is an upward shift of the aggregate (real) demand line in Figure 11-5c back to $D_1 D_1$. As the **LM** curve shifts to the right, the interest rate falls. The falling interest rate causes the aggregate demand line in Figure 11-5c to shift back to $D_1 D_1$. When real output and expenditures have returned to Q_f, the actual demand for labor will equal both the planned demand for and the supply of labor at N_f (point T), and involuntary unemployment will again be zero. The decrease in W and P will have restored general equilibrium.

ANALYSIS VIA EXCESS DEMAND AND EXCESS SUPPLY

We can follow the process using an excess demand table as we did in the last chapter. Now we are considering four markets—bonds, money, commodities, and labor. We begin row 1 (Table 11-1) in general equilibrium. The Fed decreases the money base by selling bonds on the open market. This creates an excess supply of bonds accompanied by an excess demand for money (row 2); the Fed is demanding money in exchange for bonds. Next the excess supply of bonds causes bond prices to fall and interest rates to increase until the bond

Table 11-1   Excess demands in four markets

Row	Status	Bond Market	Money Market	Commodities Market	Labor Market
1	General equilibrium	0	0	0	0
2	Fed sells bonds	ES	ED	0	0
3	Bond prices fall (interest rate rises)	0	ED	ES	0
4	Y falls (Q falls)	0	0	ED (0)	ES
5	P and W (and r) fall	0	0	0	0

market is in equilibrium. The higher rate of interest causes real demand to decline in the commodities market, creating therein an excess supply (row 3). The combination of the excess demand in the money market and the excess supply in the commodities market decreases total spending (Y), but at first all of the decrease shows up as a decline in real output (Q) rather than in P. The decline in Q implies production cutbacks and layoffs as the actual demand for labor drops below the planned demand for labor at the existing (so far unchanged) W and P. This drop creates an excess supply in the labor market.

This excess supply in the labor market must, in accordance with Say's Principle, have a corresponding excess demand somewhere. But remember that Say's Principle is about *planned* excess demands, not *actual* excess demands. The households that are unable to sell all of the labor services they would like at the existing real wage have both a planned and an actual excess supply of labor. They also have a planned excess demand for commodities in the sense that if they could sell all the labor they would like to sell (N_f), they would use the proceeds to buy all the output they would like to buy (Q_f) at the existing real wage $(W/P)_f$. But since they can sell only N_2 of labor, they can actually demand only Q_2 of real output. Actual demand and supply are equal in the commodities market at point G in Figure 11-5c. There is zero *actual* excess demand in commodities (shown as zero in parentheses in the commodities market column, row 3, of Table 11-1), but a positive *planned* excess demand in commodities (shown as ED in the commodities market column, row 3, of Table 11-1).

Finally, the unemployment ($N_f - N_2$) in the labor market and the excess capacity ($Q_f - Q_2$) in the commodities market cause W and P to fall. This decline moves the **LM** curve in Figure 11-5a back toward **LM**$_1$ as the real stock of money increases, allowing real commodity demand to shift back to D_1 in Figure 11-5c, actual labor demand to expand toward point T in Figure 11-5d, and the interest rate to fall toward r_f in Figure 11-5a. General equilibrium is restored as indicated by row 5 in Table 11-1.

THE REAL WORLD

It has been a long time since the average levels of prices and wages have fallen in the United States. This analysis may therefore seem irrelevant to the real world, but it is not. The major reason why the average levels of prices and wages have not fallen for so long is that whenever unemployment and production cutbacks emerge in the economy, the Fed usually rushes to expand the money stock to remove any downward pressure on prices and wages. The adjustment process we described above is simply not *permitted* to occur. It could occur and would if government policy did not immediately become expansionary whenever the unemployment rate goes above normal.

Of course, the exercise we just went through was initiated by a decline in the money stock starting from a position of general equilibrium. There is nothing especially commendable about forcing the economy to go through the painful adjustment of temporary production cutbacks and unemployment when it is possible to offset the decline of M with an increase of M. However, other shocks (such as huge jumps in the price of petroleum), if offset by increases of M, would merely sustain the increase in the average money price level that the petroleum price increase initially causes. In the absence of offsetting increases of M, if more money is spent on petroleum and petroleum-related products, less money must be spent on other things. Reduced spending in these other areas would mean temporary production cutbacks and layoffs until the relevant prices and wages fell. When those prices and wages fell, the average levels of prices and wages would return to what they were before. Higher oil prices cannot cause inflation unless new money is created to accommodate the higher prices.

The federal government has, by increasing M, routinely offset *any* shocks that would lead to temporary recession. As we will see in the next chapter, this routine reaction accounts for the chronic and deepening inflation the economy has suffered from since the late 1960s.

Government policymakers have had an expansionary bias because, at least until the late 1970s, the electorate seemed to dislike increases in the unemployment rate more than it disliked increases in the inflation rate. Politicians perceived that to stay in power they should combat increases in unemployment even at the cost of higher inflation. In the late 1970s, however, the fact that higher inflation led eventually to more severe unemployment became appreciated, and public opinion began to turn against the expansionary bias of the policymakers. The public seemed more and more to realize that increases in unemployment would reverse themselves if prices and wages were given time to adjust.

11-5 CHANGES IN THE COMMODITIES MARKET AND THE LABOR MARKET

In Figure 11-6 we start in general equilibrium with real income equal to $(Y/P)_f$ and the interest rate equal to r_1.

WHEN PRIVATE INVESTMENT EXPENDITURES DECREASE

Suppose investment expenditures decrease because investors become pessimistic about the future. The **IS** curve will shift to **IS**$_2$, causing real income to decrease to $(Y/P)_2$. This smaller level of real output means that there will be involuntary unemployment in the labor market and excess capacity in the commodities market. In time, money wages and prices will yield to the downward pressure on each of them. As prices fall, the **LM** curve shifts to the right. Eventually general equilibrium is reestablished. Real output will be at its full employment level and W and P will be lower, but real wages will be unchanged and

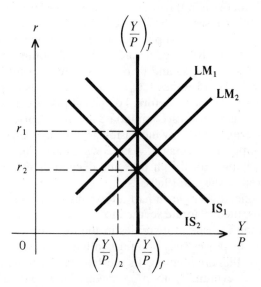

Figure 11-6 The effects of worsening profit expectations with variable prices.

real money balances will be larger. The fall in the interest rate from r_1 to r_2 induces individuals to hold the larger stock of real money balances.

Note that we say full employment will be restored "in time." Because of information costs these adjustments take time, and during this period there will be continuing involuntary unemployment. An insight from the **IS-LM** model is that we can avoid this unemployment period by taking immediate steps to counteract the initial shift in the **IS** curve. In particular, we could cause the **IS** curve to shift back to $\mathbf{IS}_1$ by increasing government expenditures to offset the decrease in private investment spending. This action would remove the necessity for prices and wages to fall.

Another feasible policy in the face of decreased private investment expenditures is to expand the money stock. In Figure 11-6 this means that as soon as **IS** shifts to $\mathbf{IS}_2$, we could cause the **LM** curve to shift *immediately* to $\mathbf{LM}_2$. We know it would eventually shift to $\mathbf{LM}_2$ as prices fell, but an increase in the money stock would remove the necessity for prices to fall by restoring aggregate demand (in nominal terms) to its previous level. The expansionary monetary policy merely offsets the decrease in nominal aggregate demand that arose because of depressed investor expectations. Existing wages and prices are made equilibrium prices and wages.[6]

WHEN GOVERNMENT EXPENDITURES INCREASE

In Figure 11-7 we again start in general equilibrium, but this time we increase government expenditures (keeping taxes unchanged), thus shifting the **IS** curve to the right, to $\mathbf{IS}_2$. The new intersection of **IS** and **LM** indicates a demand for real output in excess of the capacity to produce it. Initially, inventories will decrease. This decrease would be *unplanned*. Simultaneously, firms begin to increase prices and hire more workers. Households offer more labor for sale because as long as they do not correctly assess the increase in prices, the increased money offers for their labor services will be interpreted as an increase in the real wage rate. The rise in prices causes a shift in the **LM** curve. As workers revise their expectations about the price level (and their perceptions of the real wage rate), employment will fall. General equilibrium will be restored with a higher interest rate, higher prices, and the same level of real output.

The increase in the interest rate was brought about by two factors: increased borrowing by the government (the move from 1 to 2 on $\mathbf{IS}_2$), and the decrease in the real stock of money resulting from the increases in P (the move from 2 to 3 along $\mathbf{IS}_2$). This increase in the interest rate caused consumption and investment spending to decline in real terms until the extra government spending was exactly offset.

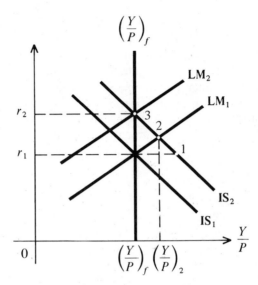

Figure 11-7 The effect of an increase in government spending with variable prices.

11-6 THE REAL BALANCE EFFECT

Thus far, our **IS-LM** curves have been drawn in such a way that the **IS** curve always intersects the full employment level of output at a positive rate of interest. Consider Figure 11-8. A shift of the **IS** curve, perhaps due to worsening profit expectations, has resulted in a circumstance where the **IS** curve no longer intersects Q_f at a positive rate of interest. A fall in prices, which would shift the **LM** curve to the right, would probably still not restore equilibrium. After all, the nominal rate of interest cannot fall below zero. (Who would lend money at a negative interest rate?) Seemingly, the only solution is a shift in the **IS** curve through fiscal policy that would restore equilibrium.

If we assume that consumption spending is affected by people's wealth as well as income, a solution can be found without resorting to fiscal policy. Consider some of the forms of wealth—real estate, art, automobiles, and wine. A general decrease in prices will result in a decrease in the dollar value of such assets but not in their real value. Some other assets, however, will actually increase in real value. In particular, the exchange value (purchasing power) of cash will increase as prices fall. As long as real consumption is a function of real wealth and real money balances are part of wealth, a decline in P will cause an increase in consumption and a corresponding shift in the **IS** curve to the right.

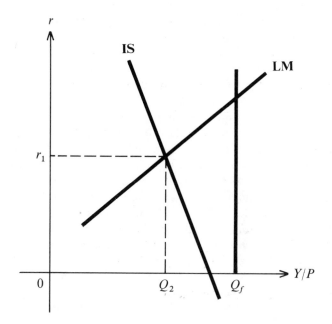

Figure 11-8 The three markets without an equilibrium at a positive interest rate.

This real balance effect has happened in the past, as demonstrated in many studies. Patinkin has summarized these results and concludes that the elasticity of aggregate consumption expenditures with respect to the price level is about −0.2.[7] The minus shows that a given percentage change in prices causes real consumption expenditures to change in the opposite direction. For every 1 percent change in P, a 0.2 percent opposite change in consumption results. This effect was significant in the years when prices actually fell during recessions. In these times the real balance effect helped to restore equilibrium by stimulating consumption expenditures. Friedman and Schwartz examined the 17 recessions in the United States from 1869 to 1932.[8] Fourteen were characterized by either falling or stable prices. Since World War II prices have been increasing through both contractions and expansions, albeit at changing rates.

Instead of a decrease in P to stimulate aggregate consumption, contractions have recently been characterized by a growth in M exceeding the growth in P. In this way, real cash balances are growing, stimulating consumption. As long as the economy is at less than full employment, this growth can lead to an increase in real income. At full employment any increase in the real money stock through increases in M will ultimately lead to rising prices as long as output cannot permanently expand to meet the increase in spending. The increase in the real money stock will be temporary.

11-7 ACTUAL TIMING IN MONETARY POLICY

One of the most important pieces of information that policymakers would like to have is a time frame for the impact of monetary policy on velocity, prices, and output. Andersen and Karnosky examined the continuing impact of a 1 percent increase in rate of growth of the money stock on these variables.[9] We already know (from Chapters 8 and 9) what should happen. Starting at full employment, real cash balances initially rise as individuals come to hold more real cash balances than they desire. They seek to balance their portfolios and begin to increase spending. Initially output expands, but ultimately output falls back (as workers and firms revise their expectations) and the full impact is felt on prices.

Andersen and Karnosky show that initially velocity falls (as cash balances increase). Real output rises as individuals adjust their cash balances. The peak in real output growth is achieved three to four quarters after the initial change in the money stock. Price effects do not occur until approximately seven quarters after the change. Almost two years pass before any inflationary effects are observed, and these effects occur very gradually. The full price effect is not reached until approximately 20 quarters after the initial change. At that point, prices are rising 1 percent more rapidly than before and the real growth rate of output is back to its original level.

Although the time frame presented above is subject to some statistical error, the sequence of events is just as expected. The results of this statistical investigation verify the theoretical conclusions of our variable price **IS-LM** model. What is most interesting is the length of time that it takes the economy to adjust fully to money stock changes. Increases in the money stock do not have immediate inflationary effects; these effects are observed after a considerable lag. Other investigators, working with statistical models that are somewhat different from that used by Andersen and Karnosky, have found shorter adjustment periods, but all such studies agree that the adjustment process is lengthy and that the time periods involved are variable.

11-8 UNION POWER AND GENERAL EQUILIBRIUM

Do unions make any difference in the analysis in Section 11-5? As we shall see in this section, they can affect the general equilibrium values of the aggregate variables only if there is one gigantic, monopolistic union that organizes the entire labor force. If such a union were capable only of resisting downward pressures on the nominal wage rate, the Fed could offset in real terms the effects of the monopoly union. If the monopoly union could set the *real* wage rate, the Fed could do nothing to offset the union's power. We must emphasize, however, that we are discussing the case of a *monopoly* union. Although some industries have only one union that organizes all labor in those industries, there is no union that organizes all labor in the entire country.

The purpose of this section is to illustrate that most popular discussions about the effects of union power implicitly assume the existence of one monopoly union. For instance, it is frequently asserted that the existence of unions makes total employment less than it would be without them. It is even more often asserted that the existence of unions makes the average price and wage levels higher than they otherwise would be. Both assertions are incorrect unless there is one monopoly union that controls the entire labor force.

We have seen in Section 11-2 that an employer, in order to maximize profits, will hire the number of labor-hours that equates the cost of a labor-hour (in real terms) to the extra (real) output produced when the additional labor-hour is employed. We have also seen that the amount of additional output produced when one more labor-hour is employed declines as an employer hires increasing amounts of labor. This relationship implies that as fewer labor-hours are employed, the amount of output produced by hiring an additional labor-hour (the marginal product of labor) increases. A firm maximizes profit by paying a real wage equal to the marginal product of labor. The only way that unions can get employers to pay a higher real wage rate is to restrict the supply of labor relative to the demand for that labor. In other words, if the amount of labor that is made available for employment decreases, employers will be forced back up along their demand for labor curves. With the labor supply restriction a higher real wage will be paid, but fewer labor-hours will be employed.

Over time the capital stock increases, technology improves, and so the marginal product of labor increases. In other words, the demand for labor increases over time. In the absence of unions, the increase in the demand for labor will (if the supply of labor doesn't increase by as much) increase real wage rates. A union in any industry can make real wage rates higher than they otherwise would be only if it restricts the supply of labor to a level below what it otherwise would be. Over time we observe increases in real wage rates along with increases in the number of workers employed even in industries that are unionized. This growth does not contradict what was said above: a union that makes real wages larger than they otherwise would be does so by reducing the number of labor-hours employed below what it otherwise would be. Employment in unionized industries grows over time, but if the real wage in these industries is higher than it would be without the unions, employment is lower than it would be without the unions.

FIXED MONEY WAGE CASE

Figure 11-9 represents the aggregate supply and demand for labor at a point in time. In the absence of a union, the real wage rate would be $(W/P)_f = W_1/P_1$. The quantities of labor demanded and supplied would be equal at N_f labor-hours. Suppose one gigantic union were formed that succeeded in obtaining an increase in the money wage rate from W_1 to W_2 and that could resist any downward pressure on this new rate. Initially the real wage rate was W_1/P_1 and now it is W_2/P_1. The supply of labor must therefore have been restricted to N_u. At the new, higher real wage rate the number of labor-hours that would be offered in an open market setting would be N_s—the union has closed the market and excluded $N_s - N_u$ labor-hours from the market. In effect, the supply of labor curve has become the dashed vertical line labeled S_u.

Figure 11-10 depicts the impact of the union on the **IS-LM** diagram. Here the "equilibrium" real output level decreases from Q_f to Q_u—the output rate when N_u labor-hours are employed with the K_0 units of capital that exist at this point in time. The (restricted) supply of labor is equal to the demand for labor,

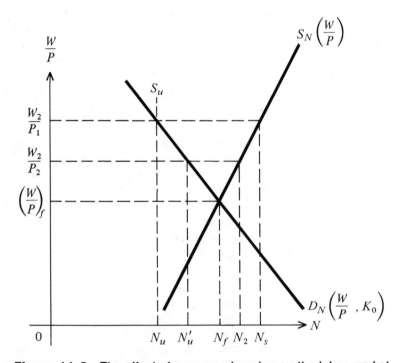

Figure 11-9   The effect of a monopoly union on the labor market.

and the labor market is in "equilibrium." Total expenditures at existing prices call for Q_f output, but only Q_u output is produced, and so prices must rise. As prices rise, two things happen: the **LM** curve shifts to the left, and the "equilibrium" real output rate increases (the Q line in the **IS-LM** diagram shifts to the right). The reason the real output rate increases is that as the average price level (P) increases, the real wage rate (W/P) decreases and more labor will be employed. In Figure 11-9 we can see that as the real wage rate declines, employers will increase the quantity of labor demanded (they will move down along their demand for labor curves). Since the union's power is, by assumption, limited to resisting reductions in the money wage rate below W_2, as the price level increases to P_2 the real wage falls to W_2/P_2 and N_u' labor-hours are demanded. The union supplies the additional labor demanded, and real output increases to Q_u' (as in Figure 11-10). Real output does not return to Q_f because the **LM** curve has been shifted to the left by the increase in P.

The new general equilibrium is at a higher real wage and lower employment level than when we started. There is, in fact, continuing involuntary unemployment. If we look back at Figure 11-9, we see that when the real wage is W_2/P_2 the number of workers who want to work is N_2. But the union permits only N_u' to work. This number is all it can permit to work if it insists on W_2 when the price level is P_2. Thus the existence of the monopoly union has resulted in the general equilibrium value of our aggregate variables being different from what they

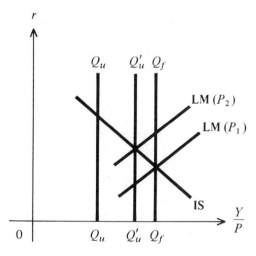

Figure 11-10 The effect of a monopoly union on general equilibrium—fixed money wage case.

would be without the union. Real output is lower, employment is lower, prices are higher, the interest rate is higher, and nominal and real wages are higher.

The Fed can, if it wishes, alter this situation. It can return the economy to where it would be (in real terms) if the union did not exist. Suppose the Fed increases the money base and therefore the money supply; the **LM** curve in Figure 11-10 will shift to the right, prices will rise above P_2, the real wage will fall, and real output will increase. The Fed could continue this inflationary policy until $(W/P)_f$ and Q_f are attained. The end result would be that labor would be no better off (in real terms) than it was without the union, but prices and money wages would be higher.

A second possibility would be a shift in the **IS** curve through an increase in government expenditures or a decrease in taxes. Either of these tactics would restore equilibrium at a higher rate of interest (assuming that the increased deficit is financed by selling bonds to the public).

In the absence of any intervention through fiscal or monetary policy, firms would be faced with excess capacity, measured as the difference between Q_f and Q_u'. In the long run, firms will seek to reduce this excess capacity by reducing their investment expenditures—they will not renew some depreciated capital equipment. This reduction will shift the full employment level of real income to Q_u', ratifying the higher wage rates of the monopoly union.

FIXED REAL WAGE CASE

We have just seen that if a monopoly union had sufficient power to fix the money wage rate, the monetary authorities would have to expand the money supply to bring about zero involuntary unemployment. If the union's monopoly power is strong enough to fix the *real* wage rate, however, and if this real wage rate is above $(W/P)_f$, continuing involuntary unemployment will be the result no matter what the monetary authorities do, as can be seen in Figure 11-11.

Suppose the real wage imposed by the union by virtue of its power to exclude workers from the effective work force is $(W/P)_u$. Any time that the price level increases, money wages increase as well. (Escalator clauses in union contracts are an example of how this may be done.) Even though N_s workers would be willing to work at $(W/P)_u$, the union keeps $N_s - N_u$ out of the market. The level of real output is Q_u. Full equilibrium is at point T in the **IS-LM** diagram no matter what the monetary authorities do. If they expand the money supply, P will increase; but W will also, and so Q remains at Q_u. The price level will rise to whatever level it must to make the **LM** curve shift back to its original position. Real income is lower, employment is lower, prices are higher, the interest rate is higher, and nominal and real wages are higher than they would be in the absence of the monopoly union. Furthermore, in this case the Fed is powerless to do anything about the decreased real income and decreased employment.

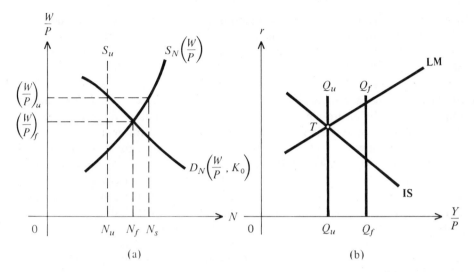

Figure 11-11   The effect of a monopoly union on general equilibrium—
fixed real wage case.

In a similar vein, an increase in the legal minimum wage could be represented by a movement from $(W/P)_f$ to $(W/P)_u$. Unemployment would increase from zero to $N_s - N_u$. The rise in unemployment would induce the government to take some action. If the Fed increased the money supply, the real wage rate would fall and equilibrium could be restored. However, if, as prices rose, Congress (acting as a monopoly union) increased the minimum wage again, the unemployment would remain.

In 1967 the federal minimum wage was $1.40 per hour. In 1979 it was $2.90 per hour, an increase of 107 percent. During that same period the average money price level rose 105 percent. Congress has been doing its share to sustain unemployment, especially among the young, unskilled, and inexperienced members of the labor force whose productivity is less than the legal minimum wage.

NONMONOPOLY UNION CASE

There is, of course, no single gigantic monopoly union in the United States. Only about 20 percent of the labor force is in unions and this membership is divided among many unions. In industries where the existence of unions makes wages higher than they otherwise would be, the unions do so by restricting the labor supply. This restriction leads to an increase in the labor supply available to nonunionized industries and thus lowers wage rates in those industries below what they otherwise would be. Either a union negotiates wage increases that would in any event have been forthcoming because of increasing demand for labor, or it gets higher wages for its members at the expense of lower wages for labor in other sectors. In the aggregate, unions will not affect the relative shares of labor and capital.

Figure 11-12 illustrates the effects of increases in the price level that are initiated by real wage increases won by unions when there is not a single union that organizes the entire labor force, i.e., when labor that is kept out of one industry by union activity is free to seek employment in other industries. Let's suppose the Steelworkers' Union gets a real wage increase for its members that they wouldn't have received without the union, and that the firms in the steel industry raise prices to attempt to cover the increased labor costs. Increases in steel prices will mean cost increases in all industries that use steel. It appears that the average price level will increase. Let's suppose that it does.

In Figure 11-12 we begin in equilibrium with an average price level equal to P_1 and a real output rate equal to Q_f. The initial **LM** curve is labeled **LM**(P_1). An increase in the average price level to P_2 would shift the curve to **LM**(P_2). Aggregate real demand would be Q_D and full employment real output would remain at Q_f. *There has been no restriction of the aggregate (or total) supply of labor.* Supply has been restricted in only one industry, and labor released from that industry is available for alternative employment. These workers will begin to search for alternative jobs. During the adjustment period while they are unemployed, only Q_D of aggregate real output will be produced, but the increase in the supply of labor to alternative industries will reduce wage rates and increase

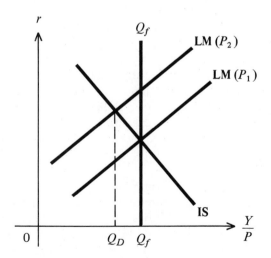

Figure 11-12   Nonmonopoly union case.

employment in those industries; eventually the average price level will return to its previous value. Relative prices will have changed—some will be higher and some lower—but the average will be back to where it was before the increase in prices in the steel industry. Thus the price rise caused unemployment, which, as usual, eventually resulted in a lower average price level. As the price level fell, the **LM** curve shifted back to its initial position.

In this case the general equilibrium value of each of the aggregate variables is unchanged by the existence of unions. Only if there were a monopoly union would there be different general equilibrium values for these aggregate variables.

11-9 FURTHER SUPPLY SIDE CONSIDERATIONS

Recent developments in macroeconomics have changed the focus of macro policy away from demand manipulation to a mixture of demand and supply considerations. In the variable price **IS-LM** model, changes in the monetary base or changes in government expenditures or taxes affect aggregate demand. Ideally, a well-conceived mixture of monetary policy and fiscal policy would bring about desired results without inflation. However, actual experience in virtually all countries in the past 15 years has been that such policies are inflationary. Why? Several possibilities suggest themselves.

INFLATION CAUSED TO INCREASE TAXES

It may be that inflation has been deliberately caused by governments. Inflation is a tax on cash balances; each year the value, in terms of purchasing power, of each unit of cash balances declines by the rate of inflation. Inflation also pushes taxpayers into higher tax brackets. As long as progressive taxation exists, any increase in income just matching the rate of inflation will result in a decrease in real disposable income because the taxpayer is paying higher rates on the higher money income. This set of circumstances allows the government to increase taxes without members of Congress having actually to vote for higher taxes. U.S. experience suggests that this may well have been significant in our continuing inflation.

Although representative democracy is the least oppressive form of government known, it has its problems. Specifically, it suffers from a built-in bias toward government spending. Each proposed government program, or proposed increase in the scope of an existing government program, has a well-defined constituency—the people who directly benefit from the program and are on the receiving end of the spending. In many cases this spending represents a large share of their disposable income, and so these beneficiaries have an intense incentive to lobby vigorously in favor of the spending. On the other hand, the tax cost of any specific program is divided among all taxpayers. Each taxpayer's share of the cost of any particular program is minuscule, and so taxpayers do not have a strong incentive to lobby against any particular spending proposal. Since spending proposals are considered one by one, the lobbying effort will almost certainly be stronger in favor of the spending than against it. Congress makes its decisions on the basis of its perceptions of the most intense feelings of the electorate. In this way government programs inexorably proliferate. The additional tax revenues collected when inflation pushes taxpayers into higher tax brackets, even when their real incomes do not increase, help to provide the wherewithal to finance this growth without Congress' having explicitly to increase taxes.

The additional tax revenue also gives Congress the opportunity occasionally to pass tax "reduction" legislation, especially around election time. All federal tax "reductions" since the huge tax cut of 1964 have actually been tax increases in the sense that they did not offset the higher taxes caused by inflation, which, in turn, was caused by government spending financed by selling government bonds to the Fed.

DATA AND TIME PROBLEMS

Monetary and fiscal policies are often difficult to apply accurately. What we can easily show in a diagram (which specifies all behavioral factors such as the marginal propensity to invest and consume, the interest and income elasticities of the demand for money, and the relationship between interest rates and the multiplier) cannot be done with nearly as much accuracy in our real world economy. There is always a problem with data. A set of data at best reflects the state of the economy when it was collected. It is dated by the very nature of the collection process. Furthermore, the adjustment process that results from fiscal or monetary policy is not instantaneous; it develops gradually through the economy.

But, most importantly, as F. A. Hayek has pointed out, the relevant data are not collected together anywhere for government policymakers to perceive, process, and act on.[10] Aggregate behavior variables (such as propensities to invest and consume and elasticities of supply and demand) are conceptually dependent on individual propensities and elasticities. Knowledge about individual propensities and elasticities, as well as knowledge about particular resource availabilities and production technologies, exists in the heads of individuals in little bits and pieces. Each individual knows about the particular circumstances of time and place that impinge on him or her. Each possesses only a tiny part of the total knowledge. This total knowledge exists in scattered form, not comprehended in its totality by anyone. By its very nature, the knowledge necessary to draw quantitatively accurate curves for the real world that correspond to our *qualitative* textbook and blackboard diagrams, and to keep them up to date, cannot be obtained.

REDUCING TAXES AND REGULATIONS

Many economists claim that demand management would not be sufficient even if these problems did not exist. They advocate the creation of conditions conducive to supply expansion. Fiscal policies cannot increase real output at full employment. Expansion in government spending will result in inflation and a redistribution of spending power from the public to the government. These economists encourage expansion of supply by reducing taxes and regulatory burdens. The objective would be to shift $(Y/P)_f$ to the right so that greater real output could be produced at full employment.

One of the major problems that could be attacked is the tax wedge. There is a growing difference between wages paid to workers and the actual cost to an employer of hiring a worker. Moreover, there is a growing difference between the wages paid to a worker and his or her actual take-home pay. Both the demand for labor and the supply of labor are affected by this tax wedge. On the demand side, firms are faced with such things as Social Security payments and (at times) extremely expensive Occupational Safety and Health Administration (OSHA) regulations. Let us assume that an employer would be willing to pay 100 workers a total of $10,000 per day based upon his perception of their productivity. Without regulation, each worker would be offered $100 per day. With regulations and taxes totaling $10 per worker, the actual wage offer would be only $90. On the supply side assume that workers are willing to work for a take-home pay of $75 per day. If Social Security taxes and state and federal taxes cost each worker $15 per day, workers will demand $90 per day for an actual salary of $75.

We can show these relationships in Figure 11-13. The lines labeled D and S represent, respectively, the aggregate demand for and supply of labor as they would exist in the absence of taxes and regulations. Under these conditions a total of N_1 workers would be hired at a daily wage of $80. Total real output would be that which is associated with N_1 labor on the aggregate production function (not shown). With the imposition of taxes and workplace regulation, the cost of a hire to an employer is no longer the wage paid. But D, since it is based on the productivity of labor, shows for each quantity of labor the *maximum* cost the employer is willing to incur to obtain the services of a worker. Thus the tax and regulation cost must be subtracted from D at each quantity of labor

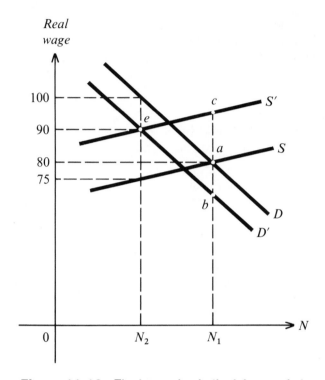

Figure 11-13 The tax wedge in the labor market.

in order to show the amounts that employers are now willing to pay the workers. D' depicts the result of that subtraction. Originally, to obtain the services of N_1 of labor, firms paid to each worker N_1a; now they are willing to pay only N_1b. Similarly, line S shows both the minimum wage that employers must pay and workers must receive in order to get each quantity of labor services offered for sale. With the advent of (or increase in) taxes on workers, the minimum wages that employers must pay rise above the (unchanged) minimum wages that employees insist on getting as a condition for offering each quantity of labor time for sale. S' depicts the minimum wage that the employer must now pay to obtain each quantity of labor. Originally, to get N_1 of labor they had to pay at least N_1a; now, to get the same quantity, they must pay at least N_1c. Labor market equilibrium is now at point e, with only N_2 of labor employed. Aggregate real output has declined to that associated with N_2 on the aggregate production function. The daily wage is $90 per day, but the cost of a hire is $100 per day, while a worker's take-home pay is $75 per day.

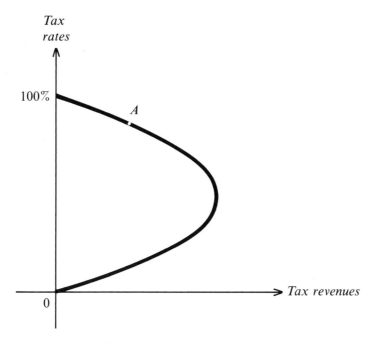

Figure 11-14   The Laffer curve.

We are not here concerned with any moral judgments on OSHA, Social Security, or taxation. We are only concerned with their economic impact on the supply side of our variable price **IS-LM** model.

Arthur Laffer has projected the tax revenues that would result if tax rates were decreased. The Laffer curve indicates that tax revenues may actually increase as tax rates decline.[11] Very high tax rates induce individuals to engage in subterranean (unrecorded) economic activities, thus avoiding taxes. A 100 percent tax rate would generate no revenue because no one would have any incentive to produce. Zero tax rates also result in zero taxes collected. According to Laffer, as tax rates rise, revenues rise up to a point. Beyond that point an increase in tax rates will reduce revenues as resources are withdrawn from the marketplace or used in a nontaxable (and possibly less efficient) manner. Figure 11-14 shows the Laffer curve. Tax revenues rise up to some point, but as tax rates continue to rise, revenues fall. Laffer believes that we are well into the backward bending part of the curve (say point *A*); thus a decrease of our high tax rates will bring resources back into the market economy, actually increasing tax revenues.

Some people argue that we cannot, in the United States, afford to cut tax rates because that would increase government deficits and make inflation worse. The analysis of the Laffer curve and the effect of taxes on employment suggest that a tax cut will raise tax revenue, make balancing the budget easier, and reduce inflation because of increases in the quantity of goods and services produced relative to the amount of money in circulation.

When thinking in terms of the Laffer curve, it is essential to understand the distinction between tax rates and tax revenues. Tax revenues are equal to the tax rate (or rates) multiplied by the tax base. The tax base is *reported* income from productive activity. Laffer and many others suggest that reductions in tax rates by X percent will cause a greater than X percent increase in the tax base; thus tax revenues will increase. The reductions in the tax rates will increase both the amount of productive activity (which will reduce inflation) and the extent to which income is reported.

11-10 CHANGES IN THE EXPECTED RATE OF INFLATION

Until now we have assumed that the expected inflation rate is zero. Although prices have changed, we have assumed that these changes have no effect on expectations. We must now drop this assumption and see what happens.

EFFECT ON THE IS CURVE

For simplicity let's assume that the **IS** curves does not shift when the money supply changes; in other words, we assume that changes in the money supply affect aggregate expenditures via changes in the interest rate. There are no direct effects.

The interest rate that has appeared on the vertical axis of all **IS-LM** diagrams up to now has been *both* the *money rate* and the *real rate of interest*. As long as the expected rate of inflation is zero, there is no difference between these two rates. Suppose, however, that a lender of money expects the price level to increase. Since each dollar can buy less at the higher price level, he will insist that the borrower compensate him for the lost purchasing power. The lender will want to make his usual interest return *plus* an amount to correct for the expected inflation. The rate of interest he will charge, r, will have two components. It will be the sum of the real rate of interest, ρ (the rate he would want if he expected prices to be constant), and the expected inflation rate, $\Delta P^e/P$. (Recall that we used this symbol to stand for the expected inflation rate in Section 8-7 of Chapter 8.) Hence the nominal rate of interest will be the sum of the real rate and the expected inflation rate. In symbols we write

$$r = \rho + \frac{\Delta P^e}{P} \qquad\qquad (11\text{-}8)$$

If borrowers agreed that the expected inflation rate is $\Delta P^e/P$, they will not mind paying the higher money rate because they recognize that each dollar will be worth less in terms of real goods. That is, if borrowers and lenders had previously agreed on ρ when both expected zero inflation, they will now agree on r if both expect that the rate of inflation will become $\Delta P^e/P$. This agreement is exactly the same as before, in real terms.

If we continue to measure r on the vertical axis of the **IS-LM** diagram, we must now recognize the difference between r and ρ. If r goes up because $\Delta P^e/P$ becomes positive, investors have no incentive to change their investment plans. While the cost of the money tied up in the investment has increased in nominal terms, the nominal amount of the returns is also expected to increase by the same percentage amount. Logically, investment spending is a function of the real interest rate. Thus if the **IS** curve is in the position labeled **IS$_1$** in Figure 11-15 when $\Delta P^e/P = 0$, it must rise to **IS$_2$** when $\Delta P^e/P = AB$. As long as ρ doesn't change, we will have the same level of investment spending. Now, however, the level of investment spending (and therefore income) is associated with a *higher* money rate of interest, r_2.

Parallel reasoning suggests that if the expected inflation rate is zero and then becomes negative, the **IS** curve will shift downward from its original position.

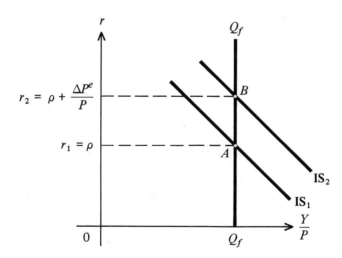

Figure 11-15 The effect of changes in the expected inflation rate on the **IS** curve.

At any income level the difference in the height of the two **IS** curves will be the expected inflation rate, whether positive or negative. Furthermore, *any* increase in the expected inflation rate will shift the **IS** curve upward. The **IS** curve when the expected inflation rate is 10 percent is 3 vertical units above the **IS** curve when the expected inflation rate is 7 percent.

EFFECT ON THE LM CURVE

The analysis of the supply and demand for money in Chapters 8 and 9 says that both are functions of the money rate of interest. Since it is the money rate that appears on the vertical axis in the **IS-LM** diagram, the effect of an increase in the expected inflation rate shows up as a *movement along, rather than a shift of, the* **LM** *curve.* We know from Chapter 8 that increases in the expected inflation rate decrease the quantity of money demanded. Physical assets become a relatively more attractive form of holding wealth, as individuals attempt to beat the expected inflation. The decrease in money demanded is shown as a movement along a given demand for money line in response to increases in the nominal interest rate.

Suppose we start in full general equilibrium in Figure 11-16, with the expected rate of inflation equal to zero. If the expected rate of inflation becomes $\Delta P^e/P$, the **IS** curve will shift to **IS$_2$**; if the expected rate of inflation does not subsequently change again, the **IS** curve will remain in its new position. Be-

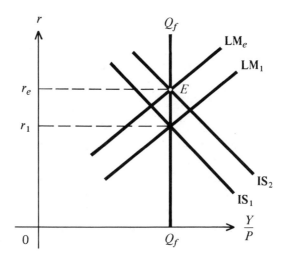

Figure 11-16 **The effect of changes in the expected inflation rate on the IS and LM curves.**

cause the intersection of **IS$_2$** and **LM$_1$** occurs at a $Q > Q_f$, prices will rise. They will continue to rise until the **LM** curve shifts to **LM$_e$**. The new equilibrium rate will be $r_e = \rho + \Delta P^e/P$.

Just the *expectation* of inflation causes a one-shot price increase but not a continuing inflation. If the expected rate of inflation continues to be $\Delta P^e/P$ and if the money supply is not altered, no further price rise will occur. When people realize that prices have stopped increasing, the expected inflation rate will become zero. This zero rate will shift the **IS** curve to the left, and a deflationary period will ensue.

The only way that point E in Figure 11-16 can be an equilibrium point is if the Fed continuously increases the money stock at the rate $\Delta P^e/P$. Only then will expectations be realized and only then will inflation be continuous. The increasing money stock will tend to shift **LM$_e$** to the right, but the rising prices will maintain it in its equilibrium position.

EFFECT ON THE MONEY MARKET

Let us consider both the initial price rise caused by the expectation of inflation and the continuous price rise caused by the continuous expansion of the money stock at the rate $\Delta P^e/P$. We can then see that the price level will have risen by a larger percentage than the increase in the money stock. Real money balances will have fallen. This decline does *not* indicate a shortage of money, as has been suggested by those who see the inflation causing the (deficient) increases in the money stock rather than the other way around. If the Fed should attempt to ameliorate the situation by increasing the money stock more rapidly, the expected rate of inflation would increase and real money balances would fall even farther. The way to increase real money balances is to *reduce* the rate of growth of the money stock, which will in turn reduce the expected inflation rate.

What goes on in the money market when the expected inflation rate changes from zero to some positive value? We have already manipulated the **IS-LM** model to analyze such a change, but let's look at the money market itself. Figure 11-17 combines the **IS-LM** diagram and the money market diagram. Initially $\Delta P^e/P = 0, r = r_1, \rho = \rho_1, Q = Q_f$, and $M/P = M/P_1$. The expected inflation rate becomes positive, causing r to change to r_2. At r_2 there is an excess supply of real money balances equal to AB. People find that they have larger real money balances than they want; hence they will spend. Since Q cannot exceed Q_f, this spending will cause prices to rise. Prices will continue to rise until the money supply function has shifted to M_s/P_2 or until the excess supply of real money balances is eliminated.

The **IS-LM** diagram shows precisely the same process. The initial excess supply of money at r_2 in the money market diagram shows up as an excess demand

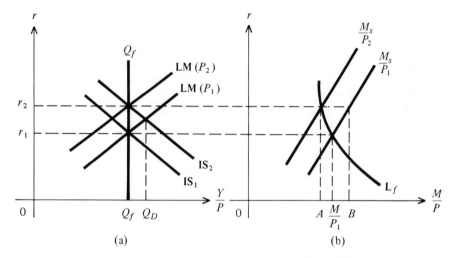

Figure 11-17   Changed expectations and the money market.

in the commodities market in the **IS-LM** diagram. This excess demand in the commodities market will increase prices until the **LM** curve shifts upward to **LM**(P_2).

The increase in the expected inflation rate caused a decrease in the quantity of real money balances demanded. Actual real money balances exceeded desired real money balances, and so spending took place. In other words, the increase in the expected inflation rate, because it caused the nominal interest rate to increase, increased velocity. The extra spending caused prices to increase and actual real money balances to decrease until desired and actual real money balances were again equal. Desired real money balances would remain at their new lower level unless inflation expectations were reversed.

11-11   EFFECTS ON INTEREST RATE OF CHANGES IN THE MONEY SUPPLY

THREE EFFECTS

When the Fed buys bonds, it drives up bond prices and drives down the rate of interest. The initial decrease in the interest rate is called the *liquidity effect* of the increased money supply. We have seen, however, that things don't stop there. The increased spending induced by the increased money supply increases the demand for loanable funds, and this increased demand tends to move the interest rate back up. This phenomenon is called the *income effect*.

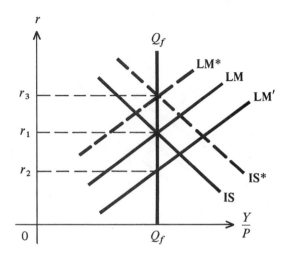

Figure 11-18   **Liquidity, income, and expectations effects on the interest rate of an increase in the money supply.**

These two effects can be seen in Figure 11-18. We start in general equilibrium with $r = r_1$ and $Y/P = Q_f$. The money supply is increased, causing the **LM** curve to shift to **LM'**. The initial impact, before anything happens to nominal income, is to reduce r to r_2. Since **IS** and **LM'** intersect at a Q greater than Q_f, prices, and therefore nominal income, rise. This rise shifts the **LM** curve back toward its initial position. When equilibrium is reattained, the income effect will have exactly offset the liquidity effect.

Suppose the increase in the price level increases the expected rate of inflation. As a result, the **IS** curve will shift upward to some position such as **IS***, and prices will increase until the **LM** curve is in the position labeled **LM***. The rate of interest will now be r_3. This rise in r from r_1 to r_3 is called the *expectations effect*. It occurs because of the change in the expected rate of inflation that was induced by the initial increase in prices. The unavoidable conclusion is that *an expansionary monetary policy will eventually cause interest rates to rise above the level they would have attained in the absence of that policy. High interest rates in this case indicate that monetary policy has recently been expansionary.*

Suppose general equilibrium is disturbed by a restrictive monetary policy. As Figure 11-19 shows, the **LM** curve will therefore shift to **LM'**. Initially the interest rate rises to r_2 due to the liquidity effect. The interest rate cannot stay there for long, however, because **IS** and **LM'** intersect at a Q less than Q_f and prices will fall until the **LM** curve returns to its initial position. This income effect brings r back down to r_1. If the falling prices reduce the expected inflation rate,

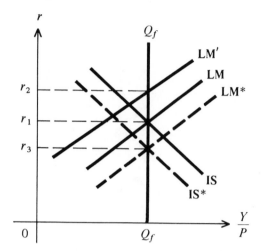

Figure 11-19 Liquidity, income, and expectations effects on the interest rate of a decrease in the money supply.

the **IS** curve will shift to **IS***, and general equilibrium can be attained only when the **LM** curve shifts to **LM***. The interest rate will fall to r_3 because of the expectations effect. The restrictive monetary policy has reduced the equilibrium rate of interest. Low interest rates in this case indicate that monetary policy has recently been restrictive.

INTEREST RATES AND MONETARY POLICY

If we forget the income and expectations effects and look only at the liquidity effect, we are led to the erroneous conclusion that high interest rates are a sign of a restrictive monetary policy and that low interest rates are a sign of an expansionary monetary policy. Consideration of the liquidity effect alone says that the money supply and interest rates move in opposite directions. This error can and sometimes does lead to unfortunate policy decisions.

Whenever the monetary authorities make the mistake of using the interest rate as the basic indicator of tightness or ease of monetary policy, the economy is in for trouble. Suppose, for instance, that the economy is in a recession and an expansionary monetary policy is undertaken. At first most of the gains in nominal income will be in real output, but prices will rise, and thus interest rates will also. If the rising interest rate is interpreted to mean that monetary policy is restrictive, the Fed will increase the money supply even more, causing excessive inflation. The interest rate illusion causes the decision makers to overshoot their objective and thus make another (restrictive) policy *change* necessary. It is precisely these *changes* in the level of nominal aggregate demand that cause our macroeconomic problems. Any level of nominal aggregate demand can be a full equilibrium one, providing that prices, wages, and interest rates adjust. Every time the level of nominal aggregate demand is changed, a new equilibrium set of wages, prices, and interest rates must be attained.

THE FED AND MONETARY GROWTH IN THE 1970s

The Fed has become increasingly concerned with the rate of growth of the money supply. Targets for monetary growth (such as between 4.5 percent and 6 percent annually) are set, and the Fed's record in achieving the targets has recently improved. Because of changes in the money multiplier, the Fed may overshoot or undershoot the target for the first few months. Given enough time, say 6 to 12 months, growth will almost certainly be within the target range. However, the Fed still shows a keen interest in interest rates. Although it has explicitly given more weight to money stock growth since the mid-1970s, it still pays too much attention to interest rates (as we saw in Figure 9-5).

As we have seen, monetary changes have long-range effects on expectations and inflation. Individuals are not always correct about their expectations and are slow to revise them. An extremely rapid expansion in the money supply in 1972 and 1973 led to a dramatic increase in interest rates. Interest rates peaked in July 1974 and then fell rapidly through 1975. During 1974 the money stock grew at a rate about half of that of 1972–73. So the rising growth rate of the money stock led to rising interest rates; then slower growth led to lower interest rates. Money stock growth rates increased in 1975. As a result, interest rates increased in 1975 and peaked in June of 1976. Beginning in mid-1976, money supply growth accelerated very rapidly until the end of 1978. This was the longest period of rapid monetary expansion since World War II. As a result, interest rates rose throughout 1977 and 1978. This six-year period was characterized by varying growth rates for the money stock and parallel changes in interest rates within approximately 6 to 12 months.

Beginning in March 1979 the money stock growth rate shot up dramatically. From March to October the annual rate of growth was over 10 percent. During the same period the federal funds rate remained almost constant, fluctuating slightly from 10 percent to 10.5 percent. At the same time, the annual rate of inflation was over 13 percent. The Fed had been claiming it was pursuing a restrictive monetary policy over all of 1979. In fact it was pushing inflation up and up as it increased the money stock in order to prevent the federal funds rate from increasing. It was ignoring its money stock growth targets in order to meet its federal funds targets. Since inflation expectations were increasing along with the actual inflation rate, it became necessary to flood the banking system with reserves to keep the federal funds rate down.

Finally, on October 6, 1979, the Federal Reserve Board of Governors voted unanimously to pay attention to its monetary growth targets and to allow the federal funds rate to become whatever the credit market called for. The immediate result was a huge jump in the federal funds rate as well as other nominal rates of interest. However, nominal rates began to come down during the first half of November, as people came to believe that the Fed was going, at last, to do something meaningful about inflation. Unfortunately, the Fed's resolve came into question in the first months of 1980 as the Fed accelerated monetary growth. The result was an explosion of nominal interest rates.

SUMMARY

In this chapter we dropped the assumption of fixed prices and wages and investigated the interaction of the commodities market, the labor market, the bond market, and the money market. Into our discussion of general equilibrium we introduced "planned" and "actual" demand—crucial ideas if we are to understand how we can have involuntary unemployment even when the real wage rate is the rate at which the supply and demand for labor are equal.

We investigated the implications of the fact that many labor unions exist and that only 20 percent of the labor force is unionized. We saw that this makes absolutely no difference to the general equilibrium values of our aggregate variables. The common assertion that the existence of unions means less employment and a higher average price level was seen to depend on the implicit assumption that there is one gigantic union that organizes the entire labor force.

We saw how inflation could be dampened by supply changes as well as demand changes. The tax wedge, which reduces both the demand and supply of labor, could be reduced. This reduction would raise the full employment level of output without corresponding demand pressures. The Laffer curve shows how tax revenues could be increased by a reduction in marginal tax rates, which would, by positively affecting incentives to produce, lead to more real economic activity and to an increase in the tax base.

Finally, we saw that when all long-run and short-run effects are taken into account, we would expect the money supply and the nominal interest rate to move in the same direction. If policymakers concentrate only on the short-run effects, they are led to equate high interest rates with a restrictive monetary policy. This error, as we saw, leads to policy decisions that have destabilizing effects on the economy.

QUESTIONS

1. Why do we say that the three unknowns in the variable price **IS-LM** model are real income, the interest rate, and the price level? Why don't we say that the three unknowns are nominal income, the price level, and the interest rate?

2. Why does the supply curve of real money balances shift to the left when P increases, but the demand curve for real money balances doesn't shift in either direction when P increases?

3. The discussion centering on Figure 11-6 asserted that the effects of decreased private investment expenditures could be offset by increases in the money stock. How is this possible? Can smaller spending on plant and equipment be offset by creating new money? Is real economic prosperity created by the monetary printing press?

4. In what sense do increases in the legal minimum wage cause inflation?

5. Why does the assertion that labor unions cause inflation rest on the implicit assumption that there exists a monopoly union? Does our analysis of monopoly and nonmonopoly unions say that unions cannot ever raise the average wage rate and the average price level, even temporarily?

6. In the text it was asserted that our earlier analysis implied that the supply of and demand for money depend on the nominal rate of interest and not on the real rate. Can you see why this is true?

7. What does Hayek's insight into the division of knowledge imply about the ability of government to fine-tune the economy?

8. How can tax rate decreases be anti-inflationary? How can tax revenue decreases be anti-inflationary?

9. In the long run the rate of inflation depends on the amount of money in circulation relative to the quantity of real goods and services the money is spent on. How have the Environmental Protection Agency and the Occupational Safety and Health Administration affected the inflation rate?

10. When taxes are taken into consideration, the nominal rate of interest will increase by more than any increase in the expected inflation rate. Why?

11. In our discussion of the price expectations effect on the nominal interest rate we added an additional unknown and an additional equation to our variable price **IS-LM** model. What are they? Is this change similar to adding the labor market equation to the model in the last chapter? Why or why not?

12. Is the price expectations effect on the nominal rate of interest a short-run or a long-run effect? Why? What do think has been happening to the time it takes for this effect to be felt? Why?

NOTES

1. Throughout the remainder of the text, boldface letters stand for real variables as opposed to nominal variables.
2. The analysis in Section 11-4 follows Don Patinkin, *Money, Interest, and Prices*, 2d ed. (New York: Harper & Row, 1965), Chapter 13.
3. Point K' in Figure 11-5a implies that the interest rate, unlike wages and prices, changes immediately, This change is likely because the decrease in the money supply is brought about through a sale of bonds by the Fed. This bond sale affects supply in the bond market—a market with lower information costs than either the commodities or labor market. Changes in supply and demand for securities show up immediately as changes in securities prices, which are quoted in the financial section of any newspaper.
4. Patinkin, *Money, Interest, and Prices*, p. 321.
5. Patinkin, *Money, Interest, and Prices*, p. 322.
6. Notice that even though initial wages and prices are ratified, the initial interest rate is not. Our analysis assumes away any inflexibility in the interest rate on the grounds that information costs are lower in the bond market than in either the commodities or the labor market. According to Axel Leijonhufvud (*Western Economic Journal*, March 1968), Keynes was most concerned with the inflexibility of the interest rate. If interest rate inflexibility is added to our analysis, the entire **IS-LM** framework must be dropped.
7. Patinkin, *Money, Interest, and Prices*, pp. 656–57.
8. Milton Friedman and Anne Schwartz, *A Monetary History of the United States, 1867–1960*, National Bureau of Economic Research (Princeton: Princeton University Press, 1963), chart between pp. 678 and 679.
9. Leonall C. Andersen and Denis S. Karnosky, "The Appropriate Time Frame for Controlling Monetary Aggregates: The St. Louis Evidence," in *Controlling Monetary Aggregates II: The Implementation*, Federal Reserve Bank of Boston (Conference Series No. 9, September 1972), pp. 147–77.
10. F. A. Hayek was the co-winner of the 1974 Nobel Prize in economic science. See, in particular, his "The Use of Knowledge in Society," *American Economic Review* (September 1945): 519–30.
11. There have been many discussions of this concept. One of the best is Barry N. Siegel, *Thoughts on the Tax Revolt*, Original Paper 21 (Los Angeles: International Institute for Economic Research, June 1979).

Inflation and
Inflationary Recession

Throughout this text we have talked about the price level. Already in Section 1 of Chapter 1 we defined inflation as a sustained increase in the average level of money prices; in Chapter 11 we saw that inflation occurs when aggregate demand in nominal terms is greater than the real productive capacity of the economy. In any real economy there are literally millions of individual prices—the price level is merely an average of these prices. At all times some prices are rising and others are falling. Those that rise rise at different rates, and those that fall fall at different rates. These movements in prices are caused by shifts in individual supply and demand curves, and they are essential to the efficient allocation of resources.

12-1 INFLATION AND RELATIVE PRICES

During an inflationary period, changes in relative prices can continue to determine the allocation of resources. Suppose tastes change and people are willing to exchange two bushels of wheat for one shirt, where before shirts were less in demand and a shirt could get only one bushel of wheat. The price of shirts relative to the price of wheat must double, but it makes no difference what the absolute level of the two prices is. During inflation the prices of shirts and wheat could both rise, with the price of shirts rising twice as much as that of wheat. In the absence of inflation the same change in relative prices could be accomplished by a fall in the price of wheat and an increase in the price of shirts.

The importance of changes in relative prices is the major reason why it is dangerous to try to control inflation by imposing legal restrictions on prices, as we will see in Sections 12-9 and 12-10. Such price controls freeze the pattern of relative prices and thus make it impossible to allocate resources efficiently. It makes more sense to control inflation by eliminating its major cause—a too rapid increase in nominal aggregate demand. Unfortunately, once an inflationary period gets started, a restrictive monetary or fiscal policy requires a great deal of time to be effective. In Section 12-8 we will discuss these lags and the resulting coexistence of inflation and recession, a condition called *stagflation* that the economy has experienced in recent years.

DISTORTION OF RELATIVE PRICES

The importance of relative prices in the allocation of scarce resources is a major reason why inflationary increases in the government-controlled money supply ought to be avoided. An implication of F. A. Hayek's analysis of the division of knowledge (Section 9 of the last chapter) is that changes in relative prices are crucial to the coordination of the plans and actions of the millions of individual decision makers in the economy.[1] If relative prices accurately reflect the constantly changing pattern of supplies and demands in the individual markets, individuals can be left to formulate their own plans based upon their own knowledge and perceived opportunities while, at the same time, all of their diverse plans and actions will be mutually consistent. Anything that distorts the pattern of relative prices will cause individual decision makers to make inconsistent plans, because relative prices will not then convey accurate information about supplies and demands.

Government-caused increases in the money supply necessarily distort the pattern of relative prices because the new money is introduced into the economy in the hands of specific people. The new money is not dropped from helicopters on the lawns of all decision makers at the same time. If, when the money stock is increased by 10 percent, each decision maker's money holdings were increased by 10 percent, there would be no necessary distortion of relative prices. Each person would simply alter his or her plans and actions to take into account the 10 percent increase in money. All suppliers and all demanders in all markets would have 10 percent more money. No one's demand price or supply price would go up relative to others' demand and supply prices. All money prices would increase by 10 percent, but relative prices would be unaffected. However, as we have seen in Section 4 of Chapter 9, the money stock is increased by the Fed by open market purchases of government securities that increase commercial bank reserves. The individuals who sell bonds to the Fed are specific people, and the individuals who borrow the increased commercial bank reserves are specific people. These are the decision makers whose plans and actions will be altered before anyone else's plans and actions. The markets in which these specific people transact will be affected before other markets.

MISDIRECTION OF RESOURCES

Since bond sellers and borrowers from commercial banks are largely business firms rather than consumers, and since business firms typically buy investment goods rather than consumption goods, the money prices of investment goods will increase relative to the money prices of consumption goods. Moreover, the initial impact of the open market purchase of bonds is to increase bond prices and lower interest rates. As we saw in Section 5 of Chapter 6, at lower interest rates the present value of investment projects with returns in the distant future will increase relative to short-term investment projects. Both of these factors will cause more resources to be drawn into capital formation (particularly long-term capital formation) than would have been the case in the absence of the increased money stock.

Such a reallocation of resources toward long-lived investment projects would be desirable only if households had decreased their current consumption spending relative to their current saving. In so doing, households would be signaling that they want to cut current consumption in favor of more consumption in the future. The correct response would be to divert resources away from the production of goods for current consumption and toward the production of investment goods that would allow additional consumption goods to be produced in the future. The increased saving would mean that households would be buying more bonds or savings passbook credits. This buying pattern would increase bond prices and lower interest rates. The lower interest rates would transmit the necessary signals.

But when the Fed increases the money stock, there is no accompanying shift of households' demands away from current consumption and toward future consumption. The same signals are generated, and so the same response will be elicited; but the reallocation of resources will be away from the true pattern of demands and supplies. In Hayek's words resources will be "misdirected."

Now, since money circulates from hand to hand and from checking account to checking account, eventually the new money will be spread more evenly among decision makers in the economy. Moreover, as the inflationary consequences of the additional money take hold, interest rates will rise. When this happens, the true pattern of demands and supplies (and, therefore, the misdirection of resources) will become evident. Then the misdirection can start to be corrected—

through production cutbacks and layoffs in those industries where production was too large relative to the actual pattern of demand. The resource owners whose resources are now unemployed will have to seek out alternative employment opportunities. This search takes time, and during it official unemployment statistics will indicate a recession.

Such a recession would occur even if the inflation continued. The recession is the period of time during which the misdirection of resources gradually becomes corrected. The correction process begins as soon as the inflation, and its price-distorting effects, become apparent. When an inflation is fully anticipated and adapted to, the recession ceases. A large amount of what has come to be called stagflation is due to the misdirection (and subsequent redirection) of resources caused by government increases in the money supply.

12-2 DO LABOR UNIONS CAUSE INFLATION?

Let's consider a widely held belief—that labor unions cause inflation because of excessive wage demands that start a wage-price spiral. Wage increases cause employers to raise product prices. The higher product prices induce unions to get even higher wage increases, which mean that prices will again increase, and so on.

UNIT LABOR COST

What is an "excessive wage demand"? As generally used, this expression means any wage increase that will increase unit labor cost. We define unit labor cost as the money wage rate divided by the average product of labor (AP_L). If $AP_L = 5$ units, then one-fifth of a labor-hour is needed to produce 1 unit. If we multiply the cost per labor-hour (the money wage rate) by this one-fifth labor-hour, we get the labor cost for that unit of output. Clearly, if the percentage increase in the money wage rate equals the percentage increase in AP_L, unit labor costs are unchanged.

The conventional wisdom is that, since it increases unit labor cost, any wage rate increase in excess of increases in productivity will force producers to increase prices. Thus excessive wage demands cause inflation. The fallacy in this line of thinking is the implicit assumption that customers will continue to buy the same amount of output as before even though prices are higher. The fact that demand curves have negative slopes belies this assumption. Sellers are constrained by the demand curves for their products. To deny this is to say that sellers can set prices as high as they wish without losing sales. If this is true, why aren't all prices higher than they are? If this is true, there can be no optimum price, and there can be no price theory. Moreover, if buyers spend more money on some specific products, while the quantity of money in circulation is unchanged, less money must be spent on other specific products.

THE WAGE-PRICE SPIRAL

Let's examine the dynamics of the wage-price spiral. Figure 12-1a depicts an aggregate demand for labor curve drawn against the real wage rate. Figure 12-1b is derived from the quantity equation of exchange (as you will recall from Section 2 of Chapter 8):

$$MV = PQ \tag{12-1}$$

Equation 12-1 can be rewritten as

$$P = \frac{MV}{Q} \tag{12-2}$$

Assume that velocity is fixed.[2] For any particular size of money stock, as P increases Q must decrease. For example, suppose the money stock is held constant at $100 and velocity is 4. If the price level is 2, Q must be 200. If the price level is 4, Q must be 100. For every price level there is a unique Q. As the price

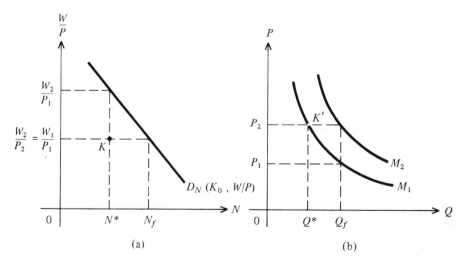

(a)

(b)

Figure 12-1   The impossibility of an unratified wage-price spiral.

level gets higher, Q decreases; at lower price levels we get larger Q's. The line labeled M_1 in Figure 12-1b shows the Q that goes with each different P when the money stock is held at M_1 dollars. This line can be regarded as an aggregate demand for output curve. As with all demand curves, the higher the price, the lower the quantity demanded. The higher the price level, with a fixed money stock, the smaller the quantity of real output demanded.

We start with $W = W_1, P = P_1$, and $M = M_1$. The real wage is W_1/P_1 and we will assume that N_f, the quantity of labor demanded at this wage, is the full employment quantity. There is no productivity advance, but wages are pushed up to W_2. This means that the real wage will rise to W_2/P_1 and only N^* labor-hours will be demanded. However, since unit labor costs have risen, prices are pushed up to P_2, where $W_2/P_2 = W_1/P_1$. Now the quantity of labor demanded rises back to N_f.

Or does it? With the money stock fixed at M_1, if P becomes P_2, the quantity of real output demanded falls to Q^*. This means that only N^* labor-hours will be demanded. The planned demand for labor is still N_f, but because producers cannot sell all they want to at the new price level, the actual demand for labor is only N^*. We will be at a point such as K in Figure 12-1a and K' in Figure 12-1b. We have higher prices (from P_1 to P_2), involuntary unemployment ($N_f - N^*$), and excess capacity ($Q_f - Q^*$). The unemployment will put downward pressure on W, and the excess capacity will put downward pressure on P. Only when W and P fall to W_1 and P_1, respectively, will we reattain equilibrium.

The time involved in getting prices and wages back to their original level may be considerable, but that is not the point. The point is that the so-called wage-price spiral contains the seeds of its own destruction. It needs outside help to continue. For example, suppose the Fed reacted to the unemployment that accompanies the increase in wages and prices by increasing the money stock to M_2. This would permit Q_f to be maintained even at the higher price level. In effect, the Fed would have ratified the wage-price spiral and made the higher prices equilibrium prices.

The same process can be depicted in a variable price **IS-LM** diagram such as Figure 12-2. As before, we begin in full equilibrium with $r = r_1$, $P = P_1$, and $Q = Q_f$. Suppose unions force wages up in excess of productivity gains and hence prices are pushed up. This wage and price rise would reduce the stock of real money balances and thus shift the **LM** curve to $\mathbf{LM}(P_2)$. This shift would mean unemployment and excess capacity ($Q_f - Q^*$), and so prices would fall back to P_1 and the **LM** curve would shift back to $\mathbf{LM}(P_1)$. If the Fed increased the money supply before prices fell, the **LM** curve would shift to the right to $LM'(P_2)$, and the downward pressure on prices would be removed. The Fed would have "ratified" the increase in prices.

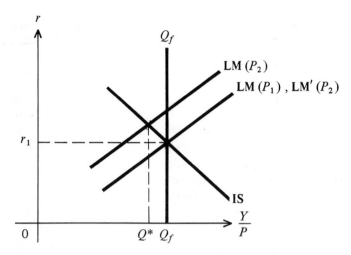

Figure 12-2 "Cost-push" inflation in an **IS-LM** diagram.

12-3 THE ILLUSION OF COST-PUSH INFLATION

It is commonly held that prices are set by costs of production and that prices go up only when costs go up.[3] In fact, most people probably think that prices are set by simply adding some markup to average cost, without any attention to demand at all. This view naturally leads to the conclusion that inflation is caused by sellers of the various inputs (such as labor) who push their selling prices higher and higher. This view is promulgated by politicians and editorial writers who constantly call for voluntary (and not so voluntary) restraints on wage and price increases.

In spite of the popularity of this view, increases in the average price level can always be traced to increases in demand, and *every* inflation in U.S. history has been associated with a too rapid expansion of nominal aggregate demand. If nominal aggregate demand (total spending) increased at the same rate as the rate of increase of real production, the average price level would not increase. However, suppose the capacity of the economy to produce real output grows at 4 percent a year. This growth is the result of increases in the capital stock, increases in the labor force, and improvements in technology. If total spending increased at 7 percent a year, the average price level would have to increase by 3 percent a year. Too rapid increases in total spending can be caused by a too rapid increase in the money stock (M) or a too rapid increase in velocity (V) brought about by an expansionary fiscal policy that increases the interest rate. *Always remember that total spending (PQ) is the product of the money stock and velocity.*

INVENTORIES

The link between increases in demand and increases in prices is obscured by the use of inventories. No seller sells at the same rate each day, week, or month. Sales rates are typically distributed around some mean (average). In order to protect against not having enough to sell on days when the sales rate is above average, a seller keeps an inventory, or a buffer, stock. Any increase in demand for the product reveals itself as a higher-than-average sales rate, but the seller does not, at least at first, realize that demand has shifted. He interprets the higher sales rate as a fortunate sampling from an unchanged sales distribution, and meets the increased demand by allowing inventories to be drawn down below normal levels. He does not change his purchase rate immediately to replenish his stock, because he thinks low sales rates will soon occur and his inventories will then return to normal. If the high sales rate persists, however, he will increase his purchase rate in order to maintain inventories at the desired level.

The firms that supply the seller will thus experience higher sales rates unless the increased demand of our seller is offset by the decreased demand of some other seller of the final product. If there is a genuine (overall) increase in demand for the final product, most sellers will have to increase their purchases from their suppliers. These suppliers, and their suppliers in turn down to the suppliers of raw materials, react to initial increases in demand by altering inventories first, not prices. There is thus a time lag between increases in demand and increases in prices. Because of this lag, people do not associate price increases with increases in demand.

AN EXAMPLE

To illustrate this process, let's suppose there is an increase in the demand for new automobiles, and that there is no corresponding decrease in the demand for any products that use the same resources. The sales rate for automobiles increases and the inventories of new car dealers are drawn down. The higher sales rates persist, and so the dealers increase their purchase rates from manufacturers. In turn, the manufacturers must eventually increase their purchase rates of steel, labor, and equipment. Manufacturers of steel will want to increase their purchases of iron, but existing supplies are insufficient to meet all the demand, and so the buyers of iron will be forced to increase their bids. Unless there is substantial unemployment, an increased demand for labor will also require buyers to increase bids for this input. Car manufacturers will therefore have to pay

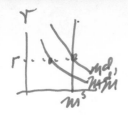

increased prices for their inputs. They will say that these higher costs make it necessary to charge the dealers higher prices. Of course, the higher dealer prices will mean that new car buyers will have to pay higher prices.

The reason prices have risen is that demand has risen. However, it appears that prices went up merely because wage rates and the price of steel went up. No amount of "jawboning" or calls for voluntary restraint in the public interest can change the fact that when resources are scarce, increases in demand cause higher prices.

If the increased demand for cars were accompanied by a decrease in demand for some other products that use the same resources, the required resources for the new cars could come from those released by the declining industries, and the price level would not be affected. If, however, the increased demand for automobiles, as well as many other products, occurred because of increases in the money supply, no resource transfer could take place, and since resources are scarce, prices must rise.

12-4   THE ESSENTIAL NATURE OF INFLATION

We have seen that the only way a cost-push inflation can endure is if it is supported by increases in aggregate demand brought about by an expansionary monetary or fiscal policy. All inflations ultimately rest on increases in nominal aggregate demand; thus the term "demand-pull inflation" is really redundant. This section will illustrate the inflation process with **LM** and **IS** curves.

SHIFTS OF THE **LM** CURVE

In Figure 12-3 we start in general equilibrium with $P = P_1, r = r_1$, and $Y/P = Q_f$. If tastes change so that, in the aggregate, people demand smaller real money balances, the **LM** curve shifts to **LM'**(P_1). Since only Q_f of real output is available and aggregate demand in base year prices is for Q_D, the price level must rise from P_1 to P_2. As it does, the **LM** curve shifts back to its original position. The price level is higher, the interest rate is back to its original value (here we are ignoring inflation expectations effects), and velocity has increased. The nominal money stock is unchanged, but nominal income has risen. As long as people's attitudes toward money balances do not change, the price level will remain at P_2.

The same diagram can be used to illustrate the effect of increases in the money supply. The increased money supply would shift the **LM** curve to the right, prices would rise, and the interest rate would eventually return to its original value (again ignoring inflation expectations effects). The only difference between the effects of a decrease in the demand for real money balances and a

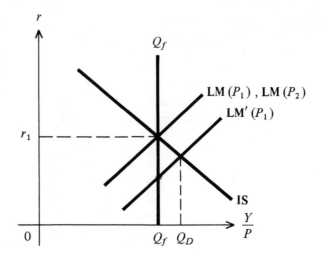

Figure 12-3 Inflation from shifts of the **LM** curve.

comparable increase in the stock of real money balances is that in the latter case velocity would be unchanged, and in the former velocity increases.

As we noted in Section 2 of Chapter 8, velocity is nominal income divided by the nominal money stock, i.e., $V = PQ/M$. We can divide both the numerator and the denominator by the price level and get

$$V = \frac{(Q)}{(M/P)} \qquad (12\text{-}3)$$

or velocity is equal to real income divided by the real money stock. In both of the cases above using Figure 12-3, the Q is constant at Q_f. In the first case, where desired real money balances decreased, when we arrive at the new equilibrium, real money balances will be lower than when we started, and so velocity will be greater. In the second case, both the numerator (real income) and the denominator (real money balances) are unchanged, and so velocity will be unchanged.

One proposal that has been advanced as a solution to inflation is an act of Congress specifying a constant rate of expansion of the money stock.[4] If real output grows at a rate of 4 percent a year, an increase in the money stock of 4 percent a year would keep the price level stable as long as velocity was unchanged. This policy would create an environment where the money growth rate is known in advance, and so new money would cause less distortion; but it would also eliminate variable monetary policy in times of expansion or contraction. Those who

feel that the Fed performs a valuable service in economic stabilization have opposed this rule, while those who feel that, on balance, the Fed destabilizes the
economy by making too many unanticipated changes of the money stock favor it.

SHIFTS OF THE IS CURVE

If the **LM** curve is not vertical, (i.e., if velocity is responsive to changes in the
interest rate), inflation can arise from nonmonetary sources. In Figure 12-4, for
example, suppose the government incurs a budget deficit at a time of full employment. Assume the money stock is constant. The **IS** curve shifts to IS_2. While
velocity is not infinitely variable, it is sufficiently variable to move the economy
from point A to point B on the **LM** curve. This increase in velocity, which was
caused by the increase in interest rate from the Treasury's borrowing, means
there will be an excess demand in nominal terms, which will cause prices to rise.
This price rise reduces the real money stock, shifting the **LM** curve to $LM(P_2)$
and causing the interest rate to increase further to r_3.

Notice that, even without a change in the money supply, prices have risen.
Corresponding to the monetary rule we discussed in the last section is a proposal
that would require a balanced federal budget; any increase in government expenditures would have to be matched by increases in taxes. Thus the **IS** curve
would not shift as in Figure 12-4. This fiscal rule would certainly reduce deficit-
induced inflation, as the proponents of the policy advocate. Opponents argue

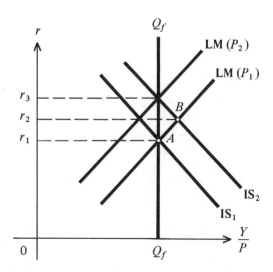

Figure 12-4 Inflation from shifts of the IS curve.

that this policy would hamper stabilization policies in times of contraction or expansion.

Opponents of both the monetary rule and the fiscal rule argue that the authorities know what policies should be pursued and are willing to pursue them for the long-term benefit of the economy. It seems clear from the experience of the 60s and 70s that this is not the case. While inflation rates were variable in both decades, the average rate of inflation was substantially higher in the latter decade. Thus the proponents of these rules can cite evidence backing up their claim that stabilization policies in the United States have been unsuccessful.

Economists who oppose monetary and fiscal policy rules believe that sometimes it is necessary to pursue expansionary policies and at other times it is necessary to pursue restrictive policies. However, policymakers implement expansionary policies much more often than they implement restrictive policies. The federal budget, for example, has been in deficit *every* year for the last 20 years except 1969. No economist argues for increasing budget deficits when inflation is accelerating, but such a policy has frequently been implemented since the mid 1960s. The reason for this, it has been suggested, is that politicians perceive greater benefits to themselves from the spending side of programs than from the taxing side. Keynesian analysis gives them a rationale to incur budget deficits, and so they are happy to do so. They spend without taxing. Politicians have no incentive to create budget surpluses even when Keynesian analysis calls for them. To do so, they would have to cut spending or increase taxes or both. As politicians see it, such actions tend not to lead to reelection.[5]

12-5 INFLATION AND VELOCITY

The shifts of the **IS** and **LM** curves discussed above do not take into account the additional economic impacts of anticipated inflation. In Section 10 of Chapter 11 we showed that anticipated inflation will shift the **IS** curve up by the rate of inflation. As interest rates rise, the demand for real cash balances falls and velocity rises. The rise in velocity continues until individuals fully adjust their cash balances to this new, higher rate of inflation. As a consequence, prices will rise more rapidly during the adjustment period than after it.

The significance of velocity changes in inflation was examined by Albert Burger.[6] He found that in the period 1953–72 the average difference between the inflation rate in any year and the average rate of monetary growth in the previous 5 years was only 0.22 percentage points. During the period 1972–78, however, the difference was 1.46 percentage points. In the first period the rate of money growth exceeded the inflation rate, while in the second period the reverse was true. Clearly, increases in velocity have become more significant. This increased significance is primarily because people are coming to expect more and more inflation, and so they spend more quickly in order to avoid even higher prices in the immediate future.

12-6 WEALTH TRANSFERS FROM UNANTICIPATED INFLATION

An unanticipated inflation is simply an unexpected sustained increase in the price level.[7] Clearly, not everyone correctly anticipates every inflation. Some economic actors (governments, firms, and individuals) gain from such an event and others lose. We can identify the gainers and the losers if we look at individual balance sheets.

MONETARY AND REAL ASSETS AND LIABILITIES

The LHS (left-hand side) of a balance sheet lists assets. The RHS (right-hand side) merely divides the dollar amount of assets into those owned outright (equity) and those owed to others (liabilities).

Assets may be monetary or nonmonetary. A monetary asset is a claim to a fixed amount of money. Cash is an example, as are bonds (once they are purchased); deposits in banks and pension plans that promise a fixed stream of income are other examples. A nonmonetary asset, sometimes called a "real" asset, represents a claim to some good or service stream that can change in money value but is fixed in real terms (e.g., a car).

A monetary liability is an obligation to pay a fixed sum of money. A mortgage on a house and a contract calling for car payments of $70 a month for three years are examples. A real liability is an obligation to give some real good or service, the money value of which can change (e.g., a home mortgage where the interest rate is varied to account for inflation).

Since the LHS and the RHS of a balance sheet must be equal, we can write:

equity = assets − liabilities

      = (real assets − real liabilities) + (monetary assets − monetary liabilities)

      = net real assets + net monetary assets

In symbols,

$$E = R + M \qquad (12\text{-}4)$$

where E is equity, R is net real assets, and M is net monetary assets.

Any changes in the price level, P, will affect the dollar value of R. Since E is in dollar terms, we must write

$$E = PR + M \qquad (12\text{-}5)$$

Suppose the initial level of prices is taken as the base (i.e., $P = 1$) and the price level increases 50 percent. Initially $E = E_1 = R + M$; now $E = E_2 = 1.5R + M$. Has E increased by a larger or smaller percentage than P? The answer to this question depends on whether M is positive or negative. If M is positive, this person or firm is a *net monetary creditor*. If M is negative, the person or firm is a *net monetary debtor*. A net monetary creditor is worse off when P increases because E increases by a smaller percentage than P, and thus the real value of equity falls. A net monetary creditor loses wealth and a net monetary debtor gains wealth during an unanticipated inflation. If M is negative, E increases by a larger percentage than P, and so real wealth has increased.

WHY THE INFLATION MUST BE UNANTICIPATED

When we say an individual's real wealth has increased (or decreased) we mean it has increased (decreased) relative to what he *thought* his real wealth position would be. Only anticipated inflation can be hedged against. If an individual anticipates the inflation, he can (by charging interest that would cover the amount lost to anticipated inflation) be a net monetary creditor and not lose real wealth relative to what he thinks his real wealth is. The wealth transfer analysis using Equations 12-4 and 12-5, however, applies only to *unanticipated* inflation.

Consider an individual who has no monetary liabilities and $10,000 in cash. He lends the money at 5 percent interest, not expecting an inflation, but an inflation takes place; our net monetary creditor has lost wealth—he has made less than what he expected. Now suppose he expects an inflation rate of 5 percent, and so he charges 10 percent on the loan. He is a net monetary creditor, and when the inflation actually takes place his balance sheet will show a loss of real wealth. However, he knew the inflation was coming and hedged against it by adding 5 points to his interest charge. Relative to what he expected, he has not lost wealth. In fact, if the expected inflation did not materialize, we would say this net monetary creditor had gained wealth because, relative to his expectations, there was an unanticipated deflation.

In this sense, "fixed income groups" lose in an actual inflation. A person on a pension has a monetary asset. Its value is the present value of the fixed pension payments that will be coming in. When this person acquired this asset, he had some expectation about inflation. If the actual rate of inflation exceeds his expectation, he has lost real wealth as far as this particular asset is concerned. Thus pension plans that contain cost-of-living escalator clauses are not monetary assets. They are claims to a stream of goods and services fixed *in real terms*.

12-7 TAX EFFECTS OF INFLATION

Inflation can create disincentives for capital formation because of tax regulations that do not permit adjustments for inflation.[8] Differing inflation rates will result in differing returns on investment.

ON BUSINESS FIRMS

We can see the effect of inflation by considering the first-year results of the following investment scheme. A firm considers buying a $300,000 asset that will yield $100,000 annually in net real income over its expected useful life of 6 years. We will look at each of four different inflation rates over the life of the asset— 0 percent, 5 percent, 10 percent, and 50 percent. We need only look at the first year because the effects observed in that year will carry through all subsequent years.

Table 12-1 presents these results. Depreciation, the expense associated with the use of the asset, is $60,000 a year ($300,000/5 years). A tax rate of 50 percent is applied to the difference between receipts and depreciation to determine taxes paid. Cash flow is the difference between receipts and taxes paid. The final two rows are taxes paid and after-tax cash flow in real terms (deflated by the rate of inflation).

As inflation accelerates, the real monetary return of the investment (the real cash flow) decreases while the real revenue received by the government increases. The culprit, of course, is the tax treatment of depreciation. The law does not permit the depreciation deduction to increase with inflation. It is tied to the initial purchase price of the asset rather than to the replacement price. If the depreciation base ($300,000 over 5 years) were to be revalued according to the rate of inflation, there would be no transfer of real wealth from firms to the government. In our example, at an inflation rate of 50 percent, if depreciation were

Table 12-1   Investment returns with differing inflation rates

| Item | Inflation Rate | | | |
	0%	5%	10%	50%
Net cash receipts	$100,000	$105,000	$110,000	$150,000
Depreciation	60,000	60,000	60,000	60,000
Taxes paid	20,000	22,500	25,000	45,000
Cash flow	80,000	82,500	85,000	105,000
Real taxes paid	20,000	21,429	22,727	30,000
Real cash flow	80,000	78,571	77,273	70,000

NOTE: To calculate real taxes paid, divide taxes paid by 1 plus the inflation rate. For example, with 5 percent inflation real taxes paid equal $21,429 (or $22,500 ÷ (1 + .05)). Similar calculations are made for real cash flow.

$90,000 (50 percent more than $60,000), taxes would be $30,000 ($20,000 in real terms) and cash flow $120,000 ($80,000 in real terms). As long as depreciation is not adjusted, investment will decrease as inflation accelerates.

ON INDIVIDUALS

Similar tax effects exist for individuals due to the progressive income tax. Suppose a woman receives $10,000 a year in income that is taxed as follows: 10 percent of the first $5,000, 20 percent of the next $5,000, and 30 percent of any income above $10,000. She would pay $1,500 in taxes and have $8,500 disposable income. If inflation is 10 percent and her money income increases 10 percent, will her real disposable income be unchanged? On an income of $11,000, she will pay $1,800 in taxes, leaving $9,200 as disposable income. In real terms, this is equal to $8,364—$136 less than the $8,500 she had the first year. Her real disposable income has decreased as a result of inflation.

Interest rates are also going to adjust to inflation. Assume that the woman above initially receives interest income (included in her original $10,000). Further, assume that she desires a 5 percent real return *after taxes*. Since she pays a marginal tax rate of 20 percent, a 6.25 percent yield provides a real return of 5 percent after taxes without any inflation. The real after-tax return equals the market rate of interest multiplied by 1 minus the marginal tax rate, or

$$6.25\% \ (1 - 20\%) = 5\%$$

Now if inflation is 10 percent, market rates of interest will rise by more than 10 percent because individuals will be pushed into higher tax brackets. The market interest rate must increase to offset the effects of inflation and taxes. In order for a person to continue to receive a 5 percent after-tax real return in the 30 percent tax bracket with inflation of 10 percent, the market interest rate must be 21.43 percent. This calculation can be broken down as follows:

$$(21.43) \ (1 - 30\%) = \quad \underline{\begin{array}{l} 15\% \text{ nominal after-tax rate} \\ -10\% \text{ inflation rate} \end{array}} \\ 5\% \text{ real after-tax rate}$$

Taxes and inflation have combined to cause the interest rates to vary by more than the rate of inflation.

Investment will be doubly affected by inflation. Understated depreciation increases real taxes, and the market rate of interest will increase. These two combined effects will substantially lower the net present value of an investment.

ON FINANCIAL INSTITUTIONS

As long as the maximum interest rates banks can pay depositors are held below rates on other securities, inflation will cause "disintermediation." In other words, individuals will withdraw savings from commercial banks, savings and loans, and the like and use these funds in financial markets where interest rates are not controlled. The Fed's Regulation Q sets upper limits on interest rates banks can pay depositors. As a result of disintermediation, the Fed has allowed commercial banks to offer other financial instruments such as Treasury market accounts. These instruments provide for the adjustment of yields according to changes in market interest rates. Savings and loans offer similar instruments. In April 1980 President Carter signed a law that repeals Regulation Q gradually over a 6-year period.

12-8 MORE ON INFLATIONARY RECESSION

At the beginning of this chapter we saw that the coexistence of inflation and recession (sometimes called "stagflation," but just as often called "inflationary recession") can be explained as a correction of a misdirection of resources caused by the distortion of relative prices that results from government-caused increases in the money supply. As soon as the inflationary consequences of such money supply increases are perceived, interest rates will adjust, and the misdirection of resources will become apparent. Production cutbacks and layoffs and alternative employment search (recession) occur even though the inflation continues. When the misdirection of resources has been corrected, it would be possible for inflation to proceed along with only normal unemployment. However, if steps were then taken to eliminate the inflation, inflationary recession would again emerge. A restrictive monetary policy, for example, designed to reduce (the rate of growth of) nominal aggregate demand would have such an effect. In our discussion of labor unions and inflation (Section 12-2) we saw that, given the level of nominal aggregate demand, there is one and only one price level that is consistent with full employment. Any higher price level will cause unemployment. In the case of cost-push inflation, the price level goes up and aggregate demand remains the same; while in the case of a restrictive policy, nominal aggregate demand goes down and (at first) the price level stays the same. The result is the same in both cases—inflationary recession.

QUANTITY EQUATION OF EXCHANGE IN RATE OF CHANGE FORM

From the quantity equation of exchange it follows that

$$\frac{\Delta M}{M} + \frac{\Delta V}{V} = \frac{\Delta P}{P} + \frac{\Delta Q}{Q} \tag{12-6}$$

That is, the sum of the percentage change in the money stock and the percentage change in velocity equals the sum of the percentage change in the price level and the percentage change in real output. We know what while there may be temporary changes in velocity after a change in monetary policy, equilibrium velocity changes very slowly over the long run. Assume that $\Delta V / V$ is constant at α percent a year. Equation 12-6 can then be rearranged to

$$\frac{\Delta P}{P} = \frac{\Delta M}{M} + \frac{\Delta V}{V} - \frac{\Delta Q}{Q}$$

or

$$\frac{\Delta P}{P} = \frac{\Delta M}{M} + \alpha - \frac{\Delta Q}{Q} \qquad (12\text{-}7)$$

Equation 12-7 says that if the money stock is growing at 4 percent a year ($\Delta M / M = 4\%$), and if velocity increases at 1 percent a year ($\alpha = 1\%$), the rate of growth of the average price level ($\Delta P / P$) will be the difference between 5 percent ($\Delta M / M + \alpha$) and the rate of growth of real output ($\Delta Q / Q$). If the rate of growth of real output is 3 percent, the rate of growth of prices will be 2 percent; if the rate of growth of real output is 1 percent, the rate of growth of prices will be 4 percent, and so on. Look at Figure 12-5. Suppose the sum of the rate of growth of the money stock and the rate of increase in velocity ($\Delta M / M + \alpha$) is equal to $0C$ on the vertical axis or $0C'$ on the horizontal axis ($0C$ equals $0C'$). If the rate of growth of real output is zero, the rate of growth of prices will equal the sum of the rate of growth of the money stock and velocity ($0C$). The economy would be at point C in the diagram.

If the rate of growth of real output were $0C'$ (equal to $\Delta M / M + \alpha$), the rate of growth of the price level would have to be zero. The economy would be at point C' in the diagram. If the rate of growth of real output were $0B$, the rate of growth of prices would be $0E$. The line CC' is made up of points whose coordinates must add up to ($\Delta M / M + \alpha$). Any time the rate of growth of the money stock increased, the economy would go to a line to the right of the original line. If the rate of growth of the money stock increased so that the sum of the new money growth rate and α were $0D$ ($= 0D'$), the economy would be on line DD'. Such lines can be regarded as aggregate demand curves for real output. With a fixed rate of growth of the money stock, as the inflation rate gets higher the rate of growth of real output decreases because the rate of growth of real money balances decreases. If the rate of growth of real money balances lags behind the growth of the capacity of the economy to produce real output, the rate of growth of purchases of real output will also lag behind capacity growth.

At any point in time there is a limit on the rate of growth of real output. The capacity of an economy to produce real output depends on the economy's labor force, capital stock, and technology, which are beyond the control of monetary

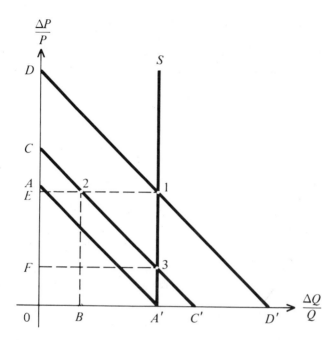

Figure 12-5 Inflationary recession from a restrictive monetary policy.

and fiscal policy. Their growth rates determine the potential growth rate of real output. Let's suppose this capacity growth rate is $0A'$. The vertical line SA' in Figure 12-5, which represents this limit, could be regarded as an aggregate supply curve. It says that the aggregate capacity supply of real output is the same, no matter what the inflation rate is. If $\Delta M/M + \alpha$ were maintained at $0A$ ($= 0A'$), the aggregate demand line would be AA'. Aggregate demand and aggregate supply intersect at A', indicating a steady average price level ($\Delta P/P = 0$) and real output growth equal to $0A'$. Unemployment would be at its natural rate since purchases are keeping up with capacity growth.

Suppose that the rate of growth of the money stock increased so that aggregate demand shifted to DD'. Since real output growth cannot exceed $0A'$, the inflation rate would have to become $0E$. The economy would be at point 1 in Figure 12-5. For example, if the money stock growth rate were 9 percent, velocity increased by 1 percent a year, and the capacity growth rate were 3.5 percent, inflation would have to be 6.5 percent a year. Total spending would be increasing at 10 percent a year, and the rate of increase of real things available for purchase would be only 3.5 percent a year. The difference must show up as inflation.

CONSEQUENCES OF REDUCED MONEY STOCK GROWTH

Suppose that the money stock growth rate decreases so that CC' becomes the aggregate demand curve. If the inflation rate immediately fell to $0F$, the rate of growth of real output could be maintained at $0A'$ and no unemployment would result. The economy would be at point 3 in the figure.

But we know that the rate of growth of prices does not immediately respond to decreases in the rate of growth of the money stock. Thus the economy will move to position 2 in Figure 12-5. Real output growth is $0B$ and inflation is $0E$. Total spending has stopped growing as fast as it had been. But prices continue to grow at the same rate, and so total purchases of real output must grow at a slower rate. For example, if total spending had been growing at 10 percent and prices had been growing at 6.5 percent, purchases of real things must have been increasing at 3.5 percent — the rate of increase in the capacity supply of real things. If total spending should now begin to grow by only 8 percent, and if prices continued to increase by 6.5 percent, the rate of increase in purchases of real things would be reduced to 1.5 percent. This is considerably below the rate of increase in the capacity supply of real things, and thus unemployment would increase above its natural rate.

The rate of change in prices does not decrease immediately for the following reasons:

1. The position of the demand curve faced by any seller is not known with certainty. Each seller's sales rate fluctuates from day to day. For a given set of demand conditions these sales rates are distributed around some mean (average). If this sales distribution shifts to the left because of a restrictive monetary policy, at first the lower sales rates will be interpreted as coming from the lower end of an unchanged distribution. Only after time will the seller become convinced that his demand curve has shifted down.

   If there has recently been a prolonged period of demand shifts to the right caused by a too rapid expansion of the money supply, it will be difficult to convince sellers that their demand curves are now shifting to the left or at least have stopped shifting to the right. Sellers must *perceive* that demand conditions have changed. The longer the period of inflation that has just transpired, the more upward biased will be the sellers' estimates of the positions of their demand curves. Sellers' expectations about the future are determined by what has happened in the recent past.

2. Once sellers recognize that their demand curves have shifted downward, they must determine what their new wealth-maximizing prices are. It is easy for an economist to draw a demand curve, a marginal revenue curve, and a marginal cost curve and to immediately identify the new wealth-

maximizing price. Unfortunately, only academic economists have zero information costs in this regard. Real economic actors must discover the position of these curves through trial and error; only then will they be able to set the wealth-maximizing price. For this reason, after a restrictive monetary policy, we witness many special deals or sales on individual commodities. Since firms lose goodwill when they raise prices, they want to avoid lowering any price that they may have to raise again. Rather than announcing decreases in regular prices, firms will announce sales prices in order to "test the water." If they discover that lower prices make them better off, they will announce the lowering of regular prices. The prices that get included in the price indices are the regular prices or catalog prices, not sales prices.

3. The terms of many exchanges are settled over specified time periods by contract. These prices change only at the end of the contract period. Furthermore, when contracts come up for renewal, the terms that are settled on are based on expectations formed by recent experience. If the inflation rate has been 13 percent for the last year, the expectation will be that inflation will continue at a rate not too different from 13 percent. When a restrictive monetary policy is implemented, this inflation rate will cause unemployment, since it takes time for the resulting downward pressure on the increase of prices and wages to affect expectations.

4. If it is widely believed that the unemployment, which is the first effect of the restrictive monetary policy, will result in the Fed's not sticking to the restrictive policy, sellers will have no incentive to change their pricing policies. In other words, since everyone knows that increasing unemployment rates give rise to numerous complaints, it pays, even if you know that your new wealth-maximizing price increases are lower, to wait and see whether the restrictive policy is reversed.

When the inflation rate finally decreases, the economy will move along line CC' in Figure 12-5, from point 2 to point 3. As it does, unemployment will decrease to its natural level.

1967–69 AND 1973–75

We can examine inflationary recession by looking at two recent experiences of it. From 1/67 (first quarter, 1967) to 1/69 monetary growth rates averaged 7.3 percent a year—a higher rate than in the early 1960s. Initially output expanded rapidly, but eventually higher rates of inflation occurred. The numbers look like this:

Time Period	Inflation Rate
2/67–3/68	4.5%
3/68–2/69	4.8%
2/69–1/70	6.0%

In 1/69 the Fed began restrictive monetary policies designed to give the economy a "soft landing"—reduced inflation without a corresponding recession. In fact, by the third quarter of 1969 a mild recession was occurring; it lasted until 4/70. Real output fell at a rate of 1.1 percent during that time. In time the rate of inflation began to fall. The rate was down to 4.9 percent from 1/70 to 2/71. However, this rate was still unacceptably high and President Nixon imposed wage and price controls in August 1971.

What was most interesting was that restrictive monetary policy was abandoned when the recession began. Apparently the Fed was unwilling to allow a protracted but mild recession that would have resulted in a substantial reduction in inflation. So the economy received a renewed spurt of demand pressure, which would be expected to manifest itself in price rises within about seven quarters (recall our discussion of this in Section 7 of the previous chapter). Wage and price controls were an attempt to reduce inflation by fiat. It worked, temporarily. The rate of inflation fell to 3.9 percent in the period from 2/71 to 4/72.

As the controls were gradually relaxed, inflation surged. From 4/72 to 4/73 it stood at 7.4 percent and from 4/73 to 1/75, 11.3 percent. It peaked in 3/74 at a rate of 12.6 percent. Monetary expansion was rapid during this period, reaching a peak during the national election year. Immediately after the election, growth rates were sharply reduced. The record speaks for itself—1/72–4/72, 8.5 percent increase in the money stock; 1/73–4/73, 6.0 percent increase. The reduced rate of expansion of the money stock led (along with other factors) to the most severe recession in the United States since the 1930s. It began in 4/73 and lasted until 1/75. The recession was divided into two distinct parts; the first, lasting three quarters, was relatively mild. Real output declined at an annual rate of 2.7 percent. The next three quarters were much worse and real output declined by 7.3 percent. During the latter period, inventories rose dramatically as a percentage of sales. Firms grossly underanticipated the recession. They initially did not cut back production and thus purposefully increased inventories. When they finally did try to cut back, the severe recession hit.

Monetary expansion, which had been reduced in 1973, was still further reduced in 1974. From 2/74 through 4/74 the growth was down to 3.4 percent. In a period of less than two years, the rate of expansion in the money stock had fallen by more than half. Yet inflation was still rampant. This inflation in the face of restricted money stock growth deepened the 4/73–1/75 recession, which didn't ebb until inflation came in line with money growth. Inflation was lower in 1975 and lower still in 1976.

12-9 OPEN VERSUS REPRESSED INFLATION

Superficially, the most direct way to deal with inflation seems to be to make it illegal—in other words, to institute wage and price controls and simply to "freeze" prices. What could be more simple?

Since there are millions of prices in any real economy, wage and price controls would mean that each one of these prices would have to be controlled. If buyers' tastes change and so they want to buy less of product A and more of product B, at the frozen prices there will be an excess supply of A and an excess demand for B. If prices were free to move in response to market forces, the price of A would decrease relative to the price of B. This change in relative price would signal resources into industry B and out of industry A as producers sought maximum profits. In the absence of direct controls on prices, with the money stock increasing at a rate in excess of the potential real output growth rate, this change in relative prices would be brought about by increases in both prices, but the price of B would rise more than the price of A. This type of inflation would be *open*. Resources would still be allocated by individual responses to changing relative prices.

With direct price controls, relative prices could not change. The individuals in charge of the prices of A and B may recognize the excess supply of A and the excess demand for B and know that the price of B should rise relative to the price of A, but by how much? How do they know what the market clearing price is? If they did know the market clearing price and permitted the price to rise to that level, the controls would be ineffective because in the absence of controls the price would have risen by precisely the same amount.

Many people forget that prices are not arbitrarily set in the absence of controls. Any seller is constrained by the demand curve he faces. Prices go up when these demand curves shift upward. Inflation happens when many of these demand curves shift upward at the same time, and that happens only when nominal aggregate demand is increased too rapidly by, for example, excessive rates of growth of the money supply. Whether a firm is a perfect competitor, a pure monopolist, or an oligopolist, when its demand curve shifts upward, its profit-maximizing price increases; when its demand curve shifts downward, its profit-maximizing price decreases.

In a *repressed inflation*, where prices are not free to change in response to market forces, resources are misallocated because *relative prices cannot change*.

Misallocated resources result in lower real growth rates. West Germany is an excellent example. After World War II, price and wage controls were imposed; prices were not permitted to allocate resources. The effect was to cut real output in half relative to its level when the war ended. Wage-price controls prevented optimal resource allocation because they severely constrained incentives for individuals to search for the highest valued uses of resources. In 1948 the wage-price controls were removed and the price system was allowed to work. The German economic miracle began with an abrupt increase in the rate of growth of real output.[9]

Direct wage-price controls also encourage lawlessness. If a commodity is in excess demand and its price cannot rise, how is the scarce supply rationed? Usually this rationing is accomplished through side payments of various kinds. (For instance, rent gets paid with a check and a case of bourbon.) Paradoxically, because to evade the controls is to allow relative prices to change and therefore to permit efficient resource allocation, acting unlawfully becomes beneficial, both privately and socially.

12-10 WAGE-PRICE GUIDELINES AND CONTROLS

In the 1962 *Economic Report of the President*, the Council of Economic Advisors proposed a set of wage-price guidelines as an answer to inflation. These guidelines were needed, it was argued, because large segments of the U.S. economy had become noncompetitive. Large corporations, it was said, could pass on any cost increases to their customers without any decrease in sales, simply because of their market power. Large labor unions could demand and get whatever real wage they wanted because of their monopolistic power. These economic giants must be made aware of their social responsibility; to help them steer a proper course, the guidelines were set forth.

ECONOMIC POWER IN THE UNITED STATES TODAY

Perhaps the most widely held belief about the U.S. economy is that economic power is becoming more and more concentrated. The evidence casts doubt on the validity of this belief. A greater percentage of the labor force was unionized in 1953 than is the case today. Between 1953 and 1968 the total labor force in unions declined from 25 percent to 23 percent; in 1979 it was 20 percent. The same is true on the output side of the market.

The four-firm concentration ratio in an industry is the percentage of total sales in the industry made by the industry's largest four firms. Let us look at the percentage of value added in the private sector that is generated in industries with four-firm concentration ratios in excess of 50 percent; if there is any significant change at all, it is that the relative importance of such industries is declining. For example, in 1954 the percentage of value added generated by such industries was 29.9 percent; in 1958 it was 30.2 percent; in 1966 it was 28.6 percent; and in 1970 it was 26.3 percent.[10] These figures do not suggest an increasing concentration of economic power.

The only relevant measure of market power of a firm is its market share. The reason many individuals think that market power is increasing is that they equate growing absolute size with growing market shares. The fact that the 200 largest corporations own an increasing share of manufacturing assets does not say that market power is becoming more concentrated. Many of these corporations are conglomerates, and a conglomerate sells in many *unrelated* product markets at the same time. Clearly, an economy with only 200 corporations, each selling in money markets so that in each market there are at least 10 sellers, is more competitive than an economy with 1000 markets and 1000 firms, each with a monopoly in one of the 1000 markets.

THE 1962 GUIDELINES

To help us understand the guidelines, let's consider some elementary arithmetic. If we divide the dollar value of total output (PQ) into the part going to labor (N) and the part going to other factors that we shall lump together under the name of capital (K), we can write:

$$PQ = WN + \pi K \qquad (12\text{-}8)$$

where W is the wage rate and π is total nonlabor income divided by the dollar value of nonlabor inputs. "Labor's share" of total output is WN/PQ and "capital's share" is $\pi K/PQ$. These two shares remain constant if WN and πK each grow by the same percentage amount as PQ.

If we divide Equation 12-8 by N we get:

$$P\frac{Q}{N} = W + \pi\frac{K}{N} \qquad (12\text{-}9)$$

Relative shares of total output will be constant if each term in Equation 12-9 is increased by the same percentage. Suppose Q/N, the average productivity of labor, increases by 10 percent. If relative factor shares are to be held constant, the wage rate (W) and *profit per labor-hour* $(\pi \cdot K/N)$ must be increased by 10 percent. (Note that it is *not* total profits or the profit rate that must be increased with the wage rate. The relevant comparison is between the wage rate and profit per labor-hour.) If Q/N increases, the wage rate and profit per labor-hour can both increase without anything happening to prices.

The guidelines said that an industry that has experienced a gain in productivity (Q/N) equal to the average gain of all industries should increase its wage rates by the same percentage as that productivity gain and leave prices unchanged. These actions will keep relative factor shares constant. An industry that lags behind the national average productivity gain should also grant wage increases equal to the national average productivity gain and, in order to keep relative factor shares constant, it should raise prices. An industry that registered productivity gains in excess of the national average would still increase wages by an amount equal to the national average productivity gain, and it would lower prices to maintain relative factor shares.

CRITICISMS OF THE GUIDELINES

The effects of the guidelines are to make wage rates equal in all industries, to make the general wage level increase at a rate equal to the national average gain in productivity, to make prices in industries with low gains in productivity rise, and to make prices in industries with high gains in productivity fall. Some claim that these effects duplicate the results of perfect labor and commodity markets. It is true that with homogeneous labor and perfect labor markets, wage rates would tend toward equality. *However, they are made equal in perfect markets by resource transfers responding to differences in wages.* The guidelines would never permit any wage differences, and so this movement or reallocation could not take place. The guidelines would give us equal wage rates between industries, but the equality would be *imposed* rather than the *result* of resource reallocation. Guidelines, just like direct wage-price controls, prevent the price mechanism from allocating resources, and they provide no alternative mechanism for resource allocation.

In perfectly competitive markets, prices would not necessarily rise in industries with measured productivity gains less than the national average. Prices are established by the interaction of cost and demand. Cost curves could be shifting upward because of lagging productivity gains, and prices could still fall if demand for the product fell. The guidelines completely ignored the demand side of price determination.

Finally, under a regime of wage and price controls or guidelines it becomes easy for government decision makers to ignore the rate of growth of the money stock. Indeed, in order to keep interest rates down, the Fed may increase the rate of growth of the money stock. As we saw in Section 11 of Chapter 11, the short-run effect (the liquidity effect) of increases in the money stock is to lower interest rates. The Fed typically pays attention to the liquidity effect only, completely ignoring the longer run income and inflation expectation effects. These increases in the money growth rate will mean higher aggregate demand in nominal terms, and so inflationary pressure will build up. The controlled prices will become more and more unrealistic, and the distortion of resource allocation will worsen.

THE GUIDELINES AND CONTROLS IN PRACTICE

Distortion of resource allocation occurred during the period of wage and price controls from 1971 to 1974. Strict controls did not allow consumers to bid the price of desired products up. Of course, this kind of control led to shortages in some products whose relative prices should have been rising, and surpluses in the opposite cases. Gas lines were common, as were lines for certain meat products. If the cost of a buyer's time is included in purchase prices, the purchase price of gasoline, for example, was astronomical even though the money price was held down by government control.

When controls were lifted in 1974, the economy experienced a spurt in money prices and wages as they caught up to where they would have been without the controls. In fact, in many cases in the absence of controls prices would have been lower than what they became in 1974, because the controls decreased the supply of many goods.

Many economists feel that controls will reduce inflationary expectations and thus reduce inflation. Our analysis suggests that this is wrong. Inflationary expectations can cause a one-shot increase in prices, but this increase cannot continue unless the inflation is "ratified" by shifts in either the **LM** curve (monetary expansion) or the **IS** curve (fiscal expansion). Similarly, a reduction in inflationary expectations can cause a decrease in prices; but prices will rise again unless monetary and fiscal restraints are subsequently pursued. In the United States during 1971–73 apparently no restraint was in sight. In fact, 1972 was a year of extremely rapid monetary expansion, which could only continue to fan the flames of inflation.

In the late 1970s, President Carter returned to a policy of guidelines. These guidelines were somewhat different from those of Presidents Kennedy and Johnson, but the intent was the same. Initially, wage and fringe benefit guidelines were set at a maximum of 7 percent, and price increases were limited to 0.5 percent less than the rate of increase in 1976–77. Other parts of the program included a profit ceiling of 6.5 percent above prior years unless accounted for by volume increases, policies that would minimize the inflationary impact of government regulations, and allowances for wage increases greater than 7 percent (but not more than 8 percent) in multiyear wage contracts as long as the average increase did not exceed 7 percent.[11] The success of these programs is questionable. The rate of inflation for 1978, which was forecasted to be 7 percent by government economists, was just a little less than 10 percent. This experience was repeated in 1979 with actual price increases far exceeding government predictions. The actual rate of inflation in 1979 was 13.2 percent, compared to a forecasted rate of 7 percent. By the end of the first quarter of 1980 the inflation rate was over 18 percent. Since the inflation rate was under 5 percent when President Carter took office, it seems that his guidelines have not done much good.

TIP

The notable lack of success of all of these programs led to the proposal of TIP — tax-based incomes policies.[12] In fact, all controls, guidelines, and guideposts are incomes policies since incomes policies are defined as policies where price and wage changes are determined by government decree, thus circumventing the market process. The TIP program would set a guideline for wages based on the actual increase in productivity of the economy and the rate of inflation. Firms that allowed wage increases beyond the wage guideline rate would find their profit tax increased over the base rate. For example, if the guideline wage increase is 7 percent and a firm allowed wage increases of 10 percent, the 3 percent difference would be subject to a penalty. If the penalty was set at 1.5, the profit tax for the corporation would increase by 4.5 percent ($3\% \times$ penalty rate). In this way, corporations, worried about their competitive positions and the value of their stock, would be induced to stay within the guidelines.

TIP has the same defects as other incomes policies; it does not attack the cause of inflation, and it interferes with the functioning of the price mechanism in the market. The first objection is obvious; there are no restrictions on budget deficits or monetary expansion. The proponents assume a cost-push inflation, which we have shown (Section 12-3) to be an illusion. The second objection stems from the assignment of one standard. If all wages are mandated to rise by a maximum of, say, 7 percent, how are firms in expanding markets going to bid away workers from other industries? With guidelines the ability to attract workers is much reduced.

As long as we recognize that inflation is caused by a growth in monetary demand exceeding the growth in real production, the cause can be attacked. Monetary and fiscal restraint, not cosmetic incomes policies, are the solutions. Restrictive policies do have economic and social costs, but so does inflation. The further we allow inflation and inflationary expectations to rise, the greater are the costs, and the more difficult it is to get rid of the problem. The economic attitudes of the public have already drastically changed. What was looked at with alarm in the 1950s, a 2 to 3 percent rate of inflation, is now viewed as virtually impossible to achieve. Only positive steps will work to reduce our expectations.

SUMMARY

In this chapter we have seen the importance of the fact that the "price level" is actually only the average of many individual prices. We have stressed the dangers inherent in attempts to control this average price level by imposing direct controls on the individual prices that make it up. All inflation ultimately rests on excessive growth of nominal aggregate demand (total spending); hence any inflation that is initiated by cost increases must be supported by increases in aggregate demand.

During an unanticipated inflation wealth is transferred from net monetary creditors to net monetary debtors. Even anticipated inflation has adverse economic effects: investment is reduced, real income taxes rise, and market rates of interest rise by more than the expected rate of inflation.

Inflationary recession results from the misdirection of resources during inflation and the time lags involved in restrictive policy. After a restrictive monetary policy is implemented, a new equilibrium set of prices, wages, and interest rates must be attained in order to reestablish equilibrium. This equilibrium set must be searched for, and in the interim the unemployment rate will rise above its natural level.

To the extent that the imposition of price and wage controls reduces the expected inflation rate, the time lags involved in a restrictive monetary policy may be reduced. The controls by themselves cannot reduce the equilibrium inflation rate; only an appropriately restrictive monetary (or fiscal) policy can do that.

Wage and price controls, whether direct as in the period 1971–74 or indirect in the form of guidelines and/or incomes policies, make it impossible for changes in relative prices to coordinate the plans and actions of the multitude of individual transactors in an economy. If changes in relative prices do not coordinate the plans and actions of all transactors, those plans and actions must be either uncoordinated (shortages or surpluses existing in most markets) or coordinated by authority (government deciding what gets produced and for whom). There is either chaos or loss of freedom.

QUESTIONS

1. The Hayekian analysis of misdirected resources implies that only an accelerating inflation can postpone the recession that a prior inflation has made necessary. Why?
2. Using Hayek's analysis, figure out what happens when an existing inflation continues at a steady pace and becomes fully anticipated by all transactors.

3. Using diagrams like Figures 12-1 and 12-2, analyze the "inflationary" consequences of a large increase in the price of oil declared by the international oil cartel, OPEC. Why do you think President Carter frequently tried to blame the inflation that existed from 1977 to 1980 on OPEC? Why do you think so many people believed him?
4. During an inflation the claim is frequently made that if real money balances are declining, there is actually a scarcity of money. What do you think of that claim?
5. Evaluate the fixed money growth rate rule in light of Hayek's model of misdirection of resources from inflation.
6. The federal government is a net monetary debtor. Do you think this fact has anything to do with its propensity toward creating inflation? Why or why not?
7. In 1979 and 1980 there was much hand-wringing over the decline of productivity in the United States. New capital formation was lagging behind historical norms. What do these two facts have to do with inflation?
8. What does inflation have to do with people's willingness to save? What does inflation have to do with people's willingness to save in banks and savings and loan associations? What does your answer imply about the housing market?
9. Would an inflationary recession that results from a restrictive monetary policy aimed at an existing anticipated inflation be complicated by misdirections of resources induced by the restrictive monetary policy? Why?
10. One of the excuses given by the Nixon administration for implementing wage and price controls was that such controls would reduce inflationary expectations and thus make inflation easier to control. Evaluate that claim both theoretically and historically. Could it happen? Did it happen?
11. A feature of the Carter guidelines that was proposed by the administration but not implemented by Congress was real wage insurance. A worker whose wage increase remained within the 7 percent limit would receive a tax benefit to reimburse him if inflation exceeded 7 percent. What effect would this scheme have on the allocation of resources?

NOTES

1. See note 10 in the last chapter. The analysis in this section is based on F. A. Hayek, *Prices and Production* (New York: Augustus M. Kelly, Publishers, 1967).
2. In fact, however, ever since World War II velocity has been gradually increasing. This upward trend does not change the analysis above, since the

change is gradual and predictable. A given money stock can support an increased price level if and only if velocity rises to accommodate the increase. The empirical fact is that velocity does not change value whenever some union is granted an "excessive wage demand."

3. The discussion in Section 12-3 follows Armen A. Alchian and William R. Allen, *University Economics: Elements of Inquiry*, 3d ed. (Belmont, Calif.: Wadsworth Publishing, 1972), pp. 95–97.

4. Milton Friedman has been a long-time advocate of this position. See, for example, *A Program for Monetary Stability* (New York: Fordham University Press, 1960), pp. 90–99.

5. James M. Buchanan and Richard E. Wagner, *Democracy in Deficit* (New York: Academic Press, 1977).

6. Albert E. Burger, "Is Inflation All Due to Money?" *Federal Reserve Bank of St. Louis Review* (December 1978).

7. The discussion in Section 12-6 is based on Alchian and Allen, *University Economics*, pp. 674–77.

8. For further discussion of the ideas in Section 12-7, see John A. Tatom and James E. Turley, "Inflation and Taxes: Disincentives for Capital Formation," *Federal Reserve Bank of St. Louis Review* (January 1978).

9. Milton Friedman, *Dollars and Deficits* (Englewood Cliffs, N.J.: Prentice-Hall, 1968), pp. 51–52.

10. *Federal Reserve Bank of St. Louis Review* (July 1971), p. 28.

11. White Paper: The President's Anti-Inflation Program (October 24, 1978).

12. Nancy Ammon Jianakoplos, "A Tax-Based Incomes Policy (TIP): What's It All About?" *Federal Reserve Bank of St. Louis Review* (February 1978).

PART

6

RECENT THEORETICAL INNOVATIONS

The New Quantity Theory
and Phillips Curves

The **IS-LM** models we have used in this textbook were developed before the modern reformulation of the quantity theory. Nevertheless, we have used them to analyze the modern quantity theory. Suppose we didn't have these models and wanted to devise a geometric representation of the modern quantity theory. What would we come up with? The main task of this chapter is to construct a new set of models that can be used to represent the modern quantity theory on its own terms.

13-1 THE ST. LOUIS MODEL

The model we shall use was constructed in 1970 by two economists, L. C. Andersen and K. M. Carlson, of the Federal Reserve Bank of St. Louis.[1] The model depicts both short- and long-run effects of changes in the rate of growth of the money stock, taking positive information costs into account.

THE GEOMETRY OF THE MODEL

Figure 13-1 depicts the short-run (S) and long-run (L) relationships between the percentage rate of change in the money stock ($\Delta M/M$), the percentage rate of change in total spending ($\Delta Y/Y$), the percentage rate of change in real output ($\Delta Q/Q$), and the percentage rate of change in prices ($\Delta P/P$).

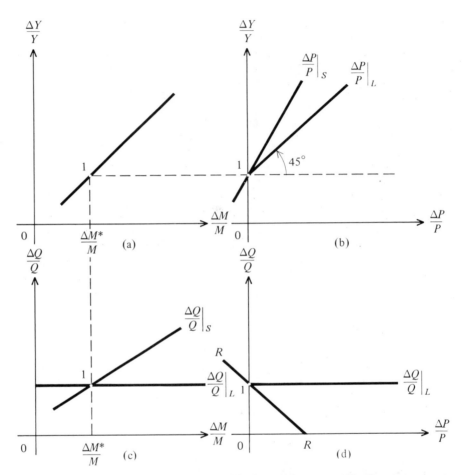

Figure 13-1   Equilibrium with the modern quantity theory.

Panel a represents the key assumption of the model, a direct and stable relationship between changes in the money stock and changes in total spending. In
other words, $\Delta V/V$ (percentage rate of change in velocity) in Equation 13-1 is
small and stable.

$$\frac{\Delta M}{M} + \frac{\Delta V}{V} = \frac{\Delta P}{P} + \frac{\Delta Q}{Q} = \frac{\Delta Y}{Y} \tag{13-1}$$

If $\Delta V/V = 0$ (i.e., if velocity were constant), the line in panel a would be 45°. If
velocity fell (rose) as the money stock increased, the line would be shallower

(steeper) than 45°. Since total spending is always equal to the product of the money stock and velocity, whenever the money stock changes we can predict the resulting change in total spending as long as velocity is predictable. As we saw in Section 6 of Chapter 9, velocity is indeed stable, changing very slowly and predictably over time.

The horizontal lines in panels c and d reflect the fact that the long-run rate of growth of real output is independent of monetary policy. It depends on the rate of growth of the labor supply and the rate of development of technology. Both of these lines are labeled $\Delta Q/Q|_L$.

Since

$$\frac{\Delta Y}{Y} = \frac{\Delta P}{P} + \frac{\Delta Q}{Q} \qquad (13\text{-}2)$$

the point labeled 1 in panel b is where the economy would be if the rate of growth of the money stock were set at the rate that caused the rate of growth of total spending to equal the long-run growth rate of real output. Under these circumstances the rate of growth of the price index would be zero. Equation 13-2 says that the rate of growth of total spending has two parts—increases in prices and increases in real output. If all of the increase in total spending is in real output, there is no total spending growth left over to be reflected in increases in prices. The height of point 1 in panel b is equal to $\Delta Q/Q|_L$. The rate of growth of the money stock associated with point 1 is labeled $\Delta M^*/M$ in panel a.

Again, since $\Delta Y/Y = \Delta P/P + \Delta Q/Q$, for every $\Delta Y/Y$ there will be a line of slope minus 1 in panel d. Such a line merely represents the fact that for a given $\Delta Y/Y$, any increase in $\Delta P/P$ must be matched by an equal decrease in $\Delta Q/Q$. In other words, if more of a given increase in spending is in the form of increases in prices, less of it can be in the form of increases in real output. The line for $\Delta Y/Y = \Delta Q/Q|_L$ is labeled RR in panel d. Point 1 in panel d is where the economy would be if the actual rate of growth of real output equaled $\Delta Q/Q|_L$ and the rate of growth of prices were zero. With an unchanged rate of growth of the money stock and therefore of total spending, $\Delta P/P$ could become positive only if the actual rate of growth of real output fell below $\Delta Q/Q|_L$.

If point 1 in panel a represents a 5 percent growth rate of the money stock, $\Delta V/V = 0\%$, and $\Delta Q/Q|_L = 5\%$, the rate of growth of nominal income would be 5 percent and the rate of change of prices would be zero. Assuming no change in velocity, if the rate of growth of the money stock is set equal to the long-run sustainable rate of growth of real income (recall our discussion of rule vs. discretion in monetary policy in Section 4 of Chapter 12), no inflation would result.

If the actual rate of growth of the money stock were larger than $\Delta M^*/M$, $\Delta Y/Y$ would exceed $\Delta Q/Q|_L$. Since $\Delta Q/Q|_L$ is the long-run ceiling on the rate of growth of real output, this situation would eventually involve $\Delta P/P$ equal to the difference between $\Delta Y/Y$ and $\Delta Q/Q|_L$. This fact is represented by the line labeled $\Delta P/P|_L$ in panel b. Note that this line must have a slope of 1. If total spending increases 10 percent and real output can grow only 4 percent in the long run, the remaining 6 percent will show up as price increases. A 6 percent increase in total spending above the long-run real growth rate results in a 6 percent increase in prices.

In the short run, however, it is possible to have actual $\Delta Q/Q$ exceed $\Delta Q/Q|_L$. If job seekers temporarily reduced the time spent in search below normal levels, we could get a *temporary* spurt in $\Delta Q/Q$. This would happen, for instance, when the accelerated rate of growth of the money stock started to increase prices and wages. The higher wages would at first be interpreted as a fortunate sampling of wage offers, and time spent in search would decrease. When the inflation rate that workers expect caught up to the actual inflation rate, the normal search time would be resumed. This means that at first when $\Delta Y/Y$ is increased, some of the increase will come in the form of increases in $\Delta Q/Q$, and so less will come in the form of $\Delta P/P$ than will in the long run. This phenomenon is represented by the line labeled $\Delta P/P|_S$ in panel b.

Since $\Delta Q/Q$ can temporarily exceed $\Delta Q/Q|_L$ when $\Delta M/M$ is increased, we must represent this relationship by a line such as that labeled $\Delta Q/Q|_S$ in panel c. The slope of this line depends on the line labeled $\Delta P/P|_S$, as will be made clear in the next series of diagrams.

INCREASE OF THE MONEY GROWTH RATE

If $\Delta M/M = \Delta M^*/M$ (that equality has been the case for some time), the economy can be pictured at each of the points labeled 1 in Figure 13-1. Suppose now that the rate of growth of M is accelerated. What would happen? Figure 13-2 duplicates Figure 13-1 as the starting point and includes the changes that would take place.

If $\Delta M/M$ is increased to $\Delta M'/M$, the rate of growth of total spending, $\Delta Y/Y$, will increase. This change will increase some prices and wages. The higher nominal wages cause less time than normal to be used in job search and the unemployment rate drops below its natural level. The economy is at point 2 in panel b. Prices are rising at the rate of $\Delta P/P_2$.

Since $\Delta Y/Y$ has increased, the line of slope minus 1 that describes the combinations of $\Delta P/P$ and $\Delta Q/Q$ consistent with a given $\Delta Y/Y$ will shift to that labeled VV in panel d. Since $\Delta P/P = \Delta P/P_2$, $\Delta Q/Q = 0T$. Since unemployment is below its natural level, the growth rate of real output can exceed $\Delta Q/Q|_L$. The economy is at point 2 in each of the diagrams.

Eventually job seekers recognize that the high nominal wage rates aren't any higher than before, in real terms. They begin to anticipate the inflation, and as

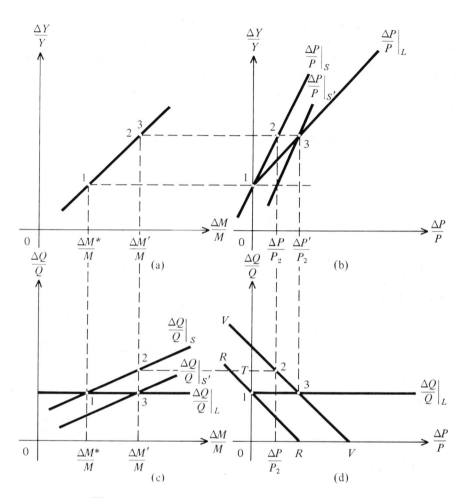

Figure 13-2 Increase in the money growth rate.

they do, search periods begin to return to normal. Since total spending is constant and since longer search times imply lower real output growth, the actual inflation rate will increase. As long as the actual inflation rate exceeds the expected inflation rate, the growth rate of real output can exceed $\Delta Q/Q|_L$. Unemployment will be below its natural level. As the expected inflation rate gets closer to the actual inflation rate, the lines labeled $\Delta P/P|_S$ and $\Delta Q/Q|_S$ in panels b and c shift toward the lines labeled $\Delta P/P|_{S'}$ and $\Delta Q/Q|_{S'}$. In panel d the economy moves from point 2 toward point 3. When the expected inflation rate

Table 13-1 Impact of an increase in the growth rate of the money stock

	1	2	3
$\Delta M/M$	5%	8%	8%
$\Delta V/V$	0%	0%	0%
$\Delta P/P$	0%	2%*	3%
$\Delta Q/Q$	5%	6%*	5%

*These are representative values. In reality $0 < \Delta P/P <$ 3%, 5% $< \Delta Q/Q <$ 8%. Any numbers falling within these ranges and summing to 8 percent would have been possible.

equals the actual inflation rate (which has been increasing), the economy will be at each of the points labeled 3 in the figure. The higher rate of growth of the money stock has eventually resulted in a higher equilibrium inflation rate than before, but the unemployment rate is at its initial (natural) level.

To illustrate, let's begin with the same basic assumptions as before: $\Delta M/M =$ 5%, $\Delta V/V = 0\%$, $\Delta P/P = 0\%$, and $\Delta Q/Q = 5\%$. Table 13-1 shows the initial, intermediate, and final positions (those we have labeled 1, 2, and 3 respectively) if $\Delta M/M$ rises to 8 percent. Try to relate the percentages in the table to Figure 13-2.

DECREASE OF THE MONEY GROWTH RATE

Suppose we start in an inflationary situation to which the economy has fully adapted and the Fed decreases the rate of growth of the money stock in order to reduce inflation. Figure 13-3 shows what would happen.

The decrease in the rate of growth of the money stock from $\Delta M/M_1$ to $\Delta M/M_2$ reduces the rate of growth of total spending and hence shifts the line of slope minus 1 in panel d from RR to VV. The rate of growth of some prices and wages decreases and this decrease has the effect of lengthening time spent in job search. The lower nominal wage offers are misinterpreted as unfortunate samples from an unchanged labor market. Unemployment rises above its natural rate, and the rate of growth of real output falls below $\Delta Q/Q|_L$ to $0T$ in panel d. The lowered rate of growth of the money stock is at first associated with a lower growth rate of real output and unemployment. The economy is at point 2 in panel c. The expected inflation rate exceeds the actual inflation rate, and so the unemployment rate rises above its natural level and the rate of growth of real output falls below its equilibrium value.

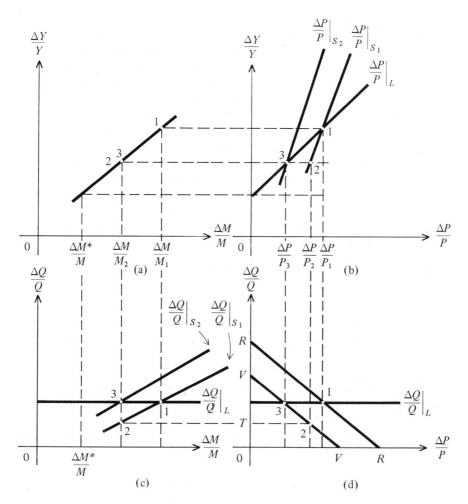

Figure 13-3 Decrease in the money growth rate.

Workers begin to anticipate the decreased inflation rate. They revise their reservation prices (the prices they hold out for in the job search process) downward. The lines labeled $\Delta P/P|_{S_1}$ and $\Delta Q/Q|_{S_1}$ shift toward those labeled $\Delta P/P|_{S_2}$ and $\Delta Q/Q|_{S_2}$ in panels b and c, respectively. The economy moves from point 2 toward point 3 in panel d. The actual inflation rate continues to decrease, but as long as this decrease is not fully anticipated, unemployment will be above its natural level. When the inflation rate has reached its new equilibrium value, $\Delta P/P_3$, and when the expected inflation rate also equals $\Delta P/P_3$, the economy will be in a new equilibrium position at the points labeled 3 in the figure. The economy will have a new lower equilibrium inflation rate and a natural unemployment rate. In the short run, however, the economy goes through a period of higher-than-normal unemployment and lower-than-normal real output growth rates.

A new table is not necessary for this case. Table 13-1, read from right to left (instead of left to right), would apply; that is, point 3 in Table 13-1 would be labeled point 1 in our current example.

IN CONCLUSION

The new quantity theory is consistent with the Keynesian analysis in the short run. The initial shock absorber is real output and employment, but the new quantity theory takes explicit account of expectations to derive the further, long-run effects. As we have seen, these long-run effects are changes in the inflation (deflation) rate rather than changes in the rate of growth of real output or employment.

Our diagrammatic representation of the St. Louis model depicts its most important features. However, the model is actually a mathematical model involving six simultaneous equations. The effects of government spending on nominal income and of monetary changes on nominal rates of interest are included in the model. In the empirical testing of the model, Andersen and Carlson found that changes in government spending have a direct effect on nominal income, but the effect lasts only two quarters and then reverses itself. After four quarters, changes in high employment government expenditures have no net effect at all. Moreover, the testing of the model verified the existence of the liquidity, income, and inflation expectation effects of monetary changes on the nominal rate of interest that we discussed in Section 11 of Chapter 11.

13-2   THE PHILLIPS CURVE AND THE ST. LOUIS MODEL

The Phillips curve is so named because of an article by A. W. Phillips, who tried to discover the exact position of such curves in the United Kingdom economy. Phillips used data on nominal wage rates and unemployment rates for three periods: 1861–1913, 1913–48, and 1948–57. He found the line that best fit the data for the first period and demonstrated that the data for the subsequent periods were close to this line. The line was interpreted to mean that there is a permanent trade-off between unemployment and inflation. Unemployment could be reduced *on a permanent basis* simply by accepting a higher permanent inflation rate. Similarly, the permanent price an economy would have to pay to reduce inflation would be a permanent increase in the unemployment rate.

The St. Louis model implies that the only way the unemployment rate can be made temporarily to fall below its natural level is to accelerate the growth rate of total spending and thus the growth rate of prices. Rising prices and rising nominal wages induce job seekers to spend less than the normal amount of time in search because they interpret the high nominal wage rate offers as fortunate samples in an unchanged labor market. Moreover, unemployment will temporarily increase relative to its natural rate when some deflation induces job seekers to spend more time than usual in search.

In Figure 13-4 the line labeled AA is the short-run Phillips curve we discussed in Section 7 of Chapter 7. The rate of inflation ($\Delta P/P$) appears on the vertical axis, and the unemployment rate (u) appears on the horizontal axis. The relationship between the inflation and unemployment rates is drawn convex toward

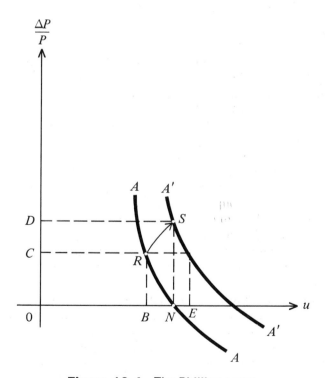

Figure 13-4   The Phillips curve.

the origin to reflect the proposition that the higher the observed rate of inflation, the more difficult it will be to trick job seekers into expecting zero inflation. Increases in the inflation rate encounter diminishing returns in terms of reductions in the unemployment rate.

Suppose the rate of growth of the money stock is held at the level that caused total spending to grow at the rate $\Delta Q/Q|_L$, and the economy has fully adapted to this growth rate. The unemployment rate would be at its natural level, $0N$ in the figure, and the rate of inflation would be zero. If the rate of growth of total spending were increased and maintained at its higher level, at first the unemployment rate would drop below $0N$ (to, say, $0B$) and this rate would be associated with inflation rate $0C$. Because the rate of change of total spending is held constant at the higher level, $0C$ is not the new long-run equilibrium inflation rate.

As workers begin to anticipate the higher inflation, unemployment will begin to increase toward its natural level. As it does (because the rate of increase of total spending is constant), the actual inflation rate increases. The economy moves along a path from point R to point S in the figure. Only when the inflation rate reaches its new equilibrium, $0D$, and this rate is fully anticipated, will unemployment return to $0N$. The line that represents the relationship between inflation and unemployment will have shifted to $A'A'$ in the figure. Each unemployment rate will be associated with a higher inflation rate than before.

If, after the economy has fully adapted to inflation rate $0D$, the rate of growth of total spending decreases to its original level, at first the unemployment rate will rise above $0N$ (to, say, $0E$), where it will stay until job seekers revise downward their estimates of best offers. This increase in unemployment to $0E$ will be accompanied by a decrease in the inflation rate to $0C$. When job seekers' expectations are revised downward, unemployment will diminish, permitting more real output growth; thus inflation will decline. Eventually, the natural rate of unemployment will be restored and inflation will stop.

The line that represents the relationship between the unemployment rate and the inflation rate shifts whenever expectations change. A given line is permanent only so long as the actual inflation rate is the equilibrium inflation rate and the inflation is fully anticipated.

13-3 PERMANENT TRADE-OFF VS. PRICE EXPECTATIONS

Consider Figure 13-5. The permanent trade-off interpretation of the Phillips curve indicates that if the economy were at point A, with zero inflation and 4 percent unemployment, the government would "buy" a reduction in the unemploy-

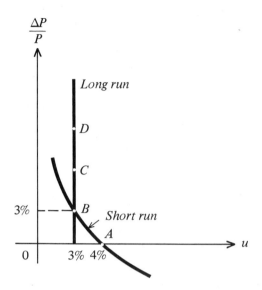

Figure 13-5 Long- and short-run Phillips curves with accelerating inflation.

ment rate from 4 percent to 3 percent by causing an inflation of 3 percent. As long as the inflation rate is maintained at 3 percent the unemployment rate will remain at 3 percent. With this interpretation the government policymakers simply need to choose which point on the fixed Phillips curve they wish to attain.

The information cost (or price expectations) interpretation of the Phillips curve indicates that the reduction in unemployment will be temporary. The temporary drop in unemployment happens because workers' expectations concerning inflation lag behind the actual inflation rate. Workers don't realize that inflation is occurring, and think that the higher nominal wage offers are lucky samples and so reduce search time below normal. As soon as they fully anticipate the price increases, they will return to normal search periods and unemployment will return to its initial level.

If government policymakers wanted to maintain the unemployment rate at 3 percent, they would have to pursue policies that *accelerated* the rate of inflation. The actual rate of inflation would have to be kept above the inflation rate that workers expect. Since workers would revise their expectations upward as actual inflation rates increased, the actual inflation rates would have to keep getting bigger and bigger. The economy would move along a vertical line to points such as C and D in Figure 13-5. The long-run Phillips curve is a vertical line. If the expected inflation rate ever caught up to the actual inflation rate, an unemployment rate of 4 percent would again be observed.

In Figure 13-6, suppose the economy is in inflationary equilibrium at point A. Unemployment is at its natural level (say 5 percent) and the inflation rate is 6 percent. The Phillips curve that exists at this point in time is drawn in the figure. If it is thought that this Phillips curve is fixed and represents a permanent tradeoff between inflation and unemployment, it will appear that the only way the inflation rate can be held to 2 percent is to increase unemployment to 7 percent.

Let's suppose that government policymakers decide to maintain an inflation rate of 2 percent. Initially the decrease in the inflation rate will not be anticipated by labor. Search times will be lengthened because labor misconstrues decreases in nominal wage offers as decreases in real wage offers. Unemployment will increase to 7 percent. The actual inflation rate is 2 percent, but the expected inflation rate is 6 percent. After some time labor's expected inflation rate will be revised downward, and normal search periods will be resumed. Unemployment will return to its natural level, and the policymakers will be pleasantly surprised. They thought the economy would have to tolerate 7 percent unemployment as the price that must be paid in order to achieve a 2 percent inflation rate.

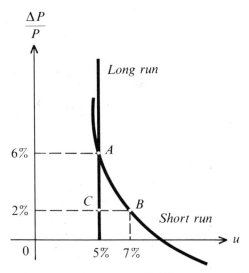

Figure 13-6   Long- and short-run Phillips curves with deflation.

Actually the economy moved from point *A* to point *B* and then, as the expected inflation rate became equal to the actual inflation rate, to point *C*. The long-run Phillips curve is again a vertical line.

The price expectations interpretation of the Phillips curve indicates that no matter what the actual inflation rate is, *if the inflation rate is maintained*, it will become expected or fully anticipated and will thus be associated with the natural rate of unemployment. The only way the unemployment rate can be reduced below its natural level for any significant period of time is to push the inflation rate up and up. The actual inflation rate may in this way be kept above the expected inflation rate. But this tactic cannot work for very long because people soon catch on to the pattern of *increasing* inflation and they then change their expectations.

Permanent reductions in unemployment simply cannot be attained by *any* amount of inflation. The permanent trade-off interpretation of the Phillips curve has been discarded by contemporary economists because the price expectations interpretation better fits the actual experience of all Western countries at least since the 1960s.

13-4 THE INFLATION–UNEMPLOYMENT TRADE-OFF IN THE UNITED STATES

We can examine the alternative interpretations of the Phillips curve by looking at the data for the United States for 1960–78. Figure 13-7 presents these data; the unemployment rate is the average for the year indicated while the inflation rate is the rate for the full year. This figure indicates that the actual nature of the unemployment–inflation trade-off is inconsistent with the permanent trade-off view of the Phillips curve. The 1960s were characterized by a relatively stable relationship, but the trade-off has clearly shifted to the right in two stages in the 1970s. Changes in price expectations (as well as technical factors discussed in Chapter 7) caused these shifts.[2]

As these shifts occur, the costs of reducing inflation to any target level rise. Economists believe that inflationary expectations change slowly. Any attempt substantially to reduce the rate of inflation will cause a more severe recession if the short-run Phillips curve is shifting to the right. It is safe to say that a reduction in the rate of inflation to a permanent 2 to 4 percent rate will require a permanently reduced monetary expansion and a lengthy, but temporary, period of above-normal unemployment.

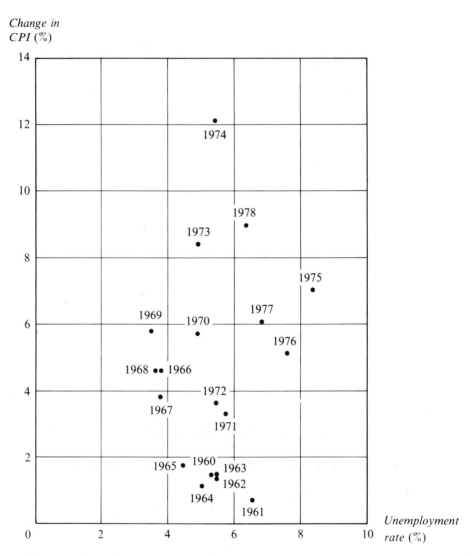

Figure 13-7 Actual "Phillips curve" data for the United States. (Data from *Survey of Current Business*, various issues)

SUMMARY

In this chapter we have developed an alternative to the **IS-LM** model. This new model is consistent with the short-run **IS-LM** model. It has the advantage of showing the long-run effects of monetary expansion as well as of being cast in terms of rates of change (rather than levels) of the variables.

Empirical testing of the St. Louis model indicates that fiscal policy has only temporary effects. After a total four quarters from the implementation of a fiscal policy change, its net effect is zero. The same empirical testing verifies the existence of the liquidity, income, and inflation expectation effects of monetary changes on the nominal rate of interest.

The approach of the St. Louis model to the trade-off between unemployment and inflation is consistent with the modern theory of the Phillips curve discussed in Chapter 7.

QUESTIONS

1. Construct an **IS-LM** diagram that incorporates the fact that the real capacity of the economy (Q_f) increases over time. Trace through the effect of an increased rate of growth of the money supply. Can you see why the **IS-LM** framework is unsatisfactory when such questions are asked?

2. Using the Andersen-Carlson diagrams, trace through the effects of an increase in the real capacity growth rate. Assume that the money stock growth rate is unchanged.

3. Do the same as in Question 2, but assume that the money stock growth rate is increased by the same amount as the increase in the real capacity growth rate.

4. If the rate of growth of total spending is increased and maintained at the higher level, this change will at first cause increased inflation and a lower unemployment rate. Soon the inflation will increase and so too will unemployment. The process stops when the inflation rate has attained its new equilibrium value and the unemployment rate has returned to its natural level. Do you agree or not? Why?

5. Represent the inflationary recession phenomenon with a Phillips curve diagram.

6. How do the results of the Andersen and Karnosky model discussed in Chapter 11 fit into the St. Louis model?

7. In a speech in 1972 at Berkeley, John Kenneth Galbraith stated that economists did not believe that a rising rate of inflation and a rising rate of unemployment could be observed simultaneously. Is this view consistent with the

permanent trade-off interpretation of the Phillips curve? Is it consistent with the price expectations interpretation of the Phillips curve? Why or why not? Is your answer symmetrical—can decreasing rates of inflation and decreasing unemployment occur simultaneously?

8. This chapter considers the effects of monetary changes on prices and output. Beginning with Figure 13-1, show the impact of a permanent increase in annual government expenditures on the rate of change of real output, prices, and the money stock. What assumptions must you make to arrive at a solution?

NOTES

1. L. C. Andersen and K. M. Carlson, "A Monetarist Model for Economic Stabilization," *Federal Reserve Bank of St. Louis Review* (April 1970), pp. 7–25.
2. Robert E. Lucas has developed and tested a model of the relationship between output changes and inflation that verifies the expectations view of the Phillips curve for 18 countries. See "Some International Evidence on the Output-Inflation Tradeoff," *American Economic Review* (June 1973), pp. 326–34.

The Reinterpretation of Keynes

Many economists think of John Maynard Keynes as the father of modern macroeconomic analysis and policy. As we saw in Chapter 3, Keynes' *General Theory of Employment, Interest, and Money*, published in 1936, marked a turning point in the way economists thought about the causes and cures of depressions and recessions. *The General Theory* itself is a very hard book to read, and it is even more difficult to understand. Soon after its appearance, a very important journal article, "Mr. Keynes and the Classics: A Suggested Interpretation," written by John R. Hicks, was published (*Econometrica*, April 1937). Hicks' interpretation of *The General Theory* became generally accepted as the correct interpretation. It is his interpretation that most economists refer to when they use the expression "Keynesian economics." Hicks' interpretation of Keynes is the basis for Chapters 4, 5, and 10 in this text.

In 1965 Robert W. Clower wrote "The Keynesian Counterrevolution: A Theoretical Appraisal" (in *The Theory of Interest Rates*, edited by F. H. Hahn and F. Brechling), in which he proposed the broad outlines of a reinterpretation of *The General Theory*. Clower's seminal suggestions were explored and developed by Axel Leijonhufvud in his 1968 book *On Keynesian Economics and the Economics of Keynes*. Clower and Leijonhufvud subsequently expanded their "new macro theory" in several journal articles. In this chapter we will examine the Clower-Leijonhufvud reinterpretation of Keynes.

14-1 WALRASIAN GENERAL EQUILIBRIUM

Look back to the tabulation of individual and market planned excess demands in Figure 3-1. In the bottom row each planned market excess demand is represented by a term like p_iX_i. The X_i is the physical quantity of the difference between the planned market demand for good i and the planned market supply for good i. By multiplying that physical quantity by p_i, the money price of good i, the planned market excess demand for good i is expressed in dollars. Now the physical quantity of the planned market demand for good i depends on the price of good i and the prices of other goods as well. So too does the physical quantity of the planned market supply. Therefore, p_iX_i is shorthand for $p_i[D_i(p_1,p_2,\ldots,p_n) - S_i(p_1,p_2,\ldots,p_n)]$, where D_i is the physical quantity of the planned market demand for good i, and S_i is the physical quantity of the planned market supply for good i.

In Section 1 of Chapter 3 we learned that general equilibrium (GE) exists when the value of p_iX_i is zero for *each* i simultaneously. In other words, GE is the name given to the situation of zero planned market excess demand in each and every market at the same time. There are n individual markets, and so there are n equations of the form

$$p_i[D_i(p_1,p_2,\ldots,p_n) - S_i(p_1,p_2,\ldots,p_n)] = 0 \qquad (14-1)$$

which together symbolically describe GE. That is, when GE exists, each of the n equations like Equation 14-1 will hold true—they each will equal zero.

Leon Walras, the economist who was the first (in the 1870s) to describe general equilibrium in these mathematical terms, taught that the prices that would make each market be in equilibrium at the same time could be found by solving a set of n simultaneous equations like Equation 14-1. That is, the n planned market excess demand equations could be solved for the set of prices $(p_1,\ldots,p_n)$ that will make each and every one of the equations equal zero simultaneously.[1] The set of prices that establishes general equilibrium is called the *general equilibrium price vector*.

From your microeconomics class you are familiar with the idea that the price of a good affects both the quantity demanded and the quantity supplied of the good. You also know that equilibrium in a particular market exists when the quantity demanded and the quantity supplied are equal. They are made equal by the price where the demand line and the supply line intersect. Walras merely extended this basic idea. He pointed out that the demand and the supply of a good are affected by the prices of other goods as well as by its own price. For example, the supply and demand for tires are affected by the price of gasoline. Because of Say's Principle that what goes on in one market must affect other markets, Walras took the general approach of thinking of each demand and supply as dependent on all prices. This approach permitted him to arrive at a set of equations, each with the same unknowns, and to depict *GE* as the simultaneous solution to those equations.

14-2 TATONNEMENT AND FALSE TRADING

When Walras was developing his approach to general equilibrium, few economists understood mathematics. Walras had to invent a way to explain his approach to nonmathematical economists. He had to describe the process of solving a set of simultaneous equations in terms that economists, who were used to thinking about demand, supply, and markets in nonmathematical terms, could appreciate. To do this, he concocted a fictional scenario he called *tatonnement* (a French word that literally means "groping").

Imagine, Walras suggested to his audience, that each transactor in the economy brings some amount (possibly zero) of each good to a central marketplace. Different people bring different amounts of different goods. (To simplify things, there is no production; people simply have what they have, like manna from heaven.) The set of goods that a person brings to the marketplace is called that person's *endowment*. The total quantity of each good available for exchange is fixed, and each person's endowment (starting amount) of each good is fixed. Each person is likely to want more of some goods than he has (he has planned excess demands for these goods), and therefore must be planning to give up other goods he has in order to pay for the goods he wants (he has planned excess supplies for these goods). But the amount of his planned excess demand or planned excess supply for any good depends on the prices that he must pay for what he acquires and the prices he can receive for what he gives up. Before anyone can decide the quantity of his planned excess demand or supply, he must know the prices of all the goods.

Imagine, Walras further suggested to his audience, that there is an auctioneer who neither buys nor sells goods, but whose job it is to call out, at random, a set of prices—one price for each good. When the auctioneer announces his arbitrarily chosen list of prices, each transactor is asked to write down the quantity he wants to acquire or give up for each good, assuming those prices existed. Each transactor then hands in his planned purchases and sales to the auctioneer, who then adds them all up for each good. That is, the auctioneer adds together all the planned purchases for each good. That sum is the planned market demand for each good. The auctioneer also adds together all the planned sales of each good to get the planned market supply for each good. Next the auctioneer compares each planned market demand with the corresponding planned market supply to see whether they match. If they match in each and every market, the price list that the auctioneer called out at random is the general equilibrium price vector. It is then announced that *GE* has been attained, and all the transactors are instructed to make the exchanges they had written down on the paper.

However, if the market planned demands and planned supplies do not match in each and every market, *no exchange takes place*, not even in those markets where demand and supply do match. In this event, the auctioneer calls out a new set of prices. In those markets where he discovered a market planned excess demand with the original price list, he will call out higher prices. In those markets where he discovered a market planned excess supply with the original price list, he will call out lower prices. Each transactor is again instructed to write out his planned purchases and planned sales of each good at the new prices and turn them in to the auctioneer. The auctioneer again adds up all the planned purchases of each good to get the planned market demand for each good, and he also adds up all the planned sales of each good to get the planned market supply for each good. If planned market demand matches planned market supply in each market, the auctioneer announces that *GE* has been established and instructs the transactors to carry out their planned exchanges. If nonzero planned excess demand exists in any markets (why did we not say any market?), no actual exchange of any good occurs. The auctioneer would then call out another price list and go through the same process. In this way the auctioneer "gropes" toward the general equilibrium price vector. Only when he finds it, in this trial-and-error manner, does any actual exchange of goods take place. The trial-and-error groping of the auctioneer is the verbal counterpart to the mathematical process of finding the general equilibrium price vector by solving a system of simultaneous equations.

False trading is defined as the actual exchange of goods at prices other than general equilibrium prices. From the above it is clear that no false trading is permitted in the Walrasian tatonnement. Actual exchange of goods is permitted only after the auctioneer has found the general equilibrium price vector. The reason Walras did not permit false trading in tatonnement is that tatonnement is supposed to correspond to the process of solving a given, and unchanging, set of simultaneous equations. The set of equations represents planned excess demands (positive and negative) at different prices but with the original pattern of individual endowments with each good. That is, given the total market supply of each good (the sum of each individual's endowment of each good), the equations tell us what the planned market excess demand for each good would be for each possible list of prices. The endowment pattern determines the forms of the equations (the coefficients and the powers attached to each unknown). Given the forms of the equations, when hypothetical values for the unknowns (the prices) are plugged in, the magnitudes of the planned market excess demands can be calculated. If false trading were permitted during the tatonnement, the pattern of holdings of the various goods by the various people would change. On the next round of the tatonnement (the next calling out of a list of prices) there would be an entirely new set of excess demand equations. Walras' mathematics called for the solution of an unchanging set of equations; so his tatonnement, which was just a verbal scenario designed to represent the mathematical process, could not include anything that would imply a changing set of equations.

14-3 EFFECTIVE DEMAND FAILURE

According to Leijonhufvud, one of Keynes' major theoretical contributions was to point out that depressions, such as the Great Depression of the 1930s, can be understood to arise from false trading. Specifically, Keynes stressed a particular kind of false trading he labeled "effective demand failure."

GENERAL EQUILIBRIUM VS. THE REAL WORLD

The prohibition against false trading in Walrasian tatonnement implies that there is no difference between planned (what Clower called "notional") market excess demands and actual or "effective" market excess demands. In general equilibrium all plans can be carried out. All plans can be effective. General equilibrium means that in every market, without exception, the amount that buyers want to acquire matches the amount that sellers want to make available. All individually made plans are mutually consistent. The economy is in what Hayek calls the fully coordinated state. If a person, at general equilibrium prices, plans to sell a specific quantity of labor time and use the proceeds of that sale to pay for four automobile tires, both plans can be executed. There will be others who plan to purchase the labor time and still others who plan to sell the tires. That is the definition of general equilibrium—no planned excess demand or excess supply for anything. Since the plans of everyone are consistent, everyone's plans can be effectively carried out. Planned excess demands, whether positive or negative, are effective excess demands.

In the real world, however, there is false trading. General equilibrium is a theoretical concept that is useful in understanding the nature of voluntary exchange economic systems, but it is scarcely imaginable that any actual economy would attain such a fully coordinated state. The basic data of the economy—tastes and preferences, resource availabilities, and production technologies—constantly change. The *GE* price vector is not a stationary target toward which actual prices move. Rather, it is a rapidly moving target, and actual prices must constantly change direction in order to stay on track. People exchange goods and services all the time without waiting for the *GE* price vector to be discovered and announced.

When there is a planned excess demand for a good, people are planning to acquire more of the good than other people are planning to make available. Not all of those who are planning to acquire some of the good will be able to do so; there will be at least some unsatisfied buyers. Similarly, when there is a planned excess supply for a good, people are planning to make available more of the good than other people are planning to acquire. Not all of those who plan to sell some of the good will be able to do so; there will be at least some unsatisfied sellers. Not all planned excess demands and planned excess supplies will be effective excess demands and effective excess supplies.

WHEN THE SUM OF EFFECTIVE EXCESS DEMANDS IS NEGATIVE

Suppose that individual households and business firms had only one source of money they could use to purchase things: the current sale of labor services in the case of households, and the current sale of the goods and services they produce in the case of firms. That is, suppose that both households and firms had used up all their ready cash and assets that could readily be converted into cash (e.g., savings accounts and other financial assets). In order to get money to buy the goods and services that firms produce, households would have to first sell some labor time for money. In order to get money to buy the labor time that households want to sell, firms would have to first sell some goods and services for money. In Clower's words, "Money buys goods, and goods buy money, but goods do not buy goods."[2] In order effectively to demand goods, you have to have money to spend.

In the real world goods are not exchanged directly for each other. As the medium of exchange, money is needed in order to make planned excess demands effective excess demands. In this situation households could have a planned excess supply of labor time (at existing, nonequilibrium prices and wages households in the aggregate plan to sell more labor services than firms in the aggregate plan to purchase) that would also be an effective excess supply (households would make offers to firms that firms would not accept). Corresponding to their planned excess supply of labor, households would have a *planned* excess demand for goods; but they would have a zero *effective* excess demand for goods. They would be saying to firms, "Look, at existing prices and wages, if you purchase the labor time we plan to sell, we plan to use the proceeds to purchase goods and services from you. But we cannot make all our purchase plans effective unless we can execute all our planned sales of labor time."

Firms, because of the disequilibrium prices and wages, plan to purchase less labor time than households want to sell. They can, therefore, purchase all the labor time they want to. (Some, but not all, households will be able to carry out their planned sales of labor time.) Firms hire the amount they want to hire, and so they have a zero planned, and effective, excess demand for labor. Moreover, they can sell all the goods and services they produce using the amount of labor they hire. Households in the aggregate plan to purchase more than firms plan to sell, but only those households that successfully sell the labor they want to sell are able to carry out their purchase plans. The amount firms plan to produce is the amount that households which successfully sell labor time plan to purchase. Firms have a zero planned and effective supply of goods.

Thus the sum of the *planned* excess demands, on the part of households and firms together, is zero; but the sum of the *effective* excess demands, on the part of households and firms together, is negative. Firms effectively sell all the goods they plan to sell and effectively hire all the labor they plan to hire; but households do not sell all the labor time they plan to sell, and so they cannot make effective all their plans to purchase goods and services from firms. Keynes labeled this situation "effective demand failure."

WALRAS' LAW VS. SAY'S PRINCIPLE

In the appendix to Chapter 3 we saw that Walras' Law is the name given to the proposition that the sum of the market excess demands for all goods and services must be zero. No distinction between planned and effective excess demands is made. We have just seen, however, that the sum of the effective excess demands for all goods and services could well be negative. Walras' Law, if it is taken to refer only to planned excess demands, is merely what Leijonhufvud and Clower call Say's Principle. But if Walras' Law is taken to refer to effective excess demands, it is simply wrong. The sum of the effective excess demands for all goods and services must be zero only in general equilibrium. According to Leijonhufvud, Keynes attacked Walras' Law (he called it Say's Law) as irrelevant to real world economies because it pertains only to general equilibrium.

It is not surprising that Walras and his followers were not careful to distinguish between planned and effective excess demands. In Walrasian theory false trading is never considered. In fact, it is explicitly forbidden. Walras' original purpose in forbidding false trading in his theoretical formulations was to permit him to work with a fixed set of general equilibrium equations. But the technique of considering only general equilibrium trading gradually became accepted as the way to proceed in all theoretical inquiry, and so economists came habitually to ignore the distinction between planned and effective excess demands. It was Keynes who, according to Leijonhufvud, first broke out of that restrictive general equilibrium approach to economic theory in *The General Theory*.

WILL PRICE AND WAGE CHANGES CORRECT
EFFECTIVE DEMAND FAILURE?

In Section 4 of Chapter 11 we discussed the effects of a decrease in the money base using the variable price **IS-LM** model (Fig. 11-5) and an excess demand table (Table 11-1). In the next to the last row of that table we depicted what we have just called an "effective demand failure." There was a planned and effective (we called it "actual") excess supply of labor services, a planned excess demand for goods, a zero effective excess demand for goods, and zero planned and effective excess demands for bonds and money. We then said that prices and wages would fall in response to the excess capacity in the commodities market and effective excess supply in the labor market. This decline in prices and wages would shift the **LM** line to the right, increasing the actual demand for labor and real expenditures until full employment real output was again attained. The decline in prices and wages, leaving the real wage unchanged, would restore general equilibrium.

According to Leijonhufvud, Keynes went further. If indeed both firms and households come to have as their only source of money the current sale of goods and labor time, there could emerge a "you go first" problem, even though prices and wages declined. Firms could say to households that they would hire all the labor households would like to sell if households would first buy some goods and services so that firms could get the money to use in the hiring. Households at the same time could say to firms that they would purchase all that the firms would like to produce but first the firms must purchase additional labor time to enable all households to make their planned excess demands effective. Figure 11-5c shows the real expenditure line in the commodities market shifting up as prices fall; but before that can happen, additional labor must be hired. Figure 11-5d shows the effective demand for labor increasing toward point K; but before that can happen, there must be an effective demand for more real output. No matter how much prices and wages fall, the coordination process may not be able to get underway. Even if prices and wages reach their GE values, general equilibrium will not be attained. The attainment of GE requires human action in response to price and wage changes. If the decline in cash and near-cash assets has been so drastic that the "you go first" problem emerges, the economy could become stuck in disequilibrium, and price and wage changes would do no good. According to Leijonhufvud, this is how Keynes explained the Great Depression of the 1930s.

Between 1929 and 1933 the money supply in the United States declined by over one-third as the result of massive failures of commercial banks. The Federal Reserve Board had the ability and the authority to prevent this drastic decline in the money supply and reduction in the number of commercial banks, but it did not use that authority; so the economy fell into a massive effective demand failure that price and wage declines could not correct. Between 1929 and 1933 the average money price level fell by 26 percent and the average money wage level fell by 22 percent. This massive deflation did not correct the situation.

THE CORRIDOR

Not every decline in the money supply is severe enough to set off an effective demand failure that deflation cannot correct. Such a situation emerges only when the stock of cash and near-cash assets has decreased so much that firms and households must rely on their current sale of goods and labor as their *only* source of effective purchasing power (money). Most of the time either firms or households (or both) have accumulated cash and near-cash assets they can use to execute their planned excess demands. The "you go first" problem will not emerge if, for example, firms have assets they can readily convert to cash in order to hire additional labor when they are confident that households will in return purchase more goods.

Leijonhufvud says there is a "safety zone" in the economy within which aggregate nominal demand may digress from its general equilibrium path over time without causing problems that changes in prices and wages won't be able to correct. He calls that safety zone "the corridor."[3] Within the corridor the normal coordinating forces of free markets are able to correct disequilibrium without explicit government intervention. If, however, the government subjects the economy to shocks that place nominal aggregate demand outside the corridor, such as it did between 1929 and 1933, countervailing government policies will be required to correct the situation. It is difficult to think of any nongovernmental shocks that could place the economy outside the corridor.

14-4 THE WICKSELLIAN THEME

So far in this chapter we have not mentioned interest rates and their role in disequilibrium. Keynes' views on interest rates were greatly affected by a Swedish economist, Knut Wicksell.[4] Wicksell's original concern was to explain the simultaneous existence of a drop in the average money price level and low interest rates. This phenomenon appeared to be a paradox because the quantity theory of money implied that a drop in the price level would be caused by a decrease in the money supply. But a decrease in the money supply was usually associated with decreased lending by commercial banks, and a reduction in the credit offered by banks would ordinarily imply higher interest rates.

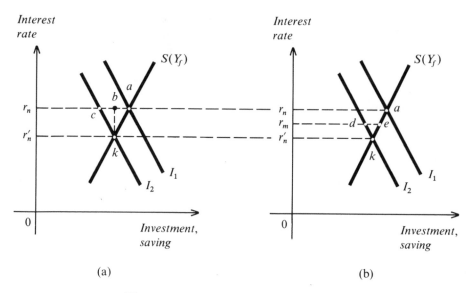

Figure 14-1   The Wicksellian theme.

Wicksell's solution to the dilemma can be understood by referring to Figure 14-1 and its associated excess demand tables. Figure 14-1 shows aggregate investment lines (labeled I) and aggregate saving lines (labeled S). From Section 6 of Chapter 6 we know that aggregate investment spending (spending by business firms on buildings, machines, and tools) increases as the rate of interest declines. This inverse relationship accounts for the negative slope of the lines labeled I. We also learned in Chapter 6 (Section 4) that as the rate of interest decreases people save less (i.e., they consume more) out of their current income. This relationship accounts for the positive slope of the lines labeled S. Both S lines are labeled $S(Y_f)$, which means that those lines would exist if nominal GNP were at its full employment level given the price level that exists. A move from point a to point k along $S(Y_f)$ in Figure 14-1a, for example, indicates both a decrease in saving and an increase in consumption of ba out of full employment nominal income (Y_f). Such a move would be depicted as a shift upward of the consumption line in a Keynesian cross (45° line) diagram.

WHEN INVESTMENT SPENDING DECLINES

Suppose that we begin in GE at point a in Figure 14-1a. Since we are discussing saving and investment, we must have the commodities market in the model;

Table 14-1 Excess demands

Row	Status	Bond Market	Commodities Market	Money Market
1	GE	0	0	0
2	Pessimism increases	ED	ES	0
3	r decreases to r'_n	0	0	0

since we are discussing an interest rate, we must have the bond market in the model; and since Wicksell was concerned with the behavior of the commercial banking system, we must include the money market in the model. The initial GE is indicated in the first row of Table 14-1. Initially the interest rate is r_n. Wicksell called the rate of interest equating the amount of saving and investment that would exist at full employment income (given the existing price level) the "natural" rate of interest.

Imagine now that for some reason investors become more pessimistic about the future profitability of current investment. At each interest rate, the amount of investment spending would be less than before. This change is shown in Figure 14-1a as a shift in the investment line from I_1 to I_2. If the interest rate did not change, investment spending would decline by ac. (The $C + I$ line in a 45° line diagram would shift downward.) This decline would reduce nominal income. In order for there to be no downward push on nominal income, the interest rate would have to fall to r'_n, which is the new natural rate. If the interest rate did fall to its new natural level, there would be a move from a to k along the S line (meaning that saving decreases and consumption increases by ab) and a move from c to k along the new I line (meaning that cb of investment will be recovered because of the fall in the interest rate). The combination of the additional consumption and investment would put the $C + I$ line in a 45° line diagram back to where it was at the start. There would be no pressure for nominal income to decline. Full employment would be maintained at the existing price level.

Row 2 of Table 14-1 shows that market forces would tend to push the interest rate toward r'_n. The increased pessimism of investors about the future profitability of current investment would mean that firms would be attempting to acquire less credit (sell fewer bonds) than before. The supply of bonds would decrease relative to the demand for bonds. The buyers of bonds are the households that save. Before the shift of the investment line to I_2, both the supply and the demand for bonds corresponded to distance $r_n a$ in Figure 14-1a. The saving line indicates the demand for bonds, and the investment line indicates the supply of bonds. Now the supply of bonds corresponds to distance $r_n c$, while the demand for bonds corresponds to distance $r_n a$. The ED for bonds is indicated in the bonds column of Table 14-1. The *ES* indicated in the commodities column is a result of the decrease in investment spending in the commodities market.

If everything went smoothly, the *ED* for bonds would raise bond prices, thus lowering the interest rate, until the bond market cleared without any involvement of commercial banks. Zero *ED* for money would be maintained throughout, and the decline in the interest rate would eliminate the *ES* in the commodities market. *GE* would be established as indicated in the third row of Table 14-1.

INTERVENTION BY THE COMMERCIAL BANKING SYSTEM

However, Wicksell argued, everything doesn't go so smoothly. The commercial banking system (whose behavior is not represented by the *S* and *I* lines) will intervene in a way that will prevent the interest rate from falling to its new natural level. Consider Figure 14-1b. As before, there is initial *GE* at point *a* (row 1 of Table 14-2). When the investment line shifts to I_2, creating the *ED* in bonds and *ES* in commodities as indicated in row 2 of the table, the interest rate begins to fall. As it does, commercial banks decrease the amount of credit they are willing to extend. Their desired excess reserves increase, and therefore the money supply decreases. The banks' decreased lending activity shows up as an *ED* in the money market. The supply of money has been cut relative to the demand for money because of the banks' actions. Households attempt to build up their money balances by cutting their spending in the commodities market. Thus the *ES* in the commodities market is not corrected.

As indicated in row 3 of Table 14-2, the banks' actions contribute to the clearing of the bond market. There was an *ED* for bonds caused by a decrease in the amount of bonds firms were attempting to sell to pay for their investment expenditures. Lenders, whether households or banks, extend credit by buying IOUs or bonds. When banks curtail their lending, they are accepting fewer IOUs (buying fewer bonds). When the rate of interest has fallen to r_m (Wicksell called it the "market" interest rate), the supply of bonds on the part of firms corresponds to distance $r_m d$, while the demand for bonds on the part of households corresponds to distance $r_m e$. The difference, *de*, is made up by the banks' reduced demand for bonds (reduction in credit supplied). Banks make up for the

Table 14-2 Excess demands

Row	Status	Bond Market	Commodities Market	Money Market
1	GE	0	0	0
2	Pessimism increases	ED	ES	0
3	r decreases to r_m	0	ES	ED

ED for bonds that would exist at r_m if there were only nonbank firms and households by reducing their own demand for bonds.

Since the banks' actions remove the ED that would otherwise exist at r_m, there is no pressure for the interest rate to fall all the way to r'_n. The banks' actions have created a wedge between the natural rate and the market rate of interest. GE will not be restored as long as the market rate exceeds the natural rate. The economy would be caught in a "cumulative process" of contraction of nominal income.

KEYNES' MODIFICATION

Wicksell constructed an analysis, based on the intervention of the money market, of an ongoing disequilibrium state in the commodities market. In 1930 Keynes published a book entitled *A Treatise on Money*, which used Wicksell's approach to ongoing disequilibrium in the commodities market but changed it somewhat. Keynes, too, talked about a divergence between the natural and market rates of interest. Look at Figure 14-1b. We begin again in GE at point a of the diagram and row 1 of Table 14-2. Again we assume that investors become more pessimistic about the future profitability of current investment. This pessimism shifts the investment line to I_2, creating an ED in bonds and an ES in commodities, as indicated in row 2 of the table. The ED for bonds raises bond prices and thus lowers the rate of interest.

Keynes assumed that the lower rate of interest would not affect the credit activities of banks, but he thought that it would increase the quantity of money some people would demand, thus creating an ED in money and preventing the commodities market from getting back into equilibrium although equilibrium was attained in the bond market. The decline in the rate of interest, Keynes argued in *A Treatise*, would make the bond buyers very leery of buying bonds. People had become accustomed to the original natural rate of interest and expected it to continue. When the market rate declines, they expect the decline to be temporary. They expect the interest rate soon to rise to its previous level (which means they expect bond prices soon to decline to their previous level). Buying bonds when their prices are unusually high and are expected soon to fall is the height of folly.

Some people become "bear speculators"; they are convinced that bond prices will soon fall, and so they not only refuse to buy bonds now, but also try to sell as many of the bonds they already have while bond prices are still above normal. They want to hold ready money instead of bonds. The ED in bonds is removed before the new natural rate is attained because, in addition to the usual supply of bonds from firms at r_m (which corresponds to distance $r_m d$), there are bonds on the market from the portfolios of bear speculators. This additional supply of bonds corresponds to distance de; since the demand for bonds from nonspeculating households corresponds to distance $r_m e$, there is zero excess demand for bonds. There is no pressure for the interest rate to fall to r_n'. It gets stuck at r_m because of the actions of bear speculators.

Although the bond market is back in equilibrium, there continues to be an ES in the commodities market because the interest rate has not fallen enough to get the sum of consumption and investment spending back to where it was before. The ED in money is a reflection of the fact that bear speculators want to sell as many bonds as possible and hold on to the money they get until bond prices return to what they think is their normal (lower) level. They want to sell bonds at today's high prices and buy them again at lower prices in the future.

14-5 THE WICKSELLIAN THEME IN *THE GENERAL THEORY*

In our earlier discussion (the first section of Chapters 12 and 14) of changes in prices as coordinators of the diverse plans and actions of individual transactors we stressed the coordination of current economic activities. There is also a problem of coordination of economic activities over time. The key price in intertemporal coordination is the interest rate. To have a smoothly functioning economic system, the plans and actions of both savers and investors must be coordinated.

INTERTEMPORAL COORDINATION

Households are the savers. They decide how much of their current income to spend on current consumption and how much of it to save in order to be able to consume more than they otherwise would in the future. Households save by purchasing financial securities such as savings account credits, stocks, and bonds. As we have seen in Section 4 of Chapter 1, all financial securities are lumped together and treated as a single financial security called a bond. "The" interest rate is the market yield on the representative security. Savers save primarily by buying bonds. (They also save by holding on to money.)

Business firms are the investors. They invest by purchasing office buildings, factories, inventories, machines, and tools. The primary source of funds for financing such expenditures is the sale of bonds (which include stocks). Firms issue bonds to raise the funds with which to make their investment expenditures. (Of course, they also generate funds internally through depreciation funds and retained earnings.)

Resources can today be used either to produce things for current consumption or to produce investment goods that can be used in the future to produce consumption goods. In order to make a profit, business firms produce those things in those quantities and with those qualities that they perceive buyers want. They also attempt to produce things that buyers want *when* the buyers want them. Households want some current consumption, but they also want to save some now in order to be able to consume more than they otherwise would in the future (e.g., during retirement). The interest rate is the signal that tells producers *when* buyers want their consumption goods.

If people increase their saving now, they are saying that they want to postpone some of their consumption. They want producers to gear up to be able to produce more consumption goods in the future. In order to do that, producers must acquire investment goods so that they will have the means to produce the additional consumption goods in the future. An increase in saving now, relative to today's investment spending (a shift of the saving line to the right against a stationary investment line), will decrease the rate of interest. The lower interest rate will increase the net present value of all potential investment projects, and so more investment projects will be undertaken. Some additional resources will be diverted from the production of consumption goods and toward the production of investment goods. (The higher investment spending would be depicted as a move downward and to the right along the stationary investment line.)

INTERTEMPORAL EFFECTIVE DEMAND FAILURE

The key question is whether the interest rate will take on the value that is necessary to send the correct signals to investors about the intertemporal consumption plans of households. And this is where the Wicksellian theme comes in. We saw in the previous section that in *A Treatise* Keynes expressed the view that the action of bear speculators could prevent the interest rate from taking on its new natural value. But in *The General Theory*, according to Leijonhufvud, Keynes went even further. Keynes explained how, if the interest rate is prevented from taking on its new natural value right away, there could be an effective demand failure even if eventually the interest rate did take on its new natural value.

There are in fact at least five markets that ought to be thought of in any macro theory—labor, bonds, money, consumption goods, and investment goods. The Hicksian interpretation of Keynes combined the latter two markets into one called the commodities market. Up to this point we have maintained that tradition. But if we are to understand correctly (according to Keynes) intertemporal effective demand failure, we must now look at how Keynes grouped the markets in *The General Theory*. According to Leijonhufvud, Keynes used a model with the following four macro markets: labor, money, consumption goods, and "assets." Bonds and investment goods were grouped together because they both are long-term claims to income streams.

Keynes also constructed a model of investment in *The General Theory* that depended on the demand price of assets (p_A) relative to the price of labor (w).[5] It is the ratio p_A/w that is crucial. For any given wage there is a critical value of p_A

that is high enough to induce sufficient investment spending to have full employment.

The demand price for assets, the maximum price that investors would be willing to pay to acquire one of such an asset, depends on investors' expectations about the future income (profit) flows from the assets, and the rate of interest that is used to discount those future flows. p_A can be too low relative to the existing wage either because investors are unduly pessimistic about the future returns or because the interest rate is too high.

Now suppose, starting from GE, that households increase the amount they save out of current income. This increase in saving relative to investment puts downward pressure on the rate of interest. Because of the actions of bear speculators, the interest rate is kept too high to permit continued full employment at the existing average money price level. A Wicksellian cumulative process of contraction gets underway. The higher saving is in fact a demand for consumption goods in the future, but no one actually places advance orders for these future consumer goods today. The future demand for consumer goods is not effectively communicated to producers because the interest rate is too high. During the cumulative contraction investors become increasingly pessimistic about the future returns from assets. The contraction could well have reduced the average money price level, the wage rate, and the interest rate to their new GE values; but because of the pessimism of investors about future returns (brought about because the demand for future consumption goods has not been an effective demand), p_A is too low relative to the GE value of w to get sufficient investment spending to establish full employment.

It is at this point that Keynes introduced the idea of government fiscal policy to "prime the pump." In this situation the interest rate is at its Wicksellian natural rate, and so there is nothing for monetary policy to do. It is merely a question of building confidence among investors so that p_A will increase relative to the wage. Keynes felt that government spending was the best way to accomplish that end. Pursuing an expansionary monetary policy would merely alter the interest rate and other prices away from their GE values and require too many other adjustments. Keynes did not prescribe fiscal policy over monetary policy because he thought the latter was ineffective. He did so merely because fiscal policy was more easily aimed at the source of the problem—overly pessimistic investors.

SUMMARY

In this, the final chapter of the text, we have discussed at some length Keynes' key concept of effective demand failure. First, we saw such an effective demand failure in the context of the problem of coordinating current economic activities. If the only source of effective purchasing power (money) that households and firms have is the current sale of labor time and goods, the sum of the effective excess demands for all goods could be negative; even changes in wages and prices could not correct the situation.

Similarly, we saw that there can be an intertemporal effective demand failure because today's savers do not today actually place orders for future consumption goods with producers. Anything, such as the behavior of bear speculators, that prevents the interest rate from immediately coordinating the plans and actions of savers and investors could result in investors' becoming so pessimistic about the future returns from current investment that even when the interest rate does take on its new *GE* value, the demand price of assets could be too low relative to the wage to call forth sufficient investment for full employment.

Along the way we saw how the mathematical tradition of Walras and the fictional scenario (tatonnement) he invented to explain his approach to non-mathematical economists led them to ignore the crucial difference between planned and effective excess demand.

QUESTIONS

1. Out of general equilibrium, in the real world, there will be many different prices for each good. Some demanders will bid higher than others and some sellers will offer to sell at lower prices than others. Why does this not alter Say's Principle?
2. In the future, with computers capable of handling much more information, could the general equilibrium price vector *actually* be discovered by solving the Walrasian excess demand equations? Why or why not?
3. What lessons can be learned from the fact that Walras' approach to general equilibrium led economists into forgetting the difference between planned and effective excess demands?
4. Can there be effective demand failure in economic systems based on barter?
5. If, subsequent to a shock, all prices immediately adjusted to their new *GE* values, effective demand failure could never emerge. Why? After some delay in price adjustments, effective demand failure can emerge even if prices do take on their new *GE* values. Why?
6. Keynes defined "involuntary unemployment" as a situation where a decline in the real wage by an increase in the money price level would increase both the quantity supplied and the quantity demanded of labor. How is this related to effective demand failure?

7. Can you think of any nongovernmental shocks that could place the United States' economy outside the corridor?
8. Draw the diagram and write out the excess demand table for (a) Wicksell's and (b) Keynes' (*Treatise*) analysis of an increase in household saving and an increase of investor optimism.
9. Why couldn't *GE* be established in the face of intertemporal effective demand failure merely by reductions in the interest rate sufficient to compensate for the excessive pessimism of investors? Would this require additional changes in wages and prices? With respect to what set of expectations is the *GE* price vector defined?

NOTES

1. Since $p_n = 1$ (the nth good is money), there are only $n-1$ unknowns—the $n-1$ other prices. But there are actually only $n-1$ independent equations since, by Say's Principle (SP), if $n-1$ of the n equations equal zero, the other one must also be zero. (Remember that SP says the sum of the equations is *always* zero.)
2. Robert W. Clower, "Foundations of Monetary Theory," *Western Economic Journal*, 1967.
3. Axel Leijonhufvud, "Effective Demand Failures," *The Swedish Journal of Economics*, 1973.
4. Knut Wicksell (1851–1926). The book from which Section 14-4 is distilled is his *Interest and Prices*, first published in 1898.
5. See Axel Leijonhufvud, *Keynes and the Classics*, Institute of Economic Affairs Occasional Paper No. 30 (London, 1969), pp. 36–40.

Index